FLIGHT THROUGH THE AGES

FLIGHT THROUGH THE AGES

A complete, illustrated chronology
from the dreams of early history
to the age of space exploration

by C. H. GIBBS-SMITH

THOMAS Y. CROWELL COMPANY, INC.

III

Copyright © 1974 by Tre Tryckare AB,
Gothenburg, Sweden. B36US21741

First published in the United States
of America in 1974 by
THOMAS Y. CROWELL COMPANY, INC.
New York, New York.

Published simultaneously in Canada by Fitz-
henry & Whiteside Limited, Toronto.

Manufactured in Spain.

Library of Congress Catalog Card Number:
74-8389

ISBN: 0-690-00607-1

1 2 3 4 5 6 7 8 9 10

FLIGHT THROUGH THE AGES

has been designed and produced by Tre Tryckare AB, Gothenburg, Sweden, and is the result of cooperation between the author and a number of internationally known aviation experts who have collaborated with the Tre Tryckare editorial and art departments under the supervision of Turlough Johnston and Einar Engelbrektson.

CHARLES H. GIBBS-SMITH,

the author, is one of the world's leading aeronautical historians and has written many widely acclaimed books on the subject. He is a member of the History Group of the Royal Aeronautical Society and holds that Society's only Honorary Companionship for history. He is also the only Englishman who has ever received the French Aero-Club Diplome de Medaille.

PETER W. BROOKS,

who is known for his books on modern aircraft, has contributed the section from 1919 to the present day and he has been advised and assisted by Kenneth Munson, himself the author of many aeronautical books.

LAYOUT AND ARTWORK

has been made by the Tre Tryckare Studios and the following artists:
John Wood Associates
Herlew Studios
Ian D. Huntley

The author and publishers would like to thank the following people and organizations for their kind assistance in providing advice, information and material:
Aer Lingus Irish
Aeroflot, USSR
Aerospacelines Inc., USA
Aerospatiale, France
Kathleen Atterton, England
Avions Marcel Dassault, France
The Boeing Company, USA
British Aircraft Corporation
British Airways
Cessna Aircraft Company, USA
Dornier, Germany
Beryl Edginton, England
Fokker-VFW, Holland
General Dynamics Corporation, USA
Grumman Corporation, USA
Hawker Siddeley Aviation, England
KLM, Holland
Lockheed Aircraft Corporation, USA
Lufthansa, Germany
McDonnell Douglas Corporation, USA
Curt Palmblad, Sweden
Piper Aircraft Corporation, USA
Saab-Scania, Sweden
Smithsonian Institute, USA
Swissair
University of Michigan, USA

contents

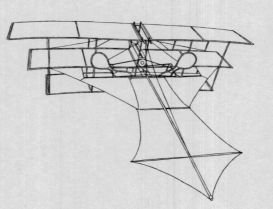

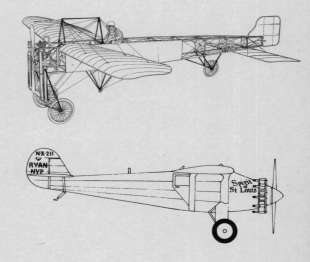

SECTION IV page 140

Development work on the jet-engine begins. Passenger routes become established. World War II and its many aircraft-fighters, light and heavy bombers, the first jet aircraft, the V-1 rocket. The first jet passenger aircraft are developed. The breaking of the sound barrier.

SECTION V page 180

The first Earth satellite goes into orbit thus signalling the start of the Space Race. The jet passenger aircraft ousts the propeller-driven. Travel by air becomes completely accepted byt the public. The supersonic military aircraft is developed. Man lands on and takes from the Moon. The era of supersonic travel begins. Men remain in space for longer and longer periods.

SECTION VI page 230

Reference and further information for the reader.

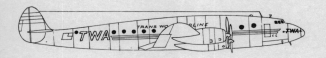

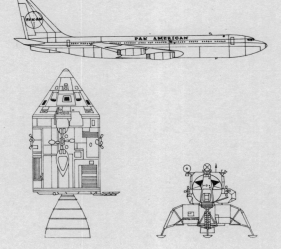

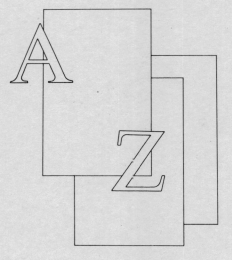

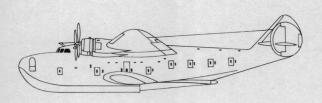

SECTION I

FROM DREAMS, MYTHS, AND THE ANCIENT WORLD TO 1859 A.D.

The wings of mythology. This illustration is based on a bas-relief dating from about 490 B.C. in the palace of Darius I in Susa. It depicts the god Ahura Masda as a winged disc guarded by two winged lions.

A

B

C

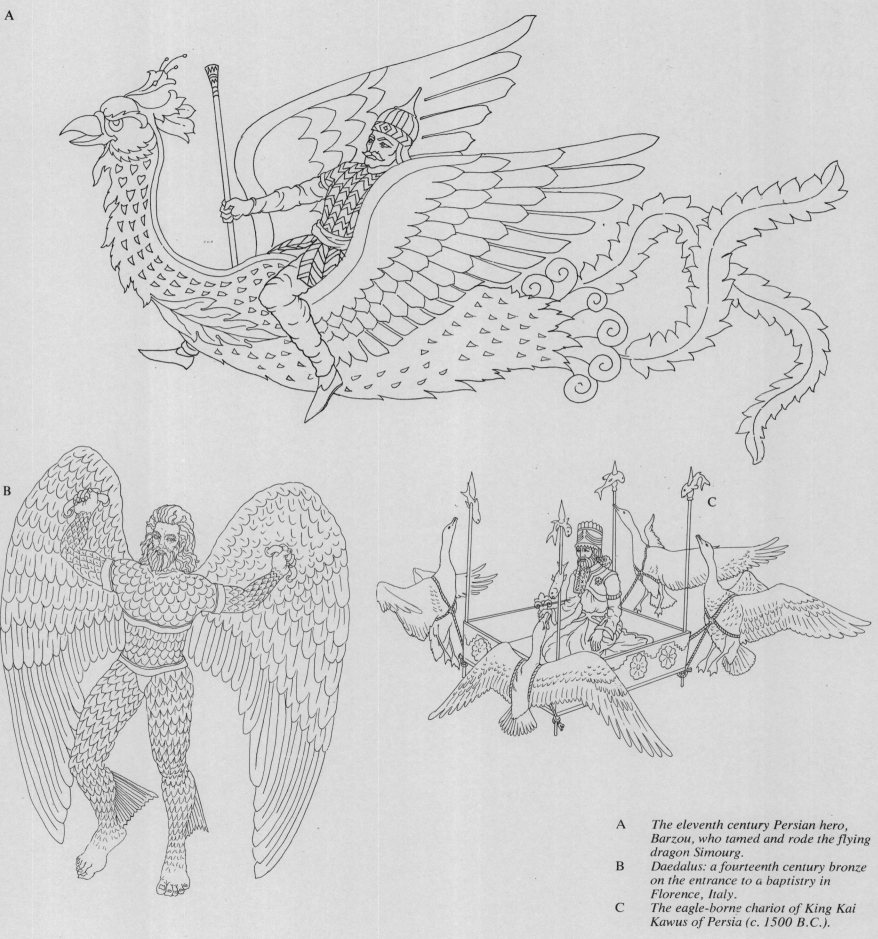

A   *The eleventh century Persian hero,*
       Barzou, who tamed and rode the flying
       dragon Simourg.

B   *Daedalus: a fourteenth century bronze*
       on the entrance to a baptistry in
       Florence, Italy.

C   *The eagle-borne chariot of King Kai*
       Kawus of Persia (c. 1500 B.C.).

A

B

C

There is a famous Greek myth which admirably symbolises the daring and danger surrounding the early aviators. Daedalus and his son Icarus had been imprisoned by King Minos in his great labyrinth on the island of Crete. Daedalus, a master craftsman, was determined to escape and so made wings of feathers for himself and his son, with which they flapped their way out of captivity and up into the freedom of the Grecian skies. But, disobeying his father's orders, Icarus flew too near the sun, with the result that the fastenings of his wings were melted, and he plunged to his death in the sea—the world's first pilot casualty.

The great perennial drama of man's striving to conquer the air stretches back to the remotest years of recorded history, and the fanciful belief that our civilisation was seeded by travellers from outer space perhaps receives its blessing from the countless winged creatures and deities that so often peopled the mythology of the ancient world and culminated in the angelic hosts of the Christian church.

It was also envy that spurred the precursors along, envy of the birds who could defy gravity and take to the air; and we find this envious feeling echoed again and again through the ages. Sometimes it drove foolhardy but daring

men to leap from cliffs and towers equipped with artificial wings, only to flounder down to death or dismemberment. All the pilots of today descend from these men of old, whose dream it was to fly like the birds; who lived in the firm belief that at some time in the distant future their descendants would fashion the necessary materials and mechanisms with which they could rise into the air and propel themselves on long journeys through space.

Curiously enough, there have existed from the earliest times three devices which utilise the properties of the air, the boomerang, the arrow—with its stabilising feathers—and the kite. These were joined, in Europe, by the

D

E

F

windmill, at some time prior to the twelfth century; and, in the Far East, by the rocket.

It is not too gross an exaggeration to say that the modern propellered aeroplane was the ultimate end-product of the kite combined with the windmill, when the latter's passive wind-turned sails became the active airscrew of the little helicopter toys that were already popular by the fourteenth century. And that the modern gas-turbine aircraft derives from the kite and the centuries-old rocket.

A *The second known illustration of a parachute: Fausto Veranzio, 1615.*

B *The gentleman parachutist. Such illustrations appeared widely after Garnerin's famous parachute descent, 1797.*

C *Foot-operated flapping-wing machine devised by J.-J. Bourcart, 1863.*

D *The flapping-board apparatus with which Besnier attempted to fly at Sablé, 1678.*

E *Thibaut de Saint-André's flying cloak, 1784.*

F *Early European diamond-form kite, 1618.*

11

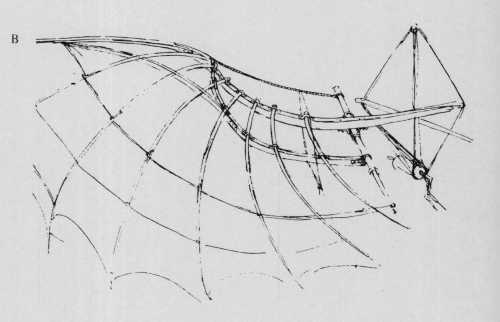

B

A

C

Apart from much fruitless speculation, and a number of broken necks, the prospect of flying remained an irking dream in the minds and imaginations of men during ancient times, during the Middle Ages, and on through the Renaissance until the end of the sixteenth century, when that giant of the arts and sciences, Leonardo da Vinci, gave part of his mind to aviation, between 1480 and 1500. At that time there still flourished the mediaeval helicopter toy—with string wound round the rotor spindle and pulled strongly away—and the plane-surface kite; but Leonardo did not exploit these prophetic playthings—let alone combine them—and pursued a largely sterile, and quite secret, programme of designing ornithopters (flapping wing aircraft): these influenced no one, either for good or evil, as they were not published until late in the nineteenth century. However, Leonardo did invent one aeronautical device, the parachute; but again he told no one, and the notion had to wait until it was re-discovered at the end of the eighteenth century, and put into practical form by the Frenchman Garnerin.

A   *Self-portrait of Leonardo da Vinci.*
B   *Sketch for a wing mechanism, based upon that of a bird, by Leonardo da Vinci.*

C   *Da Vinci design for a flapping-wing aircraft, to be worked by both arm and leg movement, c. 1485.*
D   *Ornithopter design by da Vinci, in which the pilot stood in a central structure.*

E   *The earliest design for a parachute, by Leonardo da Vinci, c. 1485.*
F   *Helix vertical take-off device, designed by Leonardo da Vinci, 1490.*

The Englishman Robert Hooke, in the second half of the seventeenth century, made some experiments with model flying-machines, but we do not know their nature. Otherwise there was a certain amount of imaginative writing thereafter, and a few more broken bodies; but little talented, sustained, or constructive thinking about aviation (heavier-than-air-flight). But in the field of aerostation (lighter-than-air-flight) there was one remarkable but fruitless suggestion in 1670 by the Jesuit Father Francesco de Lana, when he suggested a floating aircraft supported by evacuated copper spheres, which would of course have been collapsed flat by atmospheric pressure. But de Lana wrote some vivid and prophetic accounts of what bombing and aerial invasion would bring to the world.

In 1680 a severe blow was dealt to the would-be tower-jumpers by an Italian professor, G. A. Borelli, whose treatise on bird flight showed that a man's muscles, when compared with a bird's, were far too weak to lift and propel him through the air. But there would always remain a small but scattered body of men who would equip themselves with wings and try to fly.

A much publicised fantasy aeroplane was designed in 1709 by another Jesuit priest, Father Lourenço de Gusmão; but in fact we believe he made a small model which did succeed in gliding safely down from a roof-top. Gusmão also invented a small hot-air balloon about the same time, but this prophetic model was soon forgotten.

Another aerial vehicle to be mentioned is the rocket. Gunpowder rockets had been invented in China in the twelfth century and they were used at first as military weapons. They then travelled along the trade routes from China to Europe and arrived in the fourteenth century; but they were not used much as artillery because guns were improving all the time and were thought to be more effective. So rockets soon changed their main function and the art of pyrotechnics came to monopolize their role; and by the end of the eighteenth century the firework displays attained an astonishing standard of brilliance in Britain and France, where such displays became very popular. But the war-rocket, for long abandoned in Europe, was now being strongly developed by the great Indian ruler, Tippoo Sultan, and by the end of the century his rocket army numbered over a thousand men.

It seems ironic, in retrospect, that the peacefully drifting clouds inspired the first successful airmen; and the "floaters" came to beat the "flappers" into the air by more than a century. In 1783, some years before the French Revolution, both the man-carrying hot-air balloon, and the hydrogen-balloon, were born, suddenly and unexpectedly; and Man, overnight, so to say, found that he could travel through the air with ease and safety.

But balloons could not be driven or steered, and went only where the wind willed. The chance invention of the balloon at this time was a strange happening, because hot-air balloons could easily have been flown by the ancient Egyptians or anyone since their time, since all that was necessary was a reasonably airtight textile bag and a fire hung beneath it.

Within a decade and a half, balloons were ascending everywhere, and being used for adventure, for pleasure, for scientific research and even for military observation. It was to be ballooning that first accustomed men to moving through the air, and continued to foster air-mindedness among the public. In 1797, the first successful parachute descents—from balloons—commenced, and were to become very popular as a regular showman's turn throughout the nineteenth century.

A

A *Montgolfier hot-air balloon in which
   de Rozier and the Marquis d'Arlandes
   flew over Paris, 21 November 1783.*
B *De Lana's "flying boat", intended to
   be lifted by four hollow copper spheres
   from which the air had been extracted,
   1670.*

B

A

B

C

D

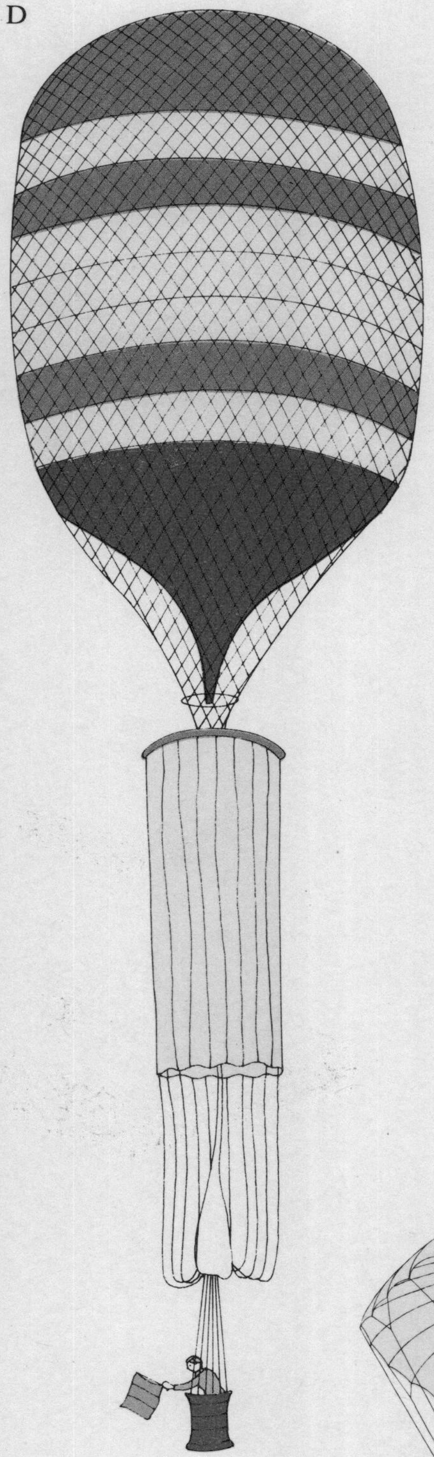

E

A   The balloon in which de Rozier and
    Romain crashed when attempting
    to fly the English Channel in 1785
    consisted of a spherical Charlière
    above a cylindrical Montgolfière.
B   General Meusnier, in France, was one
    of the many who considered the
    problem of how to find a means of
    propelling balloons. He designed this
    airship in 1785, but it was never built.
C   Henri Giffard's dirigible, 1852.
D   André-Jacques Garnerin, the pioneer
    parachutist, made the first successful
    parachute jump in 1797. He was
    carried aloft in the gondola of the
    parachute which was attached to an
    unmanned balloon.
E   The observation balloon Entreprenant
    which was used by the French Army at
    the Battle of Maubeuge, 1794.

D

Various methods of driving and steering balloons were soon attempted, but all proved unsuccessful; as with the yet undeveloped science of aviation, it was the lack of a light and powerful engine that dogged the pioneers.

The helicopter model had been in continuous use in Europe since the fourteenth century: it was now brought into a new prominence with the making, in 1784, of a twin-rotor model—operated by a bow-drill mechanism—by two Frenchmen, Launoy and Bienvenu. It was this model that Sir George Cayley, a young English baronet, saw or heard of some years later: he made a variant of it in 1796, with feathers stuck in corks for the rotor blades. Cayley's model was first published in 1809, and thereafter it gave wide and continued publicity to the helicopter principle: it is the true ancestor of every helicopter flying today.

The idea of heavier-than-air flight by flying-machines with wings had lain dormant for a long time, but had been revived at the end of the eighteenth century, spurred on by the success of the balloon. But it was the arrival in history of Sir George Cayley that was now to bring about a quiet revolution in the new field of aeroplanes. Cayley was one of the great men of his age and the greatest of all the early aeronautical pioneers: he invented the basic principles of the modern aeroplane, and is rightly called "the father of aerial navigation".

Between 1799 and 1809, Cayley laid the foundations of modern aerodynamics, a

E

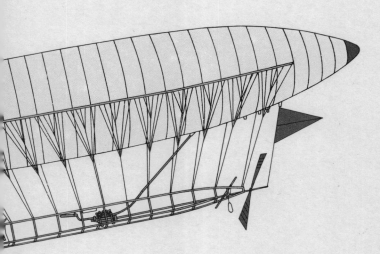

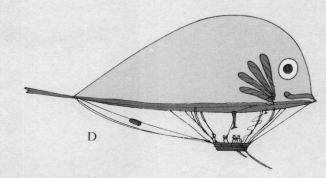

D

A   Man-powered airship of Dupuy de
    Lôme, 1872.
B   First practical airship: the Lebaudy,
    1902—1903.
C   Santos-Dumont's airship No. 6
    rounding the Eiffel Tower, 1901.
D   The fish-shaped "Egg's Folly" airship
    designed by Pauly and Egg, 1816.
E   Modern hydrogen balloon, similar in
    all essential respects to that invented
    by Professor J. A. C. Charles in 1783.

A

B

science unknown till then. He built and flight-tested both model and full-scale fixed-wing gliders, and published (1809—1810) the results of his many experiments, from which all modern aeroplanes derive. Cayley, in studying the bird, decided that the ornithopter (flapping-wing machine) must be replaced by an aircraft with fixed wings, in which the principle of lift was separated from the propulsion system, and in which inherent stability, as well as tail-unit control-surfaces, must be incorporated.

An interesting and far-reaching development occurred in rocketry early in the nineteenth century. Artillery rockets had been invented in China about 1100 A.D. and had reached Europe in the fourteenth century. As already noted, their military application declined, but their pyrotechnic use prospered. As a direct result of the effective use of war rockets by Tippoo Sultan in India against the British army at the end of the eighteenth century, Sir William Congreve in Britain was commissioned to re-invent the artillery rocket

about the year 1805. This weapon, which had marked success when correctly used, and then its successor, the finned Hale rocket, were in action on and off right through the nineteenth century. Rockets were used both by armies and navies, and had a useful range of up to a thousand yards. It was these modest weapons which were the ancestors of space flight today.

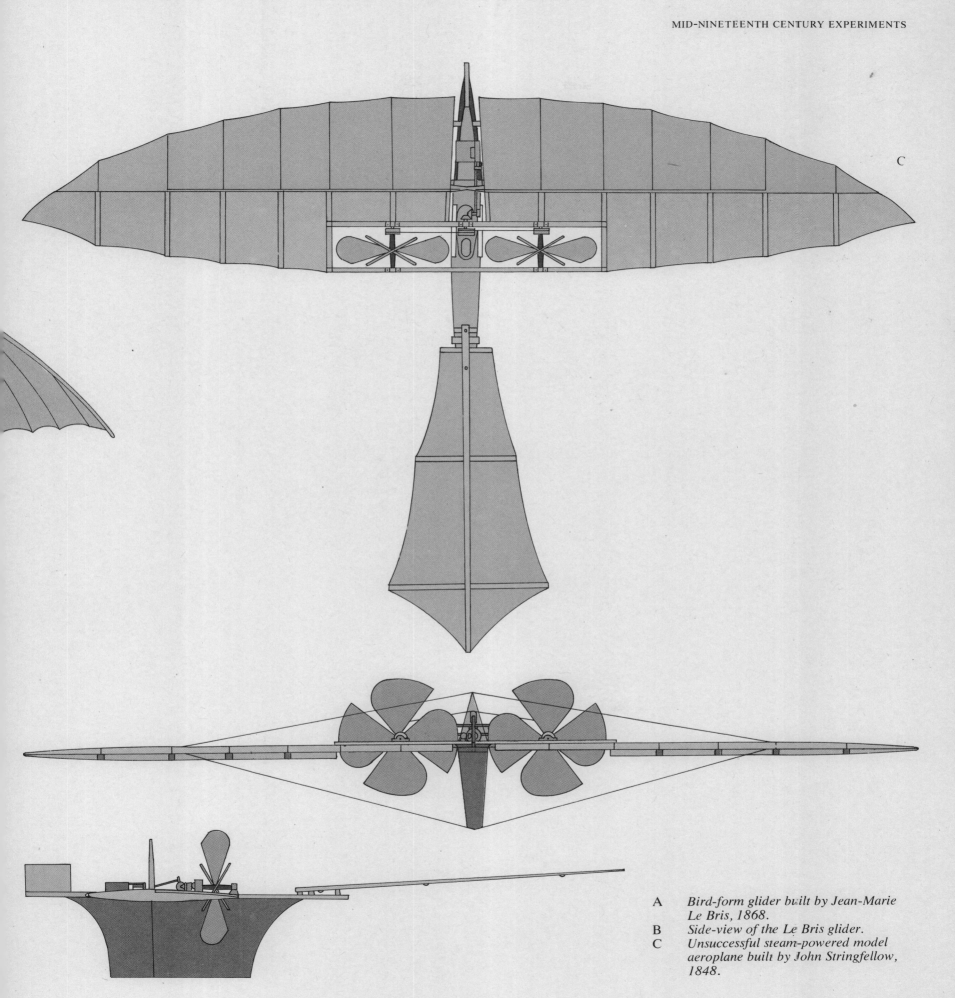

A   *Bird-form glider built by Jean-Marie Le Bris, 1868.*

B   *Side-view of the Le Bris glider.*

C   *Unsuccessful steam-powered model aeroplane built by John Stringfellow, 1848.*

A

D

B

C

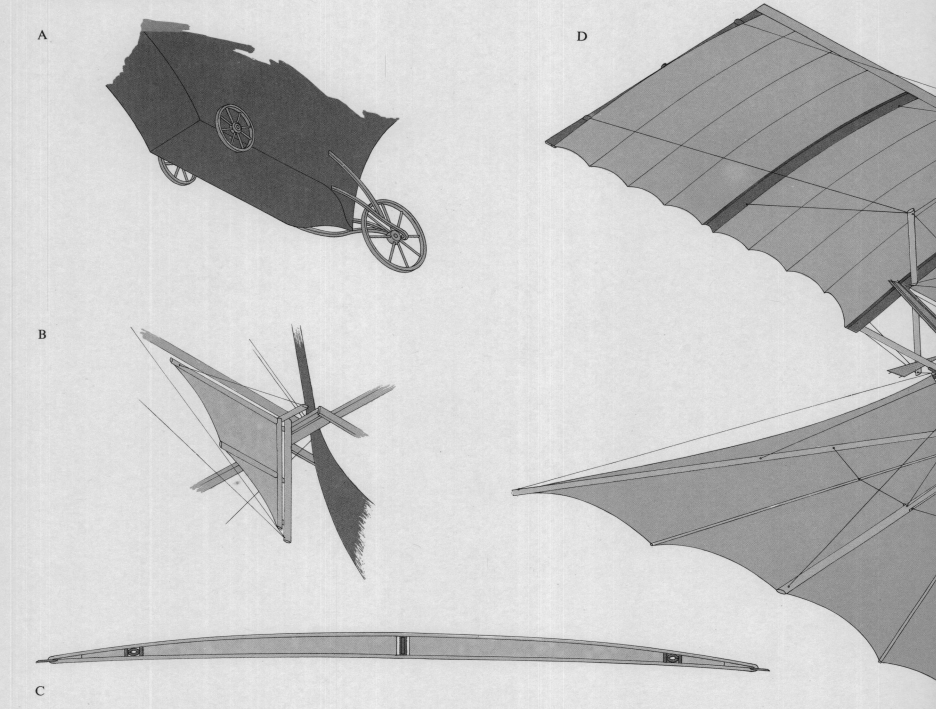

In the first half of the nineteenth century there was little useful activity in aviation except by Cayley, until W. S. Henson published his brilliantly prophetic design for a monoplane "Aerial Steam Carriage" (1843) which was widely and repeatedly republished throughout the century and did much to condition the thinking of later pioneers. This machine was drawn in dramatic pictures, as if it could really fly; these not only appeared all over the world in newspapers and magazines, but were often included in serious text-books. Henson's machine was a monoplane with two pusher propellers, a tricycle

undercarriage, elevator and rudder, and was to be driven by steam. The full-scale machine was never built; however, steam-powered models deriving from the design were built and tested, but with little success.

Meanwhile, the public's interest in the air was kept alive by balloon flights and parachute descents from balloons. Then, off the beaten track, an ominous hint of the future came with the first air-raid of history, when in 1849, pilotless hot-air balloons carrying delayed-action bombs were sent against Venice by the Austrians: luckily, little damage was done. Balloons were again used for mili-

tary observation in the American Civil War (1861—1865), this time equipped with electric telegraph wires to the ground for signalling.

This period also saw the beginnings of the practical dirigible balloon—the "airship" as it came to be called—and the first very slow and experimental flight was made in 1852 by the great French engineer Henri Giffard: his airship was driven by a steam engine, but it could only travel at about 5 mph (c. 8 km/h), and could only be navigated in dead calm weather. But this was a beginning, although the airship was to lag badly behind in the

E

aeronautical pageant, and only a few men became interested in this type of aircraft.

Probably inspired by Henson, the 1850s saw the first French designs for powered aeroplanes; Michel Loup's in 1853, and a highly sophisticated patent by Félix Du Temple in 1857, whose clockwork powered model was the first model aeroplane to fly, in or about the year 1854. In 1858—1859, F. H. Wenham in England carried out his influential tests with multiple high aspect-ratio wings (published 1866—1867), which showed that a cambered wing, at a small angle of incidence, derived most of its lift from the front portion, and hence a long narrow wing was best for lifting. This principle is well shown in nature in the seagull and the albatross, who are wonderful soaring birds equipped with long narrow wings.

Another happening of the greatest importance to future aviation was the drilling of the famous oil-well at Titusville in the United States in 1859: the object was to produce good supplies of kerosene for oil lamps. This oil production was to expand enormously; and by the time motor cars needed petroleum in the 1880s and 1890s, their fuel was ready and waiting for them.

A   *The tricycle landing gear designed by Henson for the Aerial Steam Carriage.*

B   *The aircraft's rudder, or, as Henson called it, the "lateral steering unit".*

C   *Double-surface wing-section.*

D   *The Aerial Steam Carriage, or Ariel, designed by Henson and patented in 1842—1843.*

E   *William Samuel Henson (1805—1888).*

23

The softening wax, that felt a nearer sun,
Dissolved apace, and soon began to run;
The youth in vain his melting pinions shakes,
His feathers gone, no longer air he takes;
O! father, father! as he strove to cry,
Down to the sea he tumbled from on high,
And found his fate; yet still subsists by fame
Among those waters that retain his name.

OVID, DESCRIBING THE FALL OF ICARUS
The Metamorphoses, (8 A. D.)

It is possible to make engines for flying, a man sitting in the midst thereof, by turning only about an instrument, which moves artificial wings made to beat the air, much after the fashion of a bird's flight.

ROGER BACON, *SECRETS OF ART AND NATURE, (CIRCA* 1250)

If the heavens then be penetrable, and no lets, it were not amiss to make wings and fly up; and some new-fangled wits, methinks, should some time or other find out.

ROBERT BURTON (1621)

It is impossible that men should be able to fly craftily by their own strength.

GIOVANNI BORELLI, *DE MOTU ANIMALIUM,* (1680)

CHAPTER ONE

FROM MYTHOLOGY TO 1699 A.D.

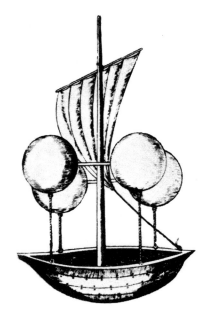

The kite is of ancient Chinese origin and was first used to ward off evil spirits.

G

c. 1483—1490

In Italy, Leonardo da Vinci conducts his experiments in aviation and designs many machines, especially ornithopters, but also including the following:
(a) clack-valve type of wing construction for ornithopters,
(b) a head-harness to operate a rear elevator-*cum*-rudder,
(c) a retractable undercarriage,
(d) a bowstring motor for operating the wing-flapping mechanism,
(e) the world's first parachute,
(f) a helical screw helicopter model operated by clockwork,
(g) finned projectiles.

1503

Giovanni Battista Danti is seriously injured when he attaches wings to his body and jumps from a tower in Perugia, Italy.

1507

John Damian, Abbot of Tungland (and an Italian emigré), attempts to fly with wings from the walls of Stirling Castle, Scotland, and is injured.

1589

First proper description in Europe of a kite by the Italian, Della Porta.

A *Child with propeller toy by Hieronymus Bosch, c. 1500.*
B *The rocket-bird illustrated by Joanes Fontana, c. 1420.*
C *The earliest illustration of a helicopter model: a painted retable in the Musée de Tessé, Le Mans, France, c. 1460.*
D *The earliest illustration of a European windmill: in the Windmill Psalter, c. 1290.*
E *A fantastic flying beast by Hieronymus Bosch, c. 1500.*
F *A helicopter toy, 1584.*
G *A winged windsock kite with a finned bomb from the manuscript of Walter de Milimete, c. 1326.*

A

B

C

D

c. 1595

Sheet- (or sail-) type of parachute is illustrated by the Italian Fausto Veranzio in his *Machinae novae*. As Leonardo's parachute is not to be published until the late 19th century, Veranzio's is the first parachute that the world saw. It derives from a ship's sail, and is here seen being used to escape from a building.
See figure A

1618

First illustration of a "standard" diamond-shaped kite, with tail, appears in a Dutch engraving.
See figure B

1638

Travel to the moon is the subject of fictional works by Bishops Francis Godwin and John Wilkins.
See figure C

c. 1655

Model ornithopters are tested by Robert Hooke, no details survive. First mention of these is published in 1705 *(Posthumous Works)*.

c. 1660

Allard, a tight-rope walker, attempts to fly, at St Germain in France, before Louis XIV, and is seriously injured.

1670

In Italy, Francisco de Lana publishes his *Prodromo*, in which appears his design for a "Flying Ship", to be raised by four vacuum spheres; and also his prophetic description of air-raids and airborne invasion.
See figure D

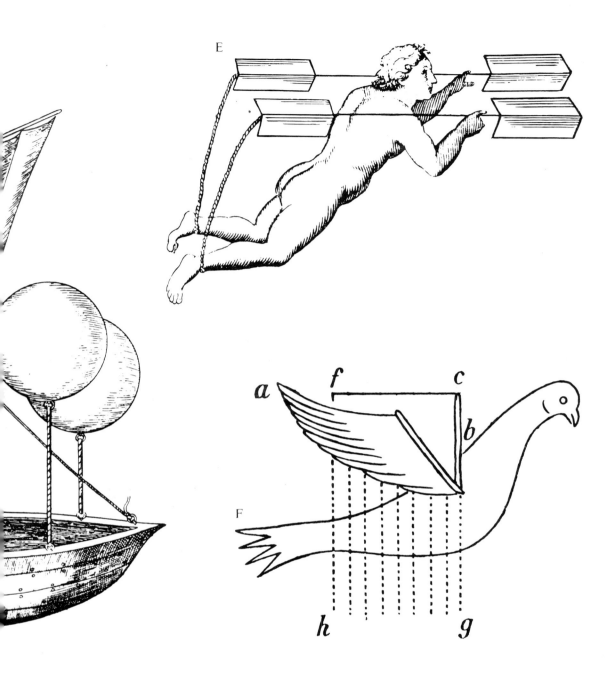

E

G

H

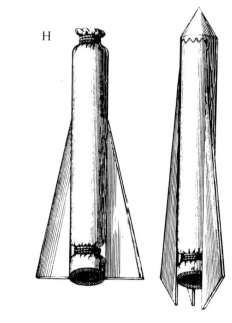

a

f

c

b

F

h

g

1673

De Bernoin attempts to fly with wings at Frankfurt-am-Main, Germany, and is killed.

1678

Besnier attempts to fly at Sablé, France; his primitive apparatus of flapping boards becomes one of the most widely illustrated "aircraft" in history.
See figure E

1680

Giovanni Alphonso Borelli, in Italy, publishes his *De Motu Animalium*, in which

he demonstrates the complete inadequacy of human muscle-power for ornithopter flight. This diagnosis is to hold good until the 1950s when, with modern knowledge of aerodynamics, and modern ultra-light materials, brief man-powered flights will be possible.
See figure F

A   *A design for a parachute by Fausto Veranzio, c. 1595.*

B   *The earliest known illustration of the conventional kite, 1618.*

C   *Domingo Gonsales, the hero of Bishop Godwin's science fiction story* The Man in the Moone, *flew in this "spacecraft", 1638.*

D   *De Lana's proposed "Aerial Ship", 1670.*

E   *Besnier attempting to fly at Sablé, 1678.*

F   *An illustration from Borelli's* De Motu Animalium, *1680.*

G   *An early European diamond-form kite, 1638.*

H   *A design for a delta-wing rocket by Siemienowiez, 1650.*

The judge, . . . when it was alleged that the priso-
ner could fly, remarked that there was no law
against flying.

The Dictionary of National Biography
(ON JANE WENHAM, ACCUSED OF WITCHCRAFT IN 1712)

The time will come, when thou shalt lift thine eyes
To watch a long-drawn battle in the skies,
While aged peasants, too amazed for words,
Stare at the flying fleets of wond'rous birds.
England, so long the mistress of the sea,
Where winds and waves confess her sovereignty,
Her ancient triumphs yet on high shall bear,
And reign, the sovereign of the conquered air.

TRANSLATED FROM GRAY'S *LUNA HABITABILIS* (1737)

"If men were all virtuous", returned the artist, "I
should with great alacrity teach them all to fly.
But what would be the security of the good, if the
bad could at pleasure invade them from the sky?
Against an army sailing through the clouds neither
walls, nor mountains, nor seas, could afford any
security. A flight of northern savages might hover
in the wind, and light at once with irresistible
violence upon the capital of a fruitful region that
was rolling under them."

SAMUEL JOHNSON (1759)

In amusement, mere amusement, I am afraid it
[the air balloon] must end, for I do not find that
its course can be directed so that it should serve
any purpose of communication; and it can give
no new intelligence of the state of the air at
different heights, till they have ascended above
the heights of mountains, which they never seem
likely to do.

SAMUEL JOHNSON (1784)

CHAPTER TWO

FROM 1700 A.D. TO 1792 A.D.

Gusmao's Passarola *was probably far more practical than this contemporary artist's impression would have one believe.*

A

B

C

1709

Bartolomeu Lourenço de Gusmao, the Brazilian Jesuit, at Lisbon, Portugal, probably tests with some success a model glider version of his *Passarola*, misleading illustrations of which are first published during the same year 1709. They later become one of the most widely published aeronautical items in history, and receive much ridicule; but the published illustrations are obviously done by ignorant artists, and the basic design was probably sound.
See opposite

c. 1742

The Marquis de Bacqueville attempts to fly with wings across the River Seine in Paris. He crashes on a washerwoman's barge, and breaks a leg.
See figure A

1764

Melchior Bauer designs an aeroplane propelled by means of eight rows of blades.
See figure B

1766

Henry Cavendish, the English scientist, isolates and describes hydrogen. He calls it "inflammable air".

1768

In France, Alexis Paucton suggests a helical-screw helicopter called a "ptérophore", with another screw to propel it. It is never built.

c. 1772

Canon Desforges builds his winged *"voiture volante"* at Etampes, France; it remains earthbound.

1781

The Frenchman, Jean-Pierre Blanchard, builds his full-size *"vaisseau volant"* (a car to be lifted and propelled by huge man-powered paddles) without success.

1781

Tiberius Cavallo, a Neapolitan living in London, experiments with hydrogen-filled soap-bubbles.

1781

Karl Friedrich Meerwein, architect to the Prince of Baden, tests at Giessen in Germany his ornithopter-*cum*-glider, and almost certainly succeeds in making brief glides.
See figure C

A   *The Marquis de Bacqueville's attempted flight across the Seine, c. 1742.*

B   *Melchior Bauer's design for a flying machine, 1764.*

C   *Meerwein's glider-cum-ornithopter, 1781.*

A

B

4 JUNE 1783

At Annonay in France the Montgolfier brothers, Etienne and Joseph, give the first public demonstration of their hot-air balloon by sending up a large model of linen lined with paper. They believe that the lifting agent is a peculiar form of gas caused by burning chopped straw and wool, and do not realise that the effect is caused by the heating of air.

News of the Montgolfier balloon prompts the Académie des Sciences in Paris to commission the physicist J. A. C. Charles to construct a hydrogen balloon, since the then mysterious Montgolfier "*gas*" seems to exert less lift than hydrogen.
The Académie also commission the Robert brothers to produce a gas-tight balloon fabric for the Charles balloon, which they do rapidly by varnishing lutestring (silk) with dissolved rubber.

27 AUGUST 1783

J. A. C. Charles sends up from the Champ de Mars at Paris his first (small) unmanned hydrogen balloon made of the Roberts' rubberised fabric. It flies for 15 miles (*c.* 24 km) to Gonesse, and there causes a panic, the villagers attacking it with pitchforks and tying it to the tail of a running horse. Hydrogen balloons now often become known as *"Charlières"*.

19 SEPTEMBER 1783

The so-called "*animal ascent*" takes place before the court of Louis XVI at Versailles, France, when the Montgolfiers send up their hot-air balloon carrying a cock, a duck and a sheep in a basket slung beneath it. This is the first aerial voyage in history of living animals; they land safely about 2 miles (3 km) away.
See figure B

OCTOBER 1783

Jet-propulsion of aircraft is first suggested by Joseph Montgolfier: i.e. hot-air to be expelled from a hot-air balloon.

21 NOVEMBER 1783

THE FIRST HUMAN AERIAL VOYAGE IN HISTORY

Pilâtre de Rozier and the Marquis d'Arlandes fly 5 miles (8 km) across Paris in a Montgolfier hot-air balloon, starting from the Château de la Muette in the Bois de Boulogne.
See figure A

DECEMBER 1783

Various theories for the propulsion of balloons are put forward in France; Bulliard

and Seconds favour rocket propulsion while l'Abbé Bertholon suggests compressed air.

1 DECEMBER 1783

J. A. C. Charles and one of the Robert brothers make the first voyage in a hydrogen balloon, designed by Charles, from Paris to Nesle, 27 miles (*c.* 43 km). Modern ballooning derives from this "Charlière", which is fitted with a net, a car, a valve in the crown, ballast and a barometer to act as altimeter. A crowd of 400,000 watch the ascent from the gardens of the Tuileries. *See figure F*

JANUARY 1784

In France, Brisson and Robert independently suggest steam jet-propulsion for balloons.

19 JANUARY 1784

The largest Montgolfière ever made, *Le Fleselle* of 700,000 cubic feet (*c.* 23,000 cubic metres) makes an ascent at Lyon with seven aboard, including Joseph Montgolfier (this was the only ascent by one of the brothers) and De Rozier. Flesselle was the name of the Governor of Lyon.

25 FEBRUARY 1784

First balloon ascent takes place in Italy, when Paul Andreani goes up with the brothers, Agostino and Carlo Gerli, in a Montgolfière from the grounds of his villa at Moncuco near Milan.

28 APRIL 1784

The model helicopter is re-invented by the French scientists Launoy and Bienvenu and is presented before the Académie des Sciences. It takes the form of two contra-rotating-twin-blade rotors operated by a bowstring. It is this device that Cayley copies in 1796 and which—through his publication of it in 1809—leads directly to the whole of modern helicopter development (see 1796).

A   *The first aerial flight of human beings: de Rozier and d'Arlandes, 1783.*
B   *The Montgolfiers send up a sheep, a cock, and a duck in one of their balloons, 1783.*
C   *Etienne and Joseph Montgolfier.*
D   *J. A. C. Charles.*
E   *M. N. Robert.*
F   *The first voyage in a hydrogen balloon, 1783.*
G   *A contra-rotating model helicopter by Launoy and Bienvenu (modern reconstruction), 1784.*

4 JUNE 1784

First woman to make an aerial voyage: Madame Thible ascends at Lyon in the hot-air balloon *Le Gustave* with Fleurant as pilot. They sing to one another as they ascend. Gustav III, King of Sweden, is among the spectators.

7 JULY 1784

First balloon ascent in Austria is made by an Austrian, J. G. Stuver, in a hydrogen balloon at Vienna.

11 JULY 1784

Abbé Miolan and Janinet construct a hot-air balloon to be propelled by the emission of hot-air, but it is destroyed by the crowd on the ground before take-off.

15 SEPTEMBER 1784

First aerial voyage in Britain by the Tuscan Vincenzo Lunardi, an employee of the Italian embassy in London, from the Artillery Ground at Moorfields, London, to Standon (near Ware) in Hertfordshire, a distance of 24 miles (*c.* 38 km).
See figure A

4 OCTOBER 1784

First balloon ascent by a Briton is made by James Sadler in a Montgolfière at Oxford.

16 OCTOBER 1784

First airborne application of the airscrew by Jean-Pierre Blanchard on the car of his balloon when he ascends from Chelsea, London, with Dr John Sheldon. It is hand-operated and ineffective.
See figure C

30 NOVEMBER 1784

First scientific observations made in the air by Dr John Jeffries with Jean-Pierre Blanchard as pilot, in the latter's balloon. They ascend from London. Dr Jeffries is an expatriate physician from America.

1785

General Jean-Baptiste Marie Meusnier in France designs but does not build a remarkably prophetic airship with many modern features, including an ovaloid

envelope, interior ballonet to preserve the shape, a car slung beneath, three man-powered airscrews, etc.
See figure B

7 JANUARY 1785

First crossing of the English Channel by air: Dr John Jeffries and J.-P. Blanchard (piloting his own balloon) from Dover to the forest of Guines near Calais.
See figure D

15 JUNE 1785

First aerial fatalities: Pilâtre de Rozier and Pierre-Ange Romain are killed near Boulogne in attempting a France-to-England Channel crossing, when their combination hot-air and hydrogen balloon catches fire and crashes. A spherical hydrogen balloon was placed on top of a cylindrical hot-air balloon, a highly dangerous combination.

12 JULY 1785

First balloon ascent in Holland is made by J.-P. Blanchard at the Hague.

3 OCTOBER 1785

First balloon ascent in Germany is made by J.-P. Blanchard at Frankfurt-am-Main.

20 NOVEMBER 1785

First balloon ascent in Belgium is made by J.-P. Blanchard at Ghent.

A   *The first aerial voyage in England, by Lunardi, 1784.*
B   *A prophetic design for an airship, by General Meusnier, 1785.*
C   *The first use of an airscrew on a full-size aircraft, by Blanchard, on his balloon, 1784.*
D   *The first Channel crossing by balloon, 1785.*

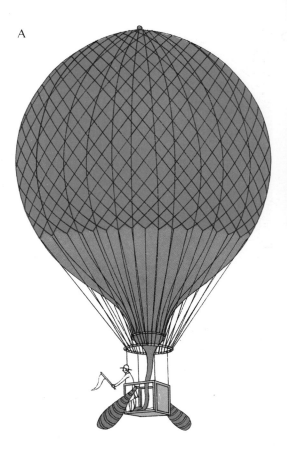

A

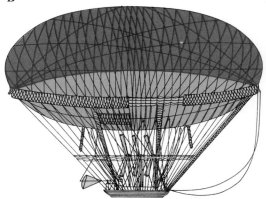

B

C

D

The whole problem is confined within these limits, viz.—To make a surface support a given weight by the application of power to the resistance of air.

SIR GEORGE CAYLEY (1809)

I may be expediting the attainment of an object that will in time be found of great importance to mankind; so much so, that a new era in society will commence from the moment that aerial navigation is familiarly realised.... I feel perfectly confident, however, that this noble art will soon be brought home to man's convenience, and that we shall be able to transport ourselves and families, and their goods and chattels, more securely by air than by water, and with a velocity of from 20 to 100 miles per hour.

SIR GEORGE CAYLEY (1809)

An uninterrupted navigable ocean, that comes to the threshold of every man's door, ought not to be neglected as a source of human gratification and advantage.

SIR GEORGE CAYLEY (1816)

I suppose we shall soon travel by air-vessels; make air instead of sea-voyages; and at length find our way to the moon, in spite of the want of atmosphere.

LORD BYRON (1822)

CHAPTER THREE

FROM 1793 A.D. TO 1834 A.D.

Archiv Aero-Club der Schweiz

"Egg's Folly" was the nickname of this
dolphin-shaped balloon which was designed
by S.J. Pauly and Durs Egg, two Swiss
armourers living in London.

A

B

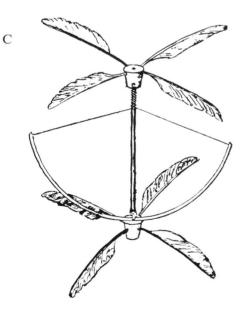

C

9 JANUARY 1793

First balloon ascent in America is made by J.-P. Blanchard at Philadelphia.
See figure B

2 JUNE 1794

First military aerial reconnaissance by J.M.J. Coutelle for the French army at Maubeuge from the balloon *Entreprenant*, which was captive. Later, on June 26, observations were also effectively made against the Austrians at the Battle of Fleurus.
See figure A

1796

Sir George Cayley, an English baronet, copying the type of model helicopter made by Launoy and Bienvenu (see 1784), makes a model consisting of two bowstring-operated contra-rotating rotors, each composed of corks stuck with four feathers: this is to be published by Sir George in 1809, and will directly influence the whole of subsequent helicopter development.
See figure C

22 OCTOBER 1797

First human parachute drop from the air is made by André-Jacques Garnerin from an unpiloted hydrogen balloon over what is today the Parc Monceau at Paris. The parachute is of the ribbed parasol-type.

16 OCTOBER 1798

Pierre Tétu-Brissy makes the first balloon ascent on horseback in France.

A   *The first military aerial reconnaissance by the French Army at Maubeuge, 1794.*
B   *The first aerial voyage in the United States, by Blanchard, 1793.*
C   *Cayley's helicopter model, based on that of Launoy and Bienvenu, 1796.*

1799

First design for modern configuration aeroplane i.e. with fixed main wings, and tail-unit comprising rudder and elevator, by Sir George Cayley. This is also the first design for a fixed-wing powered aeroplane (using flappers).
See figure A

1799

Rockets used by the Indian army of Tippoo Sahib against the British Army in India. This leads to Congreve's work (see 1805).

1804

First flight of an aeroplane of modern configuration, i.e. with fixed wings and tail-unit comprising stabilising and control surfaces: Sir George Cayley's model glider.
See figure C

Also in this year, Cayley makes the first use of a whirling arm for aeronautical research, to test aerofoils.
See figure B

23 AUGUST 1804

Balloon ascent to make scientific observations, by Gay-Lussac and his assistant Biot, from Paris.

1805

First realisation of the laterally stabilising effect of the dihedral angle, and its incorporation in an aeroplane design and probably a model, by Sir George Cayley.

1805

William Congreve achieves a practical war rocket at Woolwich in London and is officially encouraged to proceed; this is the start of all modern rocketry.
See figure E

1806

First modern European war rockets in action. These are Congreve rockets fired by the British Navy against Boulogne.

1807

Sir George Cayley is the first to realise that a cambered aerofoil provides more lift than a flat one.

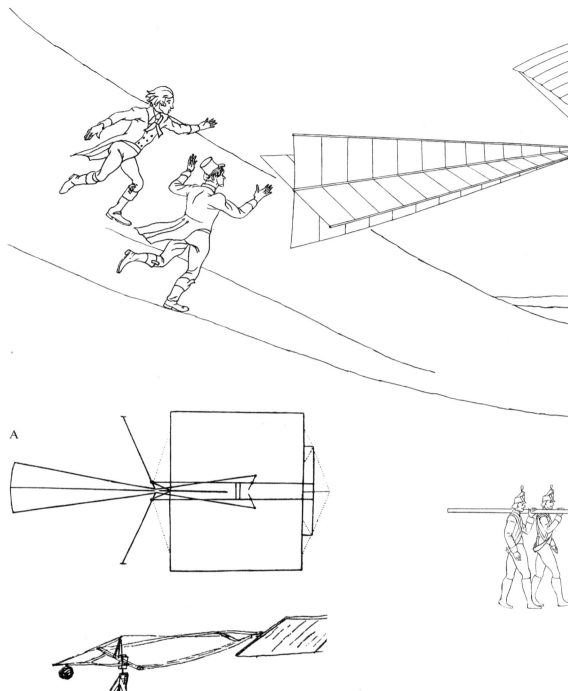

A

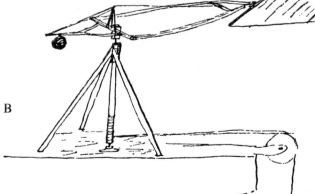

B

C

D

E

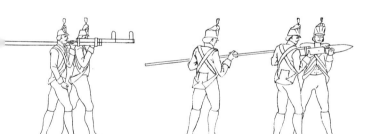

4 AUGUST 1807

First night ascent in a balloon by André Jacques Garnerin at Paris.

2—5 SEPTEMBER 1807

Copenhagen is partially destroyed by Congreve rockets fired by the British Navy during the siege.

1808—1809

During the next two years, Sir George Cayley's experiments in aeronautics lead him to the following achievements:

1808

1. First proper application of the dihedral angle for lateral stability in aviation in a kite and in a model aeroplane.
2. First proper understanding and description of the technique of bird propulsion, i.e. the propeller action of the outer primary feathers.
3. Invention of the cycle-type tension wheel, and the suggestion that it should be applied to aeroplane under-carriages.
4. First investigation of the movement of the centre of pressure on an aerofoil.

1809

5. First full-size modern configuration aeroplane flies, mostly unmanned, but on occasion carrying a man for several yards: Cayley's first aero-plane, which is equipped with propulsive flappers, but is only tested as a glider.
6. First investigation of aeronautical streamlining and the design of a solid of least resistance based on the shape of the trout.
7. First realisation that there is an area of low pressure above a cambered wing which contributes to the lift; Cayley publishes this in 1810.
8. First suggestion of an internal combustion engine for aircraft and publication of this.

1809

Jacob Degen's tests in Vienna with his balloon-supported ornithopter are widely reported in the Press, and are the direct cause of Cayley publishing his classic triple paper "On Aerial Navigation".
See figure C

1809—1810

Cayley publishes his triple paper "On Aerial Navigation" (in Nicholson's *Journal of Natural Philosophy*), which lays the foundations of modern aerodynamics. It deals with longitudinal and lateral stability, movement of the centre of pressure, cambered wings, streamlining, etc., etc.

31 MAY 1811

Berblinger, the "Tailor of Ulm" attempts to fly at Ulm in Germany using a Degen-type ornithopter, but without the supporting balloon; he crashes into the River Danube, but is unhurt.

JUNE 1813

The Rocket Brigade founded in the British Army. It first goes into action against Napoleon's army at the Battle of Göhrde on 16 September 1813. This is the first modern military rocket unit.

c. 1816

First balloon is sent up in the Arctic, by the explorer Clarke in the presence of Lapps, at Enontekiö, Sweden. It is an unmanned Montgolfière.

1816

First design for a streamlined airship also the first design for a semi-rigid airship; by Sir George Cayley.

27 AUGUST 1816

The pirate fleet and base at Algiers are bombarded and destroyed by the British Navy, much of the damage to the ships being done by Congreve rockets.
See figure D

1816—1817

Two expatriate Swiss, S.J. Pauly and Durs Egg, partially complete their fish-form airship at Knightsbridge, London. It is abandoned when Pauly dies; there is a famous colour print of this machine.

1817

First proposal for compartmentation into separate gas cells in an airship; by Sir George Cayley.

19 JULY 1821

Coal-gas first used for inflating balloons by Charles Green in London: this ascent is Green's first, and is part of the coronation festivities of George IV.
See figure A

c. 1825

George Pocock sends up the first woman to fly beneath a kite; Martha Pocock, his daughter, who is to become the mother of W. G. Grace, the famous English cricketer.

8 JANUARY 1827

George Pocock successfully demonstrates his "char-volant"—a kite-drawn carriage—on the road between Bristol and Marlborough in England.

1831

First fixed tandem-wing aeroplane design published, in the second edition of his *Treatise upon the Art of Flying*, by Walker. This design, which has propulsive flappers amidships, but is never built, will almost certainly influence D. S. Brown (see 1873—1874), and, through him, Langley.
See figure B

17 AUGUST 1834

Comte de Lennox builds his airship *L'Aigle* in Paris. It is to be propelled by eight manually-operated flappers. When being inflated for the first time it escapes from its net, rises, bursts, and is destroyed by the crowd.

A   *Charles Green.*
B   *Walker's design for a tandem-wing monoplane, 1831.*
C   *Degen's flap-valve ornithopter without its balloon assistance, 1813.*
D   *The bombardment of the pirate fleet and base at Algiers by the British Navy using Congreve rockets, 1816.*

A

D

B

C

For I dipt into the future, far as human eye
    could see,
Saw the Vision of the world, and all the wonder
    that would be;
Saw the heavens fill with commerce, argosies of
    magic sails,
Pilots of the purple twilight, dropping down with
    costly bales;
Heard the heavens fill with shouting, and there
    rain'd a ghastly dew
From the nations' airy navies grappling in the
    central blue;
Far along the world-wide whisper of the south-
    wind rushing warm,
With the standards of the peoples plunging
    thro' the thunder-storm;·
Till the war-drum throbb'd no longer, and the
    battle-flags were furl'd
In the Parliament of man the Federation of
    the World.

                      LORD TENNYSON (1842)

By land let them travel, as many as list.
And by sea, those who like the hard fare,
In an airy balloon, whilst I sit at my ease,
And pleasantly glide through the air!
Round this globe, the farthest they can reach,
Let them travel night, morning and noon;
Such excursions as these are but bagatelles,
When compared with a trip to the moon!

                   LITERARY WORLD, London, 1840

Astounding News! Atlantic crossing in three
    days!
Signal triumph for Mr Monck Mason's Flying
    Machine.

    A HOAX HEADLINE IN THE *NEW YORK SUN*, 13 APRIL, 1844.

CHAPTER FOUR

FROM 1835 A.D. TO 1858 A.D.

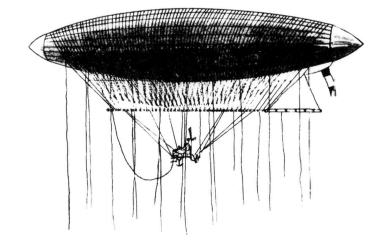

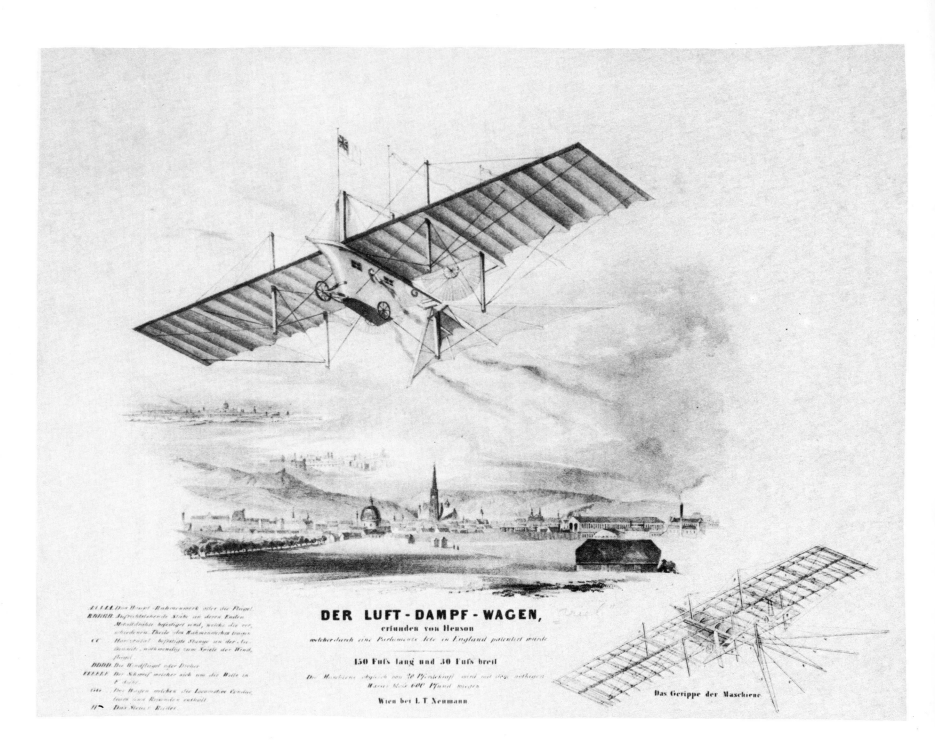

William S. Henson's Aerial Steam Carriage, *1847, had great influence on designs due to the fact that it was illustrated widely and often. (The Engineering-Transportation Library, The University of Michigan).*

A

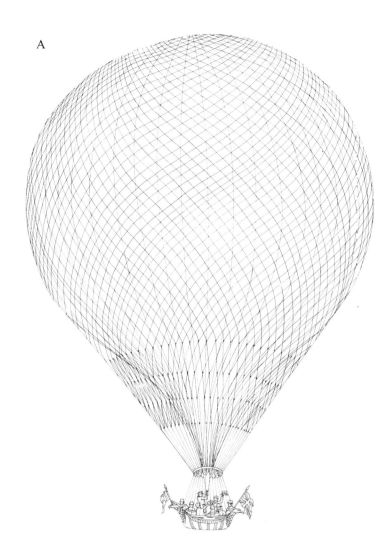

A   The Great Balloon of Nassau *which made one of the most publicised balloon flights of the 19th century.*

8 APRIL 1835

H. H. Clayton makes a balloon flight from Cincinnati to Monroe County, Virginia, USA, 350 miles (*c.* 560 km) in 9$^1/_2$ hours.

7—8 NOVEMBER 1836

Charles Green, Robert Hollond and Monck Mason fly in Green's *Vauxhall Balloon* from Vauxhall Gardens in London to Weilburg, Nassau, in Germany, 480 miles (*c.* 770 km) in 18 hours. The balloon is afterwards rechristened *The Great Balloon of Nassau*. On this voyage the trail-rope is first used by Green, following a suggestion by Thomas Baldwin in his book *Airopaidia*, published in 1786.
See figure A

24 JULY 1837

Robert Cocking is killed at Lee Green, London, on his Cayley-derived dihedral parachute. It is released from a balloon and breaks up in the air. He is the first man to be killed on a heavier-than-air-machine.

MARCH 1839

Charles Green exhibits in England a model spherical balloon equipped with a clock-work-driven propeller for both propulsion and aiding the lift.

27 APRIL 1839

The ripping-panel, for quick emptying of the balloon after landing, is first used by John Wise in the United States.

1840

Charles Green suggests and makes a model of a propeller-driven spherical balloon, with a trail-rope fitted with floats, to fly the Atlantic.

1842

In England, W. H. Phillips successfully flies a model helicopter, the blades of whose rotor are propelled from their tips by gas from the combustion of coal, saltpetre and gypsum.

A

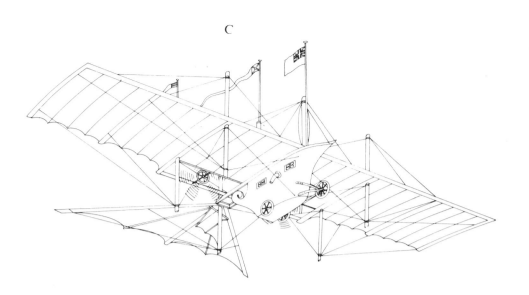

C

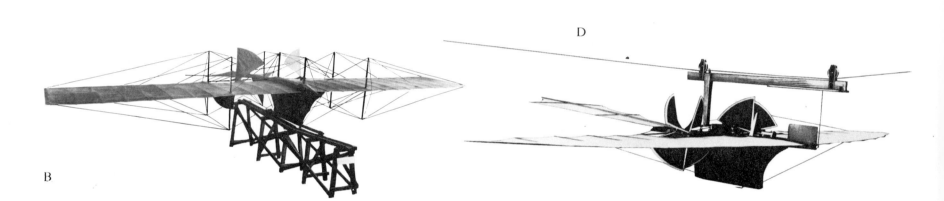

B

D

1843

In England, Monck Mason builds and tests his airscrew-driven model airship.

MARCH 1843

William Samuel Henson receives the patent, and publishes, in London, his design for an "Aerial Steam Carriage". It is the first design for an airscrew-propelled modern-configuration monoplane, and, through world-wide and oft-repeated publicity, does much to condition the basic configuration of the modern monoplane.
See figure C

APRIL 1843

Sir George Cayley publishes his design for a convertiplane, incorporating helicopter

rotors which close to form wings, and two airscrews for forward propulsion.

1846

John Wise, during the Mexican War, suggests bombarding Vera Cruz from a tethered balloon flown down wind over the city. The idea is not carried out.

2—3 SEPTEMBER 1846

The Alps are first crossed by balloon, from Marseilles to Stubini near Turin, by Francisque Arban.

1847

First airscrew-propelled aeroplane—a model—is tested: Henson's steam-driven

model, based on his *Aerial Steam Carriage* of 1843. But it fails to fly.
See figure B

6 JULY 1847

Richard Gypson, with Henry Coxwell and John Gale, makes a perilous but safe descent in his balloon over London after it bursts. He cuts the neck-line, and allows the envelope to float up into the top of the net and act as a parachute.
See figure A

1848

John Stringfellow, Henson's friend, carries on the latter's work, and tests his own steam-driven model monoplane. It is promising, but cannot make sustained flights.
See figure D

E

1849

First incorporation in an aeroplane of adjustable rear stabilising surfaces with separately operated elevator-*cum*-rudder by Sir George Cayley in his full-size triplane.

JUNE 1849

First bombing raid: pilotless hot-air balloons are sent against Venice by the Austrians, the bombs being released by timing devices. No lives are lost and little damage is done. *See figure E*

1850s

Heavier-than-air aeronautics at mid-century, and for nearly two decades thereafter, is still shunned by the established and conventional world of science. But a number of technically-minded individuals, engineers and other professional men are beginning to concern themselves with the problems of mechanical flight; and by the mid-sixties these pioneers are to make their work and interests felt by a larger professional audience, and at last begin to attract attention in the higher ranks of science.

1850

Sir George Cayley makes the first instrument to investigate aeronautical streamlining. It is a variety of whirling arm.

MAY 1850

Hugh Bell ascends in his man-powered airship with one airscrew from Kennington, London. It is called the *Locomotive Balloon*. But it cannot be propelled, and drifts for 30 miles (*c.* 48 km).

A   *The perilous descent in Gypson's balloon, 1847.*
B   *Henson's unsuccessful model monoplane, 1847.*
C   *Henson's famous design for his* Aerial Steam Carriage, *1843.*
D   *Stringfellow's steam-powered model monoplane, 1848.*
E   *The first bombing raid in history, by the Austrians against Venice, 1849.*

A   *Cayley's design for a glider, 1852.*
B   *The first feasible airship, by Henri Giffard, 1852.*
C   *Letur's parachute-type glider, 1854.*
D   *The first French design for a powered aeroplane, by Loup, 1863.*
E   *Wenham's multi-wing glider of 1859 (illustration first published in 1866).*
F   *The Le Bris glider on its launching car, 1857.*

B
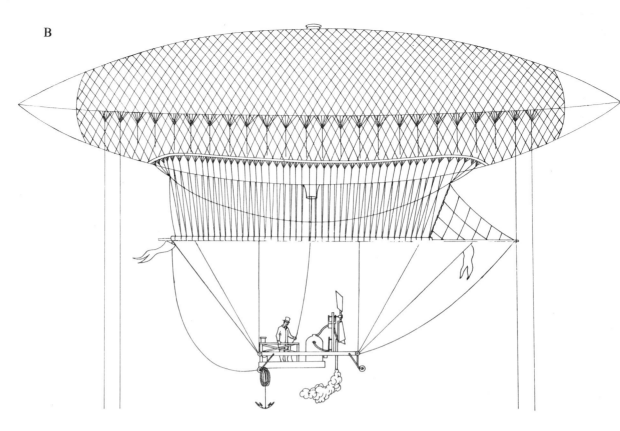

A

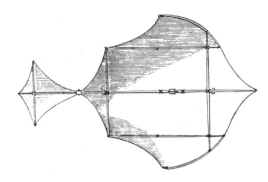

29 JUNE 1850

J. A. Barral and A. J. Bixio make the first of their balloon ascents at Paris to carry out scientific observations.

14 JULY 1850

The aeronaut Eugène Poitevin makes a balloon ascent sitting astride a horse at Paris.

9 SEPTEMBER 1850

Charles F. Durant, the first great American aeronaut, makes his first balloon ascent, from Castle Garden, New York.

NOVEMBER 1850

Pierre Jullien, a French clockmaker, in the Paris Hippodrome, successfully flies his prophetic streamlined airship model propelled by two clockwork-driven airscrews.

1852

The Société Aérostatique et Météorologique de France, the first aeronautical society in the world, is founded.

24 SEPTEMBER 1852

First powered aircraft, and first airship, to make a tentative flight: Henri Giffard's steam-powered airship, with a maximum speed of 6 mph (*c.* 10 km/h), flies 17 miles (*c.* 27 km) from Paris to Trappers. This craft is only tentative, but marks the beginning of the practical airship.
See figure B

25 SEPTEMBER 1852

Sir George Cayley publishes illustrations, a description and instructions how to fly a full-size glider, in the *Mechanics Magazine*, and calls it a "governable parachute": if this had been acted upon, successful glider

flight would have been possible by the 1860s.
See figure A

1853

First successful manned gliding flight: Cayley's third full-size aeroplane—almost certainly a triplane—is tested, and makes a flight across a small valley at Brompton Hall, near Scarborough in Yorkshire, with Cayley's coachman on board, but as a passenger rather than as pilot. It is known as the "coachman-carrier".

1853

First French design for an airscrew-propelled fixed-wing aeroplane, by Michel Loup. The two airscrews are large wing-like devices set into the wings.
See figure D

C

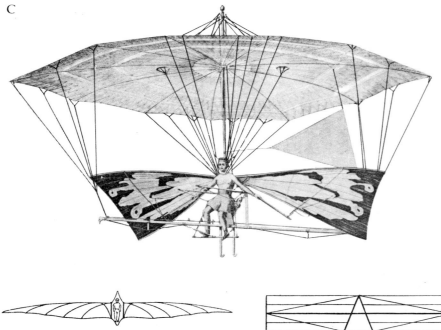

D

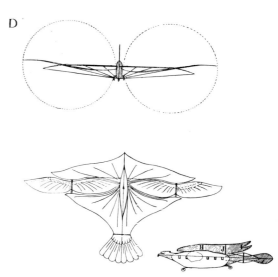

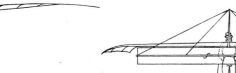

E

F

c. 1853

The Frenchman, Boquet de la Gye, tests aeroplane models propelled by rockets.

27 JUNE 1854

Louis-Charles Letur is dragged over trees, etc., in his parachute-type glider, at Tottenham, near London. He dies from his injuries on 5 July.
See figure C

1857

Jean Marie le Bris, a French sea-captain, builds and tests his first full-size glider, based on the albatross. At Tréfeuntec, near Douarnenez, France, he mounts it on a cart and releases it when the cart is drawn along at speed; he thus makes one short glide, but he crashes at the second attempt, and breaks his leg.
See figure F

c. 1857—1858

First successful flight by a powered model aeroplane, made by Félix Du Temple, a French naval officer. It was a monoplane with swept-forward wings, powered by clockwork.

2 SEPTEMBER 1858

Samuel King introduces the drag-rope in America, following Baldwin's suggestion (1786) and Charles Green's first use of it (see 1836).

OCTOBER 1858

First aerial photograph is taken by Nadar from a captive balloon over Paris by the wet-plate collodion process.

c. 1858—1859

In England, F. H. Wenham tests both models and his full-size multiplane glider, and establishes that a cambered wing derives most of its lift from the front portion, and that Cayley was correct in advocating a superposed wing structure for maximum lift with strength of structure. His resulting paper is later published (see 1866).
See figure E

2 JULY 1859

John Wise flies in his balloon with John La Mountain and two others from St Louis, Missouri to Henderson, New York State, 809 miles (*c.* 1300 km) in 20 hours.

SECTION II

FROM THE INVENTION OF THE GAS ENGINE TO THE FLIGHTS OF THE FIRST SUCCESSFUL AEROPLANES, 1860 TO 1907 A.D.

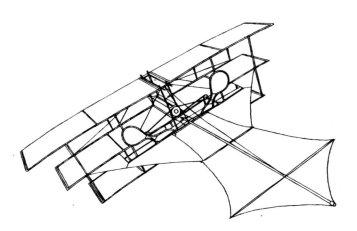

John Stringfellow exhibited his steam-powered model triplane at the Aeronautical Society's exhibition in the Crystal Palace, London, in 1868. Although-not itself successful, it was widely published and led to the growth of the biplane concept in aviation.

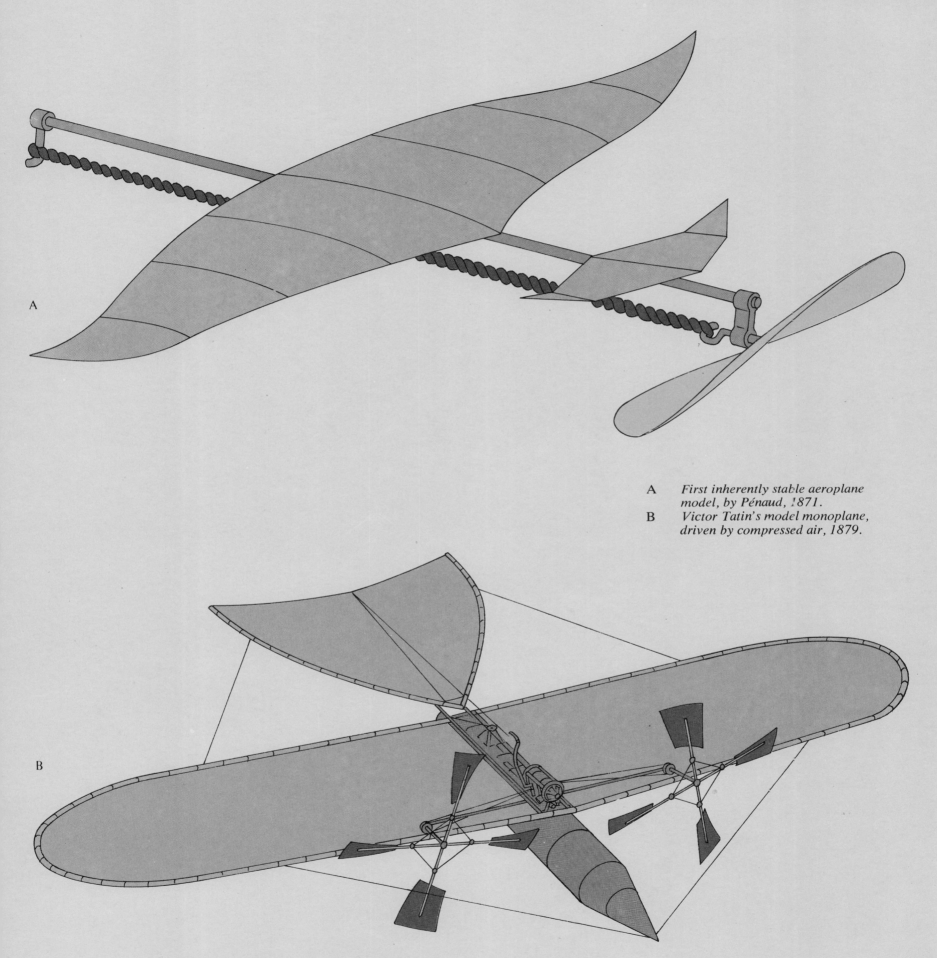

A First inherently stable aeroplane
  model, by Pénaud, 1871.
B Victor Tatin's model monoplane,
  driven by compressed air, 1879.

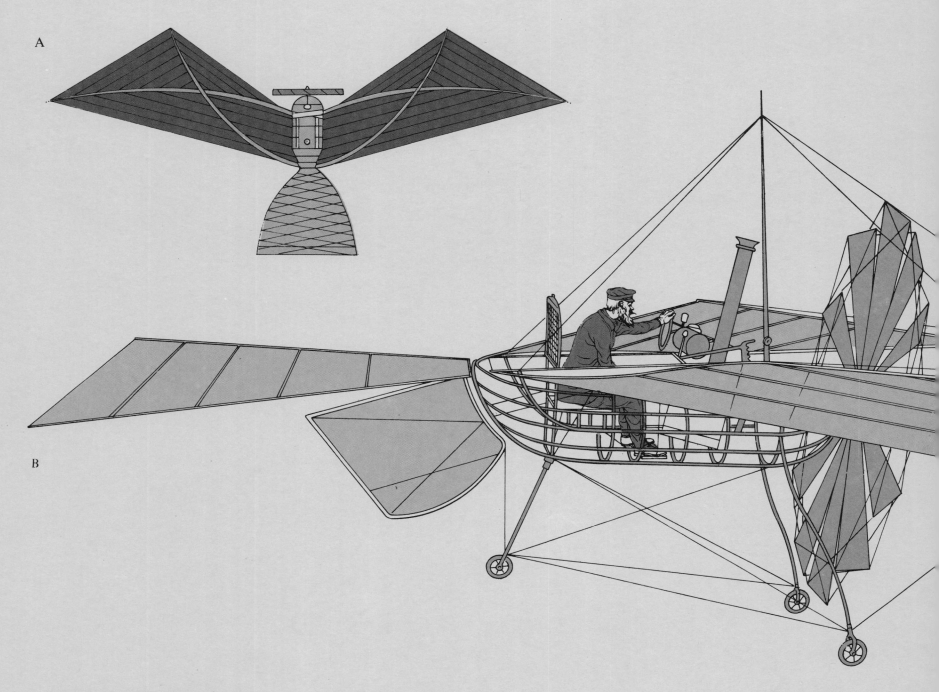

A

B

The biggest stumbling-block to progress both in airships and aeroplanes in the second half of the nineteenth century was the lack of a light and powerful engine. But in 1860 the future was ensured, for in this year the gas engine was invented in France by Lenoir, in which gas was exploded in the cylinders to drive down the pistons.

The 1860s saw an important change in the type of men taking up aviation. This subject now started attracting many more professional and mechanically-minded men, and, as if to mark this change, there came the foundation in 1863 of the Société d'Aviation in France to encourage heavier-than-air flight, followed by the Aeronautical Society (now Royal) of Great Britain in 1866. At the first meeting of the latter, in June 1866, Wenham

read his paper on "Aerial Locomotion" in which his suggestion of high aspect-ratio wings was to have a far-reaching influence. There was also much activity in France, where the first properly thought-out design for a jet-propelled aeroplane was made—but no attempt was made to build it—by Charles de Louvrié (1865). This was followed in England in 1867 by the first delta wing jet designs by J. W. Butler and E. Edwards which closely resemble the familiar classroom paper dart; but these, too, were not built. Also in France there arose a widespread addiction to making helicopter models, many of which were successful and helped promote the idea of aviation in the public mind.

Back in Britain, the Aeronautical Society

staged the world's first aeronautical exhibition at the Crystal Palace in 1868, in which Stringfellow exhibited his new steam-powered model triplane: although not itself successful, this model was widely and repeatedly published, and led directly to the growth of the superposed wing concept (biplanes, triplanes, etc.) in aviation.

The 1870s saw a significant advance in the design of aeroplanes, as well as the arrival of the popular elastic-powered model (1870), a power-unit which is still, and probably always will be, in use for model flying. It was first publicly seen (1871) in Alphonse Pénaud's model monoplane at Paris—called a "Planophore"—in which he displayed the principles of inherent stability, and with which he gave to the would-be pioneers one of the

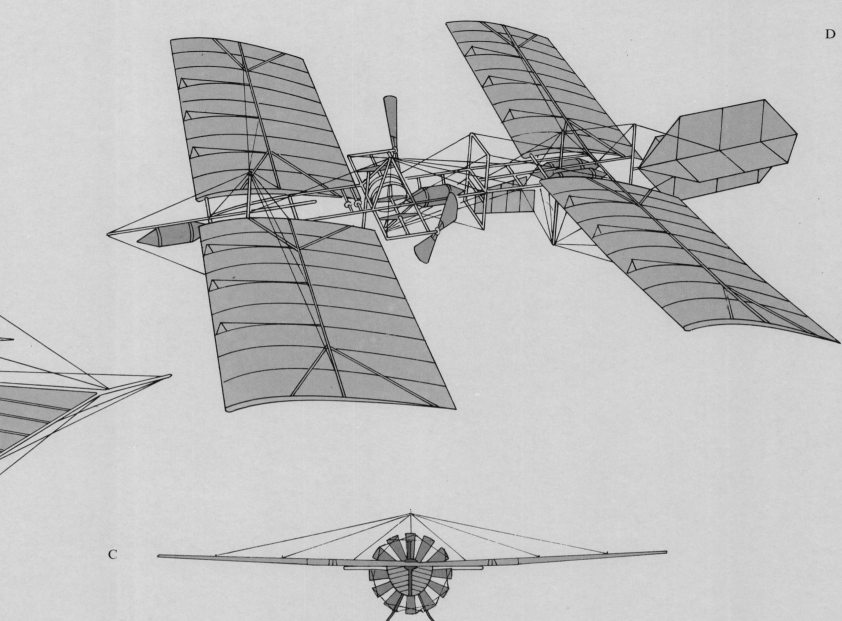

C

most important demonstrations in the history of aviation.

One of the most influential inventions of the 1870s was the four-stroke petrol engine, produced by the German engineer Otto in 1876, from which all petrol piston engines today are descended.

The 1880s provided a strange lull before the widespread inventive explosion of the next decade. But one vital illustrated and published item was issued in 1884—the Englishman Horatio Phillips' patent for his double-surface aerofoils: he was the first to demonstrate that, on a double-surface wing, with the curvature of the upper surface being greater than that of the lower, by far the major amount of lift is created by the low pressure (partial "suction") produced by the

pronounced curvature of the *upper* surface, and the lesser amount by the pressure of the air on the flatter under-surface: this was an epoch-making discovery which was to vitally influence all mature designers in the years to come.

Of the utmost future importance to aviation was the appearance in 1885 of the first practical petrol motor-car, built by Carl Benz; this was a three-wheeler, but a proper automobile. Even more important was the first Daimler car which came the following year, powered by Daimler's excellent high-speed petrol engine, derived from Otto's four-stroke cycle motor of 1876. For aviation was to call heavily on the crafts of the motor car constructor, and its driver, in the epoch shortly to open.

A Plan-view of the hot-air powered aeroplane built by the French naval officer, Felix du Temple de la Croix, and tested about 1874. It was the first aeroplane to make a powered take-off, although it was assisted by being launched down a sloping ramp.

B Side view of du Temple's aeroplane showing where the pilot sat.

C Head-on view of the same.

D The tandem-wing Aerodrome, built by Samuel Pierpont Langley and piloted by Charles Manly, which failed to fly in 1903.

A   *Percy Pilcher's hang-glider* Hawk.
B   *The Wright brothers' glider.*
C   *Sir George Cayley's full-size*
      "coachman-carrier".
D   *Otto Lilienthal's hang-glider.*
E   *Octave Chanute's hang-glider.*

A

B

C

D

E

The 1890s and the early years of this century, saw the final parting of the ways for the aviation pioneers: on the one hand there were the "power" pioneers who, like chauffeurs, believed that all they needed was lift and thrust, with the minimum of flight-control: and on the other, there were the gliding pioneers—the true airmen—who realised that they must learn to control their engine-less aircraft properly in flight before power was applied. The powered chauffeurs failed to a man. Ader just managed to take off in his steam-powered *Eole* in 1890, but could not sustain or control it. And in 1897, with his *Avion III*, he failed even to take off.

The expatriate American, Sir Hiram Maxim, in England, built and tried out his huge biplane test-rig in 1894: it would just raise itself from its rails, but that was all, and it was abandoned. And in the United States, the astronomer S. P. Langley, after some success with steam-powered models (1896), saw his full-scale petrol-driven *Aerodrome* —his misnomer for an aeroplane—crash twice at take-off in 1903. It, too, was abandoned.

The greatest pioneer of the later part of the century was the German, Otto Lilienthal, who was the first man properly to launch himself into the air in hang-gliders and fly successfully, between 1891 and 1896: his death when flying in 1896, and his outstanding example, was to inspire the Wright brothers. The Scotsman, Percy Pilcher, might have fared even better, but he was killed gliding in 1899. In 1896, the great American engineer, Octave Chanute, had brought the hang-glider to the limit of its usefulness—a hang-glider was controlled only by the pilot's body movements—before there appeared the two men who were to conquer the air, absolutely and unequivocally; these men were the American brothers, Wilbur and Orville Wright, who ran a small bicycle shop in Dayton, Ohio.

A

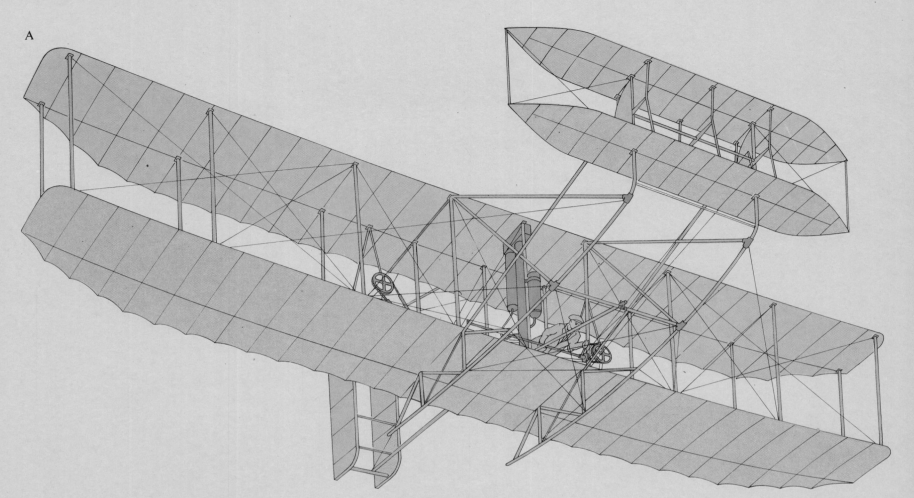

B

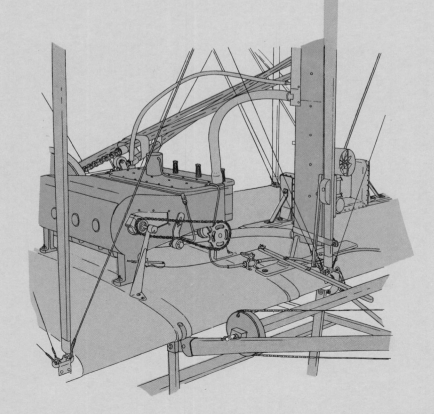

The Wrights first built and flew three biplane gliders (1900—1902), with the last of which they achieved full three-axis flight-control—control in pitch, yaw and roll—by means of movable surfaces. They went on to make the world's first powered, sustained, and controlled aeroplane flights in 1903 with their biplane *Flyer I*. They then built two more *Flyers*, and, with *Flyer III* (1905), they achieved the first practical flying-machine in history, which could be banked, turned and circled with ease, and could fly for over half an hour. The Wrights designed and built all their own aircraft, engines and propellers, with no financial assistance.

Meanwhile, Europe, after the death of Lilienthal, had become almost moribund, aeronautically speaking; but slowly—from

C

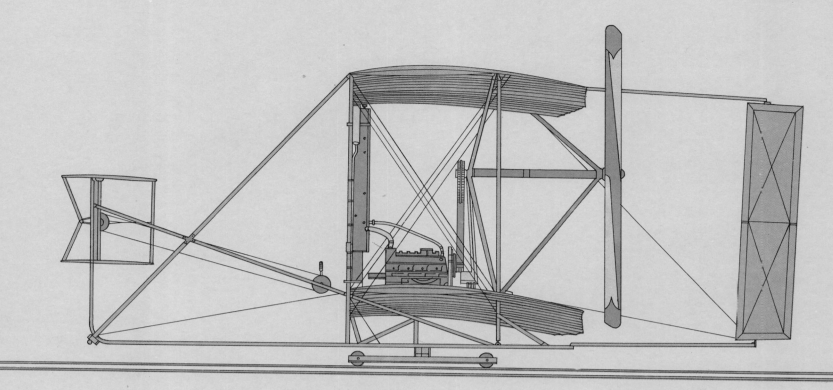

D

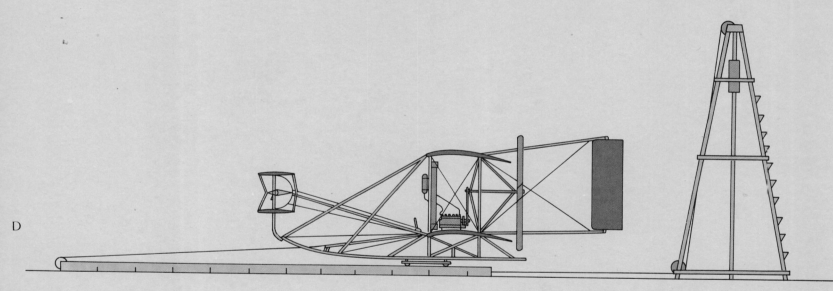

1902 to 1907—under the influence of the Wrights, her pioneers progressed from primitive gliders to primitive powered aircraft, the first powered hops in Europe being made in Paris by the Brazilian Alberto Santos-Dumont in 1906.

The airship scene had at last reached a stage of practicality with Santos-Dumont's little dirigibles—one of which circled the Eiffel Tower in 1901—and the French *Lebaudy* airship of 1902–1903. The first Zeppelin had been tentatively flown in 1900, but these craft did not become a practical proposition until later on.

In 1907, the Wrights sent one of their new and improved biplanes to France, which had to await the coming year 1908 before it was flown with brilliant success.

A *The world's first aeroplane to make a powered, sustained and controlled flight was the Wright* Flyer I, *17 December 1903. Here shown is the later* Flyer III.
Orville Wright, who piloted the aeroplane, described the occasion thus:
"The course of the flight up and down was exceedingly erratic. The control of the front rudder was difficult. As a result, the machine would rise suddenly to about ten feet, and then as suddenly dart for the ground. A sudden dart when a little over 120 feet from the point at which it rose into the air, ended the flight.

This flight lasted only twelve seconds, but it was nevertheless the the first in the history of the world in which a machine carrying a man had raised itself by its own power into the air in full flight, had sailed forward without reduction of speed, and had finally landed at a point as high as that from which it started."

B *The four-cylinder 12 h.p. petrol engine for the* Flyer I, *also designed by the Wright brothers.*

C *The 1903* Flyer I, *mounted on a small trolley fitted with two adapted bicycle wheel hubs, running on a wooden rail.*

D *The weight-and-derrick assisted take-off device for the Wright* Flyer, *first used in September 1904.*

...flying philosophers may be compared to...
the proprietors of donkeys which are announced
to ascend a ladder. The donkey never really goes
up, and the philosopher has not yet flown.

DAILY TELEGRAPH, London 1868

...it can scarcely be considered that man, even
with the help of the most ingenious wing-like
mechanism, depending upon his own muscular
force as the driving power, will be placed in a
position to be able to raise his own weight into
the air and to retain it there.

H. VON HELINHOLTZ, 1872

CHAPTER FIVE

FROM 1859 A.D. TO 1875 A.D.

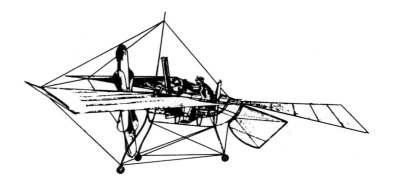

James Glaisher, a meteorologist, and Henry
Coxwell, a professional balloonist, ascended
far higher than they had intended, at
Wolverhampton, England, 1862. Lack of
oxygen caused Glaisher to pass out.

A   *Ponton d'Amécourt's steam-driven model helicopter, 1863.*
B   *Reconnaissance balloon, American Civil War, 1862.*
C   *A plan view of Etienne Lenoir's gas engine, 1860.*

B

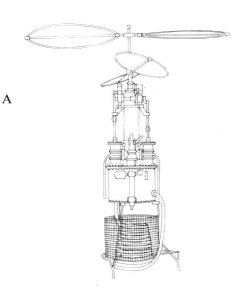

A

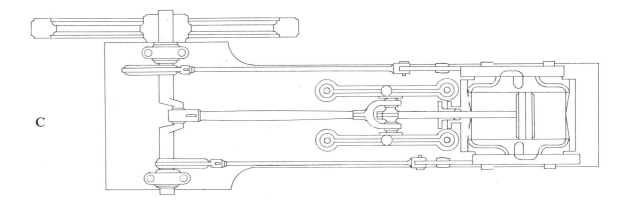

C

1860

In France, Etienne Lenoir invents the gas engine, the true ancestor of the modern petrol engine.
See figure C

1861—1863

Balloons are used for reconnaissance by both sides in the American Civil War, but chiefly by the Union forces under Thaddeus S. C. Lowe, performing valuable service. They are tethered and also connected by telegraph wire.
See figure B

NOVEMBER 1861

First aircraft-carrier in service is a converted coal-barge named *G. W. Parke Curtis*, which houses and flies a Union tethered observation balloon on the Potomac River in the American Civil War.

31 MAY 1862

Observations from a Union tethered balloon, piloted by T. S. C. Lowe, save Union forces from severe defeat at the Battle of Fair Oaks in the American Civil War.

1 JUNE 1862

T. S. C. Lowe first demonstrates military signalling by telegraph from his balloon, by means of a wire down the tethering rope, at the Battle of Fair Oaks.

5 SEPTEMBER 1862

Henry Coxwell and James Glaisher make a dramatic high altitude ascent from Wolverhampton in England in the former's balloon. Glaisher said the height reached was 36,000 ft (*c.* 11,000 m) but it was probably about 20,000 (*c.* 6100 m).
See opposite

1863

Nadar founds La Société d'Encouragement pour l'Aviation; and also founds the periodical *L'Aéronaute*, which is to become one of the world's leading aeronautical journals.

1863

Jules Verne publishes, in France, his first aeronautical novel, *Five Weeks in a Balloon*, and thus starts a notable career in the promotion of airmindedness.

31 JULY 1863

The Vicomte Gustave de Ponton d'Amécourt designs and demonstrates, in Paris, his steam-powered contra-rotating helicopter model. But it is unsuccessful.
See figure A

A   *Stringfellow's model triplane, 1868.*
B   *Harte's patent for an aileron system, 1870.*
C   *The first mature design for a jet aeroplane: by De Louvrié, 1865.*
D   *Trouvé's gunpowder ornithopter, 1870.*

C

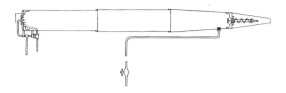

A

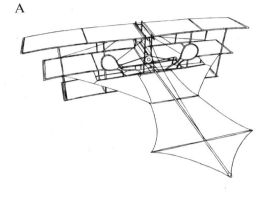

D

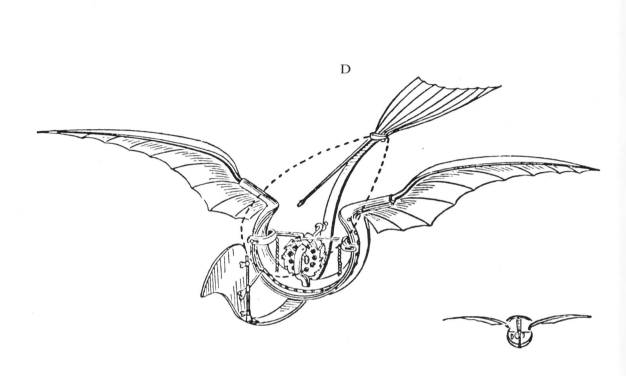

B

1865

From now on the main development of aviation is to lie in the hands of scientifically trained men. The subject of flying, to which the world has already been acclimatised through ballooning, now takes on a new meaning and a new seriousness: although man-carrying aeroplane flight will continue to be looked upon for many years as visionary, it now becomes accepted as a proper subject of investigation. Members of the newly-founded (1866) Aeronautical Society of Great Britain, with their contemporaries on the Continent, now commence the regular publication in technical journals of their researches and suggestions, and this constant dissemination of knowledge is to become of mounting importance for those engaged in the study of aeronautics.

1865

First proper jet-aeroplane design: Charles de Louvrié, in France, takes out a patent on a design of an aeroplane to be propelled by a jet of gas from the combustion of "a hydrocarbon, or better, vaporised petroleum". *See figure C*

12 JANUARY 1866

Foundation in London of the later Royal Aeronautical Society of Great Britain which has remained in flourishing existence ever since.

27 JUNE 1866

F. H. Wenham reads to the newly founded Aeronautical Society, his important and

influential paper entitled "*Aerial Locomotion*", and thus publishes the results of his researches and the work he did in c. 1858—1859 (which see).

19 JULY 1867

First delta-wing designs by the Englishmen, J. W. Butler and E. Edwards, who take out patents for designs of delta-wing monoplanes and biplanes to be propelled by jets of compressed air, steam, gas, etc., and by reaction-driven airscrews (emission from blade-tips). *See figures E and F*

1868

First suggestion and patent for ailerons by M. P. W. Boulton in England. They were to

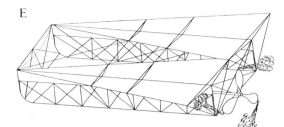

E

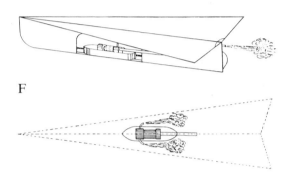

F

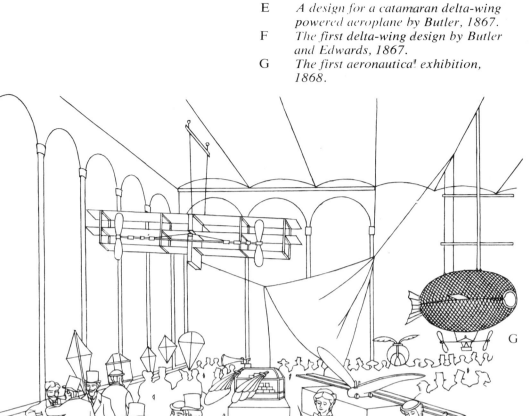

G

be used on outriggers on an ornithopter. Although Boulton thought of the simple idea of inclining the surfaces, the device as he described it would have served to upset the machine.

1868

Hunter, an Englishman, designs a jet-aeroplane, with provision also for downward jets on the wings to provide lift.

JUNE 1868

First aeronautical exhibition is held at the Crystal Palace, London, by the Aeronautical Society. The most influential exhibit is John Stringfellow's model triplane which is the first powered triplane model ever tested. Steam-powered, it is derived from a suggestion by Cayley, and although not itself successful when tested, it is to have—owing to continued and widespread publication—a profound influence in leading Chanute and others to adopt superposed planes.
See figures A and G

26 JUNE 1869

Largest hydrogen balloon ever to make a free ascent, makes a short flight; Wilfrid de Fonvielle and Gaston Tissandier in *Le Pole Nord* (formerly captive), of 424,000 cu.ft capacity (*c.* 130,000 cubic metres).

1870

Alphonse Pénaud, a Frenchman, introduces twisted (as opposed to stretched), rubber to power models—in this first case, a successful helicopter model.

1870

In France, Gustave Trouvé successfully flies his model ornithopter, which is powered by the successive force of blank cartridges firing into a Bourdon tube, to which were attached the wing-spars. It flies for some 230 ft (*c.* 70 m).
See figure D

1870

In England, Harte patents, but does not build, a tractor aeroplane, whose wings are fitted with modern-type hinged ailerons. He does not envisage proper control in roll, but suggests aileron-use (a) to counteract airscrew torque, (b) to act collectively as an elevator, and (c) to effect turning by retarding one wing. This has nothing to do with banking the machine.
See figure B

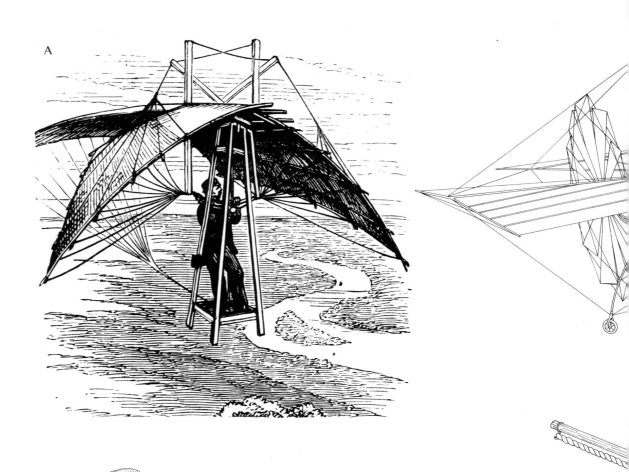

SEPTEMBER 1870—JANUARY 1871

Over 60 balloons leave Paris during its siege by the Prussians, carrying refugees, carrier pigeons and messages. The carrier pigeons return to Paris carrying thousands of messages, letters, etc., on microfilm.
See figure G

1871

The world's first wind-tunnel is built for the Aeronautical Society of Great Britain by F. H. Wenham and John Browning.

AUGUST 1871

First stable model aeroplane flies successfully for over 130 ft (*c.* 40 m). Pénaud's model monoplane, which he called a *Planophore*, propelled by twisted rubber and a pusher airscrew at the rear. This is to become one of the most influential models in history, and is widely and repeatedly published.
See figures D, E and F

2 FEBRUARY 1872

Dupuy de Lôme makes the only flight—from Fort Vincennes to Mondecourt, in France—in his man-powered airship, with eight men working the one tractor airscrew. It achieves about 5 mph (*c.* 8 km/h).

13—14 DECEMBER 1872

The Austrian, Paul Haenlein, tests his airship, but only when held captive, at Brunn in Moravia. It is the first aircraft to be powered by an internal combustion engine (i.e. a Lenoir gas engine, fed from the gas in the envelope).

1873

Etienne-Jules Marey, a French physiologist, publishes his book *La Machine Animale* (translation published in Britain in 1874 as *Animal Mechanism*). This is a stimulating work which will be read by the Wright brothers. Marey is also to lay the foundations of cinematography.

6 OCTOBER 1873

Washington Donaldson, with two companions, sets off from New York in the huge *Daily Graphic* balloon to fly the Atlantic; but they land a few hours later in the Catskills. The project is abandoned.

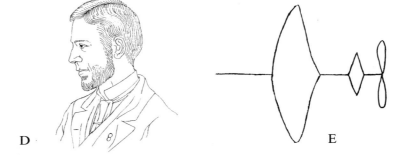

D

E

c. 1874

First test and take-off by a full-size manned aeroplane; Félix du Temple's machine is launched at Brest, France, down an inclined ramp, manned by a young sailor; no sustained flight results. This machine is believed to have been powered by a form of hot-air engine.
See figure B

1874

D. S. Brown completes the tests of his tandem-wing model gliders, and publishes the results with illustrations in the Annual Report of the Aeronautical Society for this year. He is concerned with longitudinal stability and is probably inspired by Walker (see 1831). Brown, in turn, is probably to influence Langley to choose the tandem configuration. (See 1892 and 1896.)

9 JULY 1874

Vincent de Groof, a Belgian, is killed on his ornithopter at Cremorne Gardens, London, when his machine is released from a balloon, and crashes, killing him.
See figure A

JUNE 1875

Thomas Moy flies his large tandem-wing steam-driven model tethered at the Crystal Palace, London. It is called the *Aerial Steamer*. This is the first time a steam-driven model aeroplane lifts itself off the ground.
See figure C

B

C

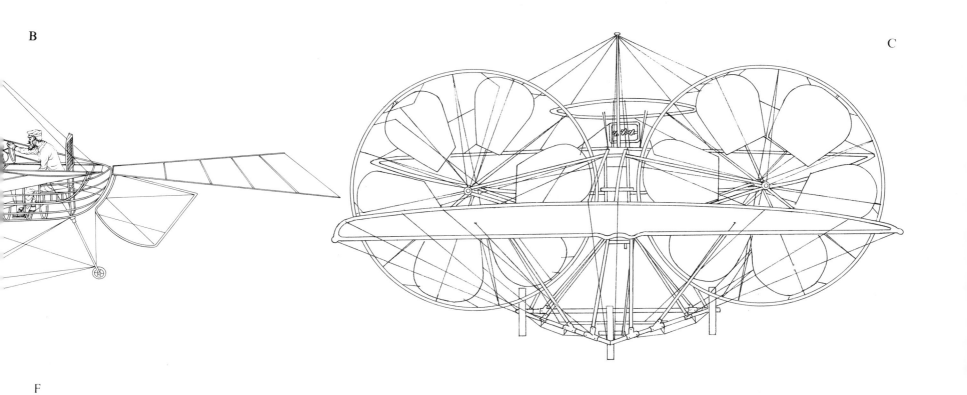

F

A   *De Groof on his ornithopter, 1874.*
B   *The first full-size powered aeroplane to take off the ground, built by du Temple, 1874.*
C   Thomas Moy's *Aerial Steamer.*
D   *Alphonse Pénaud.*
E   *Pénaud's own plan-view drawing of his* Planophore, *1871.*
F   *A reconstruction of the* Planophore.
G   *Constructing balloons on the Gare d'Orleans in Paris during the Prussian siege, 1870—1871.*

"Well, gentlemen, do you believe in the possibility of aerial locomotion by machines heavier than air?"..."You ask yourselves doubtless if this apparatus, so marvellously adapted for aerial locomotion, is susceptible of receiving greater speed. It is not worth while to conquer space if we cannot devour it. I wanted the air to be a solid support to me, and it is. I saw that to struggle against the wind I must be stronger than the wind, and I am. I had no need of sails to drive me, nor oars nor wheels to push me, nor rails to give me a faster road. Air is what I wanted, that was all. Air surrounds me as water surrounds the submarine boat, and in it my propellers act like the screws of a steamer. That is how I solved the problem of aviation. That is what a balloon will never do, nor will any machine that is lighter than air."

JULES VERNE (1886)

But we must admit the possibility that continued investigation and experience will bring us ever nearer to that solemn moment, when the first man will rise from earth by means of wings, if only for a few seconds, and marks that historical moment which heralds the inauguration of a new era in our civilization.

. . . . .

It must not remain our desire only to acquire the art of the bird; nay it is our duty not to rest until we have attained to a perfect scientific conception of the problem of flight.

OTTO LILIENTHAL (1891)

It seems, therefore, not unreasonable to entertain the hope that man may eventually achieve a mechanical success (if not a commercial one) in the attempt to compass a mode of transportation which so strongly appeals to the imagination, and that it may result in greater speeds than pertain to our present journeyings.

OCTAVE CHANUTE (1893)

CHAPTER SIX

FROM 1876 A.D. TO 1894 A.D.

*Albert and Gaston Tissandier flew the
first airship to be powered by electricity,
in 1883.*

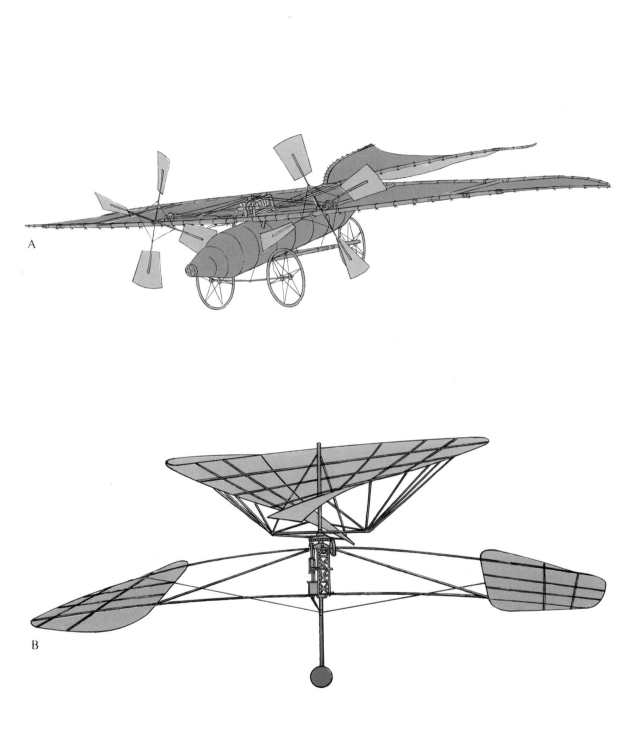

1876

In France, Alphonse Pénaud patents his remarkable design for a powered man-carrying amphibious aeroplane. It incorporates a dihedral setting of the double-surfaced wings, rear elevators, vertical rear fin and rudder, single control-column for combined operation of elevators and rudder, glass-domed cockpit, retractable under-carriage with shock-absorbers, tail-skid, etc. This machine is never built.

1876

Four-stroke petrol engine is introduced by N. A. Otto of the German firm, Otto and Langen. This type of engine is finally to make practical aviation possible.

1877

The Italian inventor Enrico Forlanini's steam-driven helicopter model flies at Alexandria, Egypt and later at Milan, Italy.
See figure B

12 JUNE 1878

Professor Ritchel, at Hartford, Connecticut, has flown (by an unknown pilot) his pedal-powered airscrew-propelled little cylindrical airship. This is, pedantically speaking, the first powered aircraft to be airborne in the United States.

1879

Victor Tatin's compressed-air model mono-plane flies in France, propelled by two tractor airscrews. This machine is a further rationalisation of the Henson concept, and helps to crystallise still further the mono-plane configuration.
See figure A

1879

J. B. Biot builds and makes a few tentative glides in his full-size glider at Clamart, France. This machine (in the Musée de l'Air, Paris) is the earliest surviving full-size aeroplane.

29 SEPTEMBER 1879

John Wise, with a companion, is drowned when his balloon force-lands in Lake Michigan in the United States.

A *Tatin's compressed air model mono-plane, 1879.*
B *Forlanini's steam helicopter model, 1877.*

75

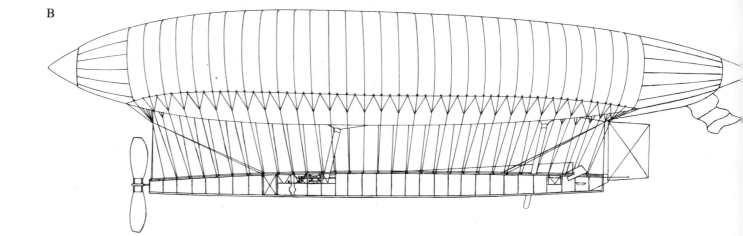

1881

Louis Pierre Mouillard publishes in Paris his *L'Empire de l'Air*, which directs attention to gliding and soaring. An abbreviated translation is to be published by the Smithsonian Institution in Washington in 1893, and is read by the Wright brothers.

1883

Alexandre Goupil constructs, in France, a remarkable monoplane, and lifts two men in it when tethered against the wind. In his published designs next year (1884) he includes primitive ailerons on the machine.

8 OCTOBER 1883

The French brothers Albert and Gaston Tissandier first fly their airship, the first to be powered by electricity (Siemens motor); but the power is too weak for proper propulsion.
See figure C

1883—1886

John J. Montgomery, in California, USA, builds and tests his first three full-size gliders. All are unsuccessful.

1884

Horatio Phillips patents and publishes in England his double-surfaced cambered aerofoils. This marks a major advance in aviation, and is to have a strong influence on future pioneers. Phillips demonstrates what Cayley surmised, i.e. that the greater part of the lift of such aerofoils comes from the area of low pressure (suction) on their upper surfaces.
See figure A

1884

The steam turbine is invented in England by Charles Parsons. This is later to provide the *modus operandi* of the turbo-jet engines.

1884

Hermann Ganswindt publishes in Germany a book proposing a giant rigid airship. This is never built, but the book probably influences Ferdinand von Zeppelin in his thinking.

JULY 1884

Second powered man-carrying aeroplane is tested and takes off. This is Alexander Mozhaiski's steam-powered monoplane, which, piloted by I. N. Golubev, is launched down a "*ski-jump*" type of ramp, near St Petersburg, Russia. It does not fly.
See figure D

AUGUST 1884

First nearly practical airship flies:
La France of Charles Renard and Arthur Krebs, powered by an 8.5-hp Gramme electric motor driving one large tractor airscrew. It first flies from Chalais-Meudon

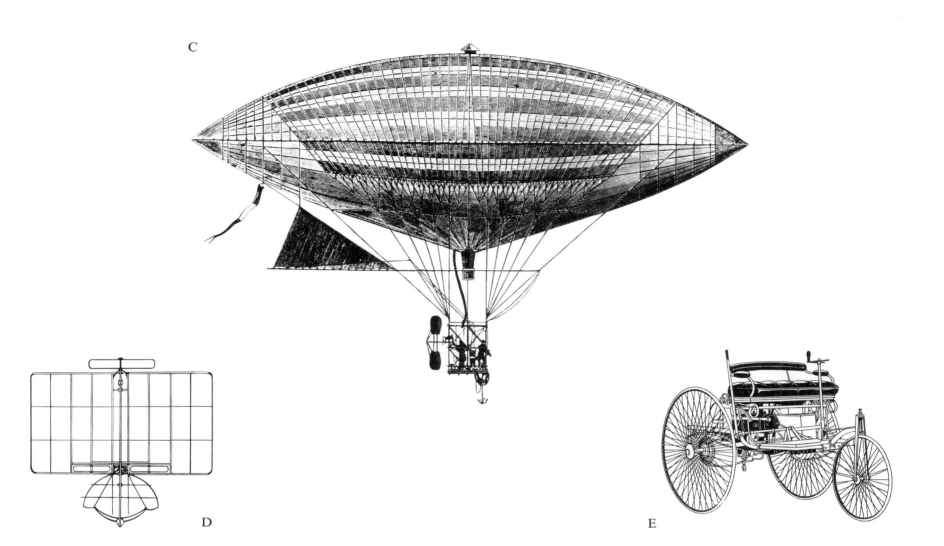

C

D

E

and returns, travelling about 5 miles at 14 $\frac{1}{2}$ mph (about 8 km at 23 km/h).
See figure B

1885

First practical petrol engines are built simultaneously and independently by Carl Benz and Gottlieb Daimler, both in Germany. It is *automobilism* which alone is to develop the petrol engine, of which aviation is later to take advantage.

1885

First practical petrol-driven automobile in action, designed and built by Carl Benz, in Mannheim, Germany.
See figure E

1887

First rotary engine is built and tested by Lawrence Hargrave in Australia. It is

driven by compressed air, but it does not influence engine history, as it is made in Australia, and communication through magazines, etc., is delayed.

12 AUGUST 1888

First petrol-engined aircraft flies: the Woelfert airship, piloted solo by Michaël, fitted with a 2-h.p. Daimler engine driving two airscrews. It flies 2 $\frac{1}{2}$ miles (*c.* 4 km) from Seelberg to Kornwestheim, Germany.

1889

Otto Lilienthal, a German civil engineer who becomes one of the great pioneers of aviation, publishes his *Der Vogelflug als Grundlage der Fliegekunst (Bird Flight as the Basis of Aviation)*. This becomes one of the classics of aviation, and includes tables of wing-area and lift. It also demonstrates what Cayley discovered, i.e. that birds are propelled by the airscrew action of their outer primary feathers.

A   *Phillips' wing-sections, 1884, 1891.*
B   *The first semi-practical airship La France by Renard and Krebs, 1884.*
C   *Tissandiers' electrically driven airship, 1883.*
D   *A design for a powered monoplane by Mozhaiski, built and tested in 1884.*
E   *Benz's experimental tricar, 1885.*

A   *The great biplane test-rig constructed by Sir Hiram Maxim, 1894.*
B   *Otto Lilienthal.*
C   *The first piloted glider flights by Lilienthal, 1891—1896.*

B

C

A

1890s

Among the aeronautical inventors there have emerged by 1890 three recognisable types of pioneer: (a) the "*academic*" inventors, whose creations, sometimes ingenious but more often wayward or visionary, are realised only on paper; (b) the "*model-makers*", who are mostly content to experiment only in miniature; and finally (c) those pioneers who are willing to risk life and limb in full-size experiments. The latter comes to divide into two vitally significant streams, the "*airmen*" and the "*chauffeurs*". Although the aeroplane is not to start proliferating until the 1890s, the attitude of the "*chauffeurs*" to aviation has been oddly evident long before. This is an attitude which regards the flying-machine as a winged motor-car, to be driven into the air by brute force, so to say, and sedately steered about the sky as if it were a land—or even marine—vehicle, which simply becomes transferred from a layer of earth to a layer of air. The true "*airman's*" attitude is evident in the pilot's desire to identify himself with his machine, or ride it like an expert horseman. The

"*chauffeurs*" come to devote themselves mainly to the pursuit of thrust and lift, and thereby prove singularly unfruitful: they invariably try to take off in powered machines before they have any true idea of flight control. The "*airmen*", on the other hand, think primarily in terms of control in the air, and quickly realise that the unpowered glider is the vehicle of choice, in which a man may emulate the technique of gliding birds, and learn to ride the air successfully before having himself precipitated into the atmosphere in a powered flying machine. This distinction between "*chauffeurs*" and "*airmen*" is to prove pivotal in the final conquest of the air.

9 OCTOBER 1890

First full-size manned aeroplane to leave the ground for about 150 ft (*c.* 55 m) under its own power: Clément Ader's steam-powered tractor *Éole*, at Armainvilliers. But it does not, and cannot, make a sustained and controlled flight.
See figure E

1891

Otto Lilienthal starts gliding in his hang-gliders at Dervitz, Germany. He is to prove one of the greatest men in aviation history. The past culminated in him. He is the first man to launch himself into the air and fly. He becomes the key figure in aviation, and is directly to inspire the Wright brothers. Excellent photographs of him gliding are published throughout the world, and are to be means of publicising his achievements.
See figures B and C

1892

Invention of the Diesel engine by the German engineer, Rudolph Diesel.

1892

Samuel Pierpont Langley, the American physicist, builds his first steam-driven aero-plane models. They are failures.

D   *Hargrave's box-kite, 1893.*
E   *The first aeroplane to leave the ground under its own power: Ader's* Eole, *1890.*
F   *Phillips' large multiplane model, 1893.*

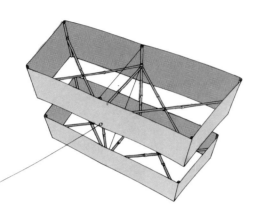

1893

Invention of the box-kite by Lawrence Hargrave in Australia. This device of Hargrave's is to be illustrated in Means's *Aeronautical Annual* for 1896, and to play a vital part in the development of the European aeroplane (see 1905).
See figure D

1893

Charles Parsons flies his steam-driven tractor aeroplane model in England. This is not published at the time, and has no influence.

21 MARCH 1893

Gustave Hermitte and Georges Besançon pioneer the use of *ballons-sonde* for meteorological recording with their *Aerophile* at Vaugirard in France.

MAY 1893

Horatio Phillips' large multi-slat machine, to test his aerofoil theories, is tested tethered to a centre-pole at Harrow, near London, and lifts itself from the track. It is powered by a steam-engine driving one pusher airscrew.
See figure F

1894

Otto Lilienthal perfects his standard monoplane hang-glider (*Normal-Segel-apparat*), a number of which he sells or presents to clients.

1894

Octave Chanute, a French-born American engineer, publishes his *Progress in Flying Machines*. This classic work is the first authoritative account of aeroplane history, and is to be widely influential in informing the early pioneers of the problems which have been solved, and those to be solved.

19 JUNE 1894

F. W. Lanchester first announces his theory of circulatory air-flow to the Birmingham Natural History and Philosophical Society in England. This theory is later to become of pivotal importance in aerodynamics (see 1907).

31 JULY 1894

Sir Hiram Maxim makes the chief test with his huge steam-powered test-rig at Baldwyns Park, Kent, England. This machine, which runs on rails, with further guard rails above, succeeds in lifting its own weight, but is brought to a stop after fouling the guard rails. It makes no free flight, nor is it capable of such flight. It influences nothing in aviation history.
See figure A

During a gliding flight taken from a great height this was the cause of my coming into a position with my arms outstretched, in which the centre of gravity lay too much to the back; at the same time I was unable—owing to fatigue—to draw the upper part of my body again towards the front. As I was then sailing at the height of about 65 feet with a velocity of about 35 miles per hour, the apparatus, overloaded in the rear, rose more and more, and finally shot, by means of its vis viva, vertically upwards. I gripped tight hold, seeing nothing but the blue sky and little white clouds above me, and so awaited the moment when the apparatus would capsize backwards, possibly ending my sailing attempts forever. Suddenly, however, the apparatus stopped in its ascent, and going backward again in a downward direction, described a short circle and steered with the rear part again upwards, owing to the horizontal tail which had an upward slant; then the machine turned bottom upwards and rushed with me vertically towards the earth from a height of about 65 feet. With my senses quite clear, my arms and my head forward, still holding the apparatus firmly with my hands, I fell towards the greensward; a shock, a crash, and I lay with the apparatus on the ground.

OTTO LILIENTHAL (1895)
(THE FIRST ACCOUNT IN HISTORY OF AN AIRCRAFT CRASH BY THE PILOT)

I have not the smallest molecule of faith in aerial navigation other than ballooning.

LORD KELVIN (1896)

Success four flights thursday morning all against twentyone mile wind started from Level with engine power alone average speed through air thirtyone miles longest 57 seconds inform Press home Christmas. Orevelle Wright.

ORVILLE WRIGHT
(THE TELEGRAM AS RECEIVED BY HIS FATHER DATED DECEMBER 17TH 1903: THROUGH ERRORS IN TRANSMISSION 57 APPEARED FOR 59 AND OREVELLE FOR ORVILLE)

CHAPTER SEVEN

FROM 1895 A.D. TO 1907 A.D.

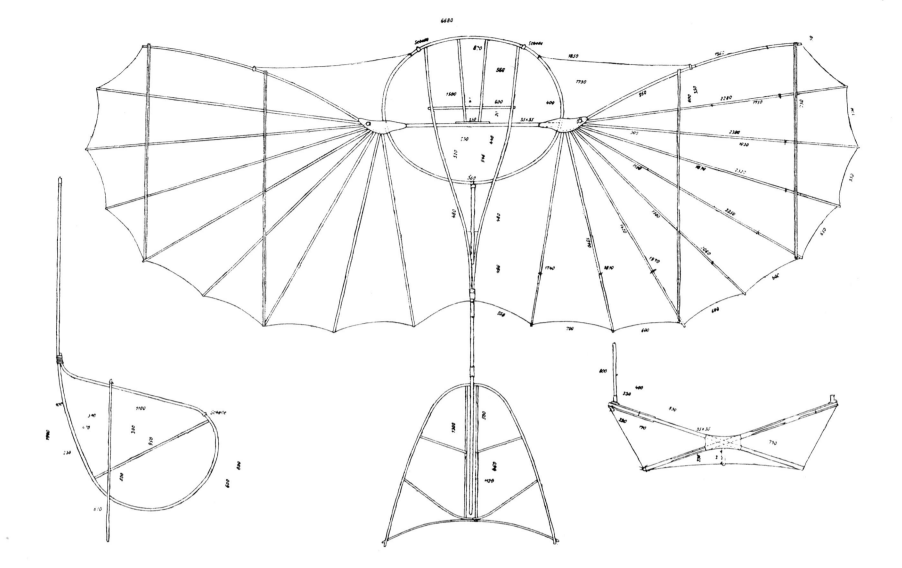

Otto Lilienthal's gliding experiments paved the way for the first successful aeroplane flights as his example influenced the Wright brothers to perfect their gliders before applying power. Illustrated is one of Lilienthal's plans for a glider. (Deutches Museum, Munich).

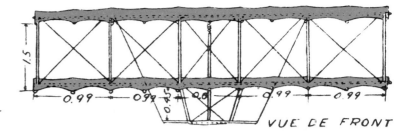

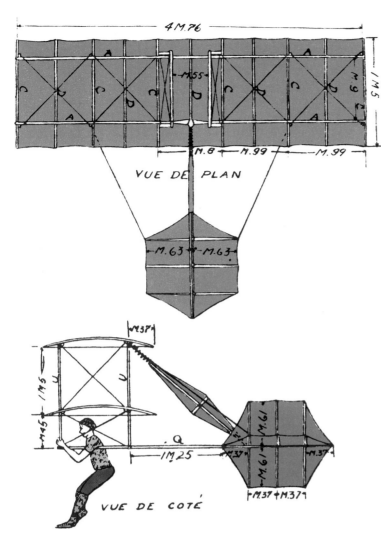

A   *The Chanute biplane glider: plan, frontal, and side views, 1896.*
B   *Octave Chanute.*

1895—1897

James Means publishes the three successive volumes of his *Aeronautical Annual* in the United States: this publication is to be of great importance in making known the work of past and present pioneers, especially Lilienthal's gliding.

1895

Percy Sinclair Pilcher builds his glider, the *Bat*, and is the first in Britain to carry out controlled glider flights like Lilienthal's and thus becomes the first true British aviator.

1895

Otto Lilienthal builds and flies successfully the first of his three biplane hang-gliders.

MAY 1895

First aeronautical society is founded in America: the Boston Aeronautical Society.

1896

Octave Chanute introduces his classic and successful type of biplane glider: this is machine whose structure is based on the Pratt-truss system of rigging; this provides the Wrights with their first rigging and general biplane structure, but does not in any other way influence them. This Chanute glider has no movable control surfaces.
See figure A

1896

Automobiles are granted the freedom of the roads in Great Britain and France, i.e. restrictions regarding accompaniment by a man with a flag, etc. are removed. This freedom immediately gives rise to a vast international surge in automobile production, the founding of automobile clubs, periodicals, etc. This universal surge is to provide the reservoir of trained engineers and mechanics which aviation will need within the next two decades.

A

B

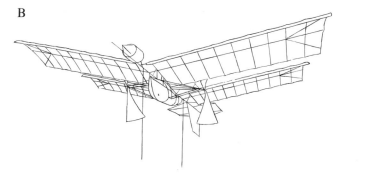

MAY 1896

Samuel P. Langley at last succeeds in obtaining good results with his Nos. 5 and 6 tandem-wing steam-powered models, which he incorrectly calls "Aerodromes". No. 5 makes a flight of 3300 ft (c. 1 km) on 6 May.
See figure B

SUMMER 1896

Percy S. Pilcher completes at Eynsford in Kent, England, and first tests, his best hang-glider, the *Hawk*; this is to prove his most successful machine. It has a wheeled under-carriage, and is often launched by being towed by men or horses.
See figure D

9 AUGUST 1896

Otto Lilienthal crashes when gliding in one of his standard monoplane hang-gliders, on the Gollenberg. He dies next day in a Berlin clinic. His influence during his life, and by his death, has been, and is to be, of profound importance.

12 JUNE 1897

Woelfert and his mechanic Robert Knabe are killed on the first flight of his new air-ship, the *Deutschland*, powered by a 6-hp Daimler engine. They leave Tempelhof, Berlin, and crash in flames soon afterwards.

11 JULY 1897

Salomon-August Andrée, the Swede, sets off with two companions in the balloon *Örnen* from Danes Island (Spitzbergen), in an attempt to fly over the North Pole. They are never seen alive again, but are found by accident beneath the ice—with their excellent photographs preserved—in 1930.

12—14 OCTOBER 1897

Clément Ader's steam-powered twin-screw *Avion III* is twice tested on a circular track at Satory near Versailles, France. It does not leave the ground on either occasion, as is made perfectly clear by the official report which, however, is not to be published until 1910.
Nine years later (in 1906) Ader is mendaciously to claim he flew for about 330 yds (300 m) on 14 October.
See figure A

NOVEMBER 1897

First all-metal (aluminium) rigid airship is tested. Designed by David Schwarz, it is powered by a 12-hp Daimler engine driving three airscrews. It rises from Tempelhof, Berlin, piloted by a mechanic, Jagels Platz, and crashes soon afterwards owing to faulty airmanship. The pilot leaps to safety at the last minute.
See figure E

1898

Aéro-Club de France is founded in Paris.

C
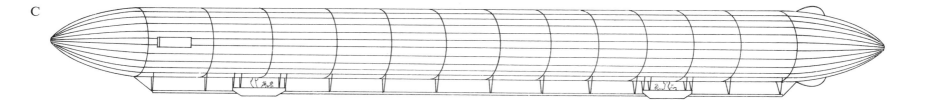

D
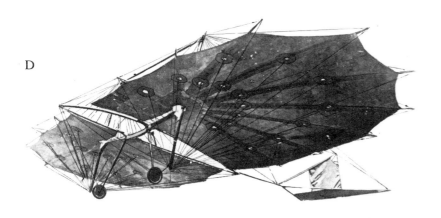

E
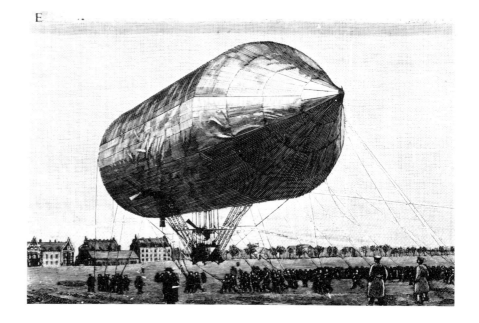

SEPTEMBER 1898

Alberto Santos-Dumont, the Brazilian, makes the first trial flights in his first small pressure airship, from Neuilly, near Paris. He is to do more than anyone to make Europe air-minded (see also 1901, 1906).

26 MAY 1899

Lawrence Hargrave, on a visit to England from Australia, demonstrates his box-kites to a meeting of the Aeronautical Society in London, and lends the kites to Percy S. Pilcher.

AUGUST 1899

In America, the Wright brothers—Wilbur and Orville—fly their warping kite, the first aircraft to have helical twisting of the wings for control in roll, which the Wrights invented.

30 SEPTEMBER 1899

Percy S. Pilcher crashes in his glider, the *Hawk*, at Stanford Park (Lord Braye's seat), Market Harborough, England. He dies from his injuries on 2 October.

2 JULY 1900

First trial of the first Zeppelin, the LZ-1 (*Luftschiff Zeppelin I*), over Lake Constance, Germany. It is tentatively successful, and attains a speed of $8\frac{1}{2}$ mph (*c*. 14 km/h). It is housed in a floating hangar, the first in history.
See figure C

OCTOBER 1900

The Wrights test their No. 1 glider at Kitty Hawk, North Carolina, USA. It has wing-warping and a forward elevator only. It is flown mostly as a kite both with, and without, a "pilot", chiefly to test the warping.

1901

The American, Samuel Franklin Cody, (later a naturalized British citizen) patents his man-lifting kite system, the kites being winged Hargrave box-kites.

A   *Ader's* Avion III *with two steam-driven propellers, 1897.*
B   *Langley's successful steam-driven model* Aerodrome No. 5, *1896.*
C   *The first Zeppelin, 1900.*
D   *Pilcher's hang glider the* Hawk, *1896.*
E   *The first all-metal airship built by Schwarz, 1897.*

A

JUNE 1901

First petrol-driven aeroplane flies
tentatively: Samuel P. Langley's quarter-
scale model *"Aerodrome"*, in the United
States.
See figure B

JULY—AUGUST 1901

The Wrights test their No. 2 glider at the
Kill Devil Hills, near Kitty Hawk: it also is
fitted with wing-warping and a forward
elevator only.

OCTOBER 1901

First full-size petrol-driven aeroplane is
destroyed while taxying: Wilhelm Kress's
tandem-wing flying-boat, on the
Tullnerbach reservoir, in Austria. Kress now
abandons his experiments.
See figure A

OCTOBER 1901

The Aero Club (later Royal Aero Club) of
Great Britain is founded, as a result of a
suggestion made by Miss Vera Hedges
Butler during a balloon voyage on 24
September 1901.

19 OCTOBER 1901

Alberto Santos-Dumont flies his airship No.
6 from St Cloud round the Eiffel Tower and
back, and wins the Deutsch prize of 100,000
francs.

5—6 NOVEMBER 1901

Samuel F. Cody is pulled across the English
Channel from Calais to Dover in a canoe by
one of his kites.

1902

The years 1902—1904 see the revival of
European aviation, moribund since the
death of Lilienthal in 1896. The true revival
of aviation in Europe is due directly to the
Wright brothers, as is clear both from the
configurations adopted, and from the
numerous contemporary statements by the
pioneers themselves. The revival is effected
through the copying of the Wright gliders by
Ferber in 1902 and by Archdeacon and
Esnault-Pelterie in 1904—1905, and by the
powerful stimulus of the news of the
Wrights' powered flying in 1903 and 1905.

JANUARY 1902

The Manly-Balzer radial engine for Samuel
P. Langley's full-size *Aerodrome* is first
tested in the United States.

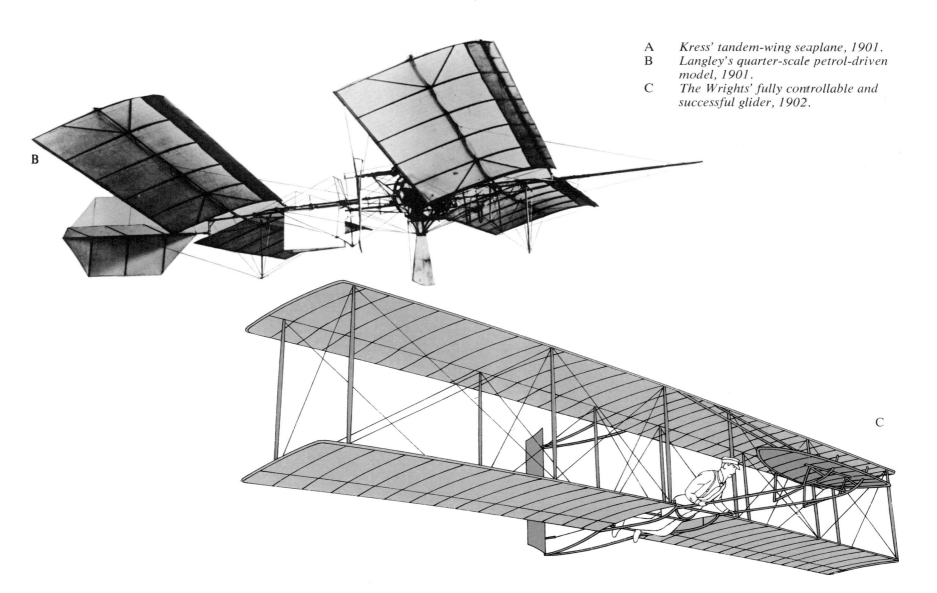

A *Kress' tandem-wing seaplane, 1901.*
B *Langley's quarter-scale petrol-driven model, 1901.*
C *The Wrights' fully controllable and successful glider, 1902.*

12 MAY 1902

August Severo and his mechanic Sachet are killed on the first flight of Severo's airship *Pax* from Vaugirard, when it explodes over Paris, and crashes into the city.

JUNE 1902

Captain Ferdinand Ferber, after receiving from Chanute descriptions and illustrations of the first two Wright gliders, now abandons his Lilienthal-type glider and adopts the Wright type, thus inaugurating the rebirth of European aviation. He first tests his Wright glider in June at Beuil, France.

22 SEPTEMBER 1902

First flight by a powered aircraft in Britain. Spencer's airship takes off from the Crystal Palace, near London, and makes a flight of some 30 miles (*c.* 48 km)

SEPTEMBER—OCTOBER 1902

The Wrights make nearly 1000 glides on their modified No. 3 glider at the Kill Devil Hills. It is this glider which incorporates, for the first time, the flight controls of the modern aeroplane i.e. control in pitch (forward elevator), in roll (wing-warping) and in yaw (rear rudder). It also incorporates the basic discovery of the Wrights, i.e. the necessity of combining control in roll (warping) with control in yaw (rudder) to counteract warp (or aileron) drag.
See figure C

13 OCTOBER 1902

Von Bradsky and his mechanic Morin are killed on the first flight of von Bradsky's airship from Vaugirard, when the car breaks away in mid-air and crashes at Stains, outside Paris.

NOVEMBER 1902

First fully practical airship completed is *Lebaudy*, commissioned by the brothers, Paul and Pierre Lebaudy, and built by Henry Juillot and Don Simoni. The first flights take place at Moisson in France with Georges Juchmés as pilot. However, the *Lebaudy's* best flights will take place the following year.

2 APRIL 1903

Octave Chanute lectures, with illustrations, to the Aéro-Club de France in Paris, paying special attention to the sophisticated No. 3 Wright glider of 1902. This lecture gives the main impetus to the rebirth of European aviation, and to the adoption in Europe of Wright-type gliders. It is Wright-type gliders which inaugurate the rebirth of European aviation. Chanute describes the simultaneous use of warping and rudder, but none of the Europeans realise the significance of these revelations.

A

Karl Jatho tests his powered aeroplane in Germany. He makes some small hops, but does not fly. He does not influence aviation.

7 OCTOBER, 8 DECEMBER 1903

Samuel P. Langley's full-size *Aerodrome*, piloted by Manly, twice crashes into the River Potomac opposite Widewater, Virginia, USA, when being launched from a houseboat. It fouls the catapult gear on each occasion. With its primitive control system, and also with probable structural weaknesses, it would not have been capable of successful flight.
See figures A and C

17 DECEMBER 1903

THE WORLDS FIRST POWERED, SUSTAINED AND CONTROLLED FLIGHTS IN AN AEROPLANE

Orville and Wilbur Wright at the Kill Devil Hills near Kitty Hawk make four flights from level ground without assisted take-off, the first (Orville) of 12 seconds, the fourth of 59 seconds, when Wilbur covers 852 ft (*c*. 260 m) and travels an air distance of half a mile (*c*. 800 m), owing to the head wind. This time of 59 seconds was not exceeded by any pilots other than the Wrights until November 1907.
See figures D, E and G

1904

First large airship is built in America. The *California Arrow* is constructed by Thomas Baldwin, with a Curtiss engine, and makes promising tests.

1904

First woman to fly in an airship: Madame Paul Lebaudy in a Lebaudy at Moisson in France.

APRIL 1904

Ernest Archdeacon, one of the founders of the Aéro-Club de France, has a Wright-type glider built for him, which Ferdinand Ferber and Gabriel Voisin fly tentatively.

MAY 1904

The Wrights start flying their powered *Flyer II* at the Huffman Prairie, near Dayton, Ohio, USA.

MAY 1904

Robert Esnault-Pelterie, the French engineer and inventor, imitates the Wright glider, but without success (see October 1904).

MAY 1904

In the United States, the St Louis International Exposition is opened at which Octave Chanute exhibits a replica of his classic 1896 biplane glider launched by an electric winch-tow. Colonel J. E. Capper from England and Alberto Santos-Dumont from France visit the show.

7 SEPTEMBER 1904

The Wrights first use their weight-and-derrick-assisted take-off device in order to make themselves independent of the weather.

20 SEPTEMBER 1904

First circle is flown by an aeroplane by Wilbur Wright on the Wright *Flyer III* at the Huffman Prairie. This is witnessed by Amos Root, and a vivid description is published by him in the magazine he edited, *Gleanings in Bee Culture*, for January 1905.

OCTOBER 1904

In France, Ferdinand Ferber takes the first important step to modify the Wright-type glider by adding a tailplane to provide longitudinal stability. This is the beginning of the stable European biplane configuration.
See figures B and F

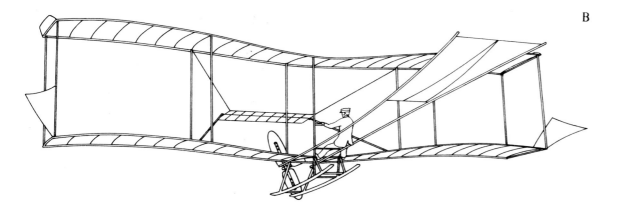

B

A   *Langley's full-size* Aerodrome *on its launching catapult, 1903.*
B   *The beginning of the European stable biplane tradition, Ferber's tailed glider, 1904.*
C   *Samuel P. Langley.*
D   *Wilbur Wright.*
E   *Orville Wright.*
F   *Ferdinand Ferber.*
G   *The first aeroplane to achieve man-carrying, sustained, powered and controlled flight is the* Flyer No. I, *with Orville Wright on board, 1903.*

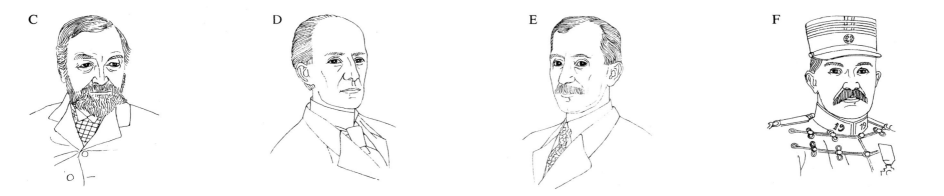

C   D   E   F

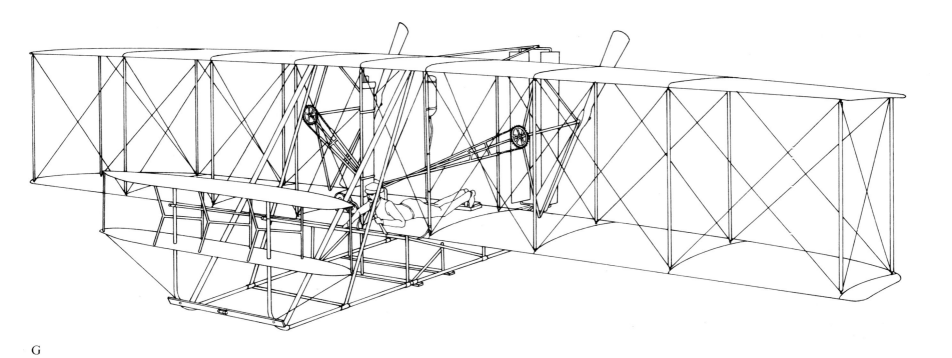

G

OCTOBER 1904

Robert Esnault-Pelterie tests, still unsuccessfully, his modified Wright glider near Boulogne, France. The important point about this machine is the ailerons, which are fitted in front of the wings. Although unsuccessful, these are the first ailerons to be fitted to an aeroplane, and will lead to the modern aileron system.
See figure A

9 NOVEMBER 1904

First flight of over 5 minutes by Wilbur Wright at the Huffman Prairie. It lasts 5 minutes 4 seconds, during which he flies 2 $^3/_4$ miles (*c.* 4.4 km). This duration will not be exceeded by any European pilot until May 1908.

1905

This year sees the Wrights in America achieve the first practical powered aeroplane in history with their *Flyer III*. Meanwhile the Europeans continue their slow and confused progression. The only significant feature of European aviation— which in practice still means French aviation—is in conception, not execution. This is the crystallising of their determination to pursue the inherently stable tailed aeroplane, rather than the inherently unstable machine espoused by the Wrights. In more detail the European situation may be itemised as follows: (*a*) the complete abandonment by the Europeans of the Wrights' doctrine of inherent instability; (*b*) the consequent settled pursuit of inherent stability; (*c*) the consequent abandonment of the pure Wright-glider configuration of forward elevator, wings, rear rudder and no rear horizontal surfaces; (*d*) the furthering— following Ferber in the cause of inherent stability—of the Wright-type-glider-plus-tailplane configuration; (*e*) the inauguration of the second type of European biplane configuration, i.e. the Wright-type-glider-*cum*-Hargrave-box-kite; (*f*) the final and still tentative European attempts to fly gliders; (*g*) the abandonment of this basic flight philosophy of Lilienthal and the Wrights, which postulated that mastery of glider flight should precede attempts at powered flight; (*h*) the tentative application of power to the first European biplane configuration.

MARCH 1905

First use as an aerodrome of the military ground at Issy-les-Moulineaux, Paris; by Ernest Archdeacon, to test his second glider.

This aerodrome becomes the site of many famous aeronautical events.

16 MARCH 1905

First glider descent from a balloon: Maloney on a Montgomery tandem-wing glider at Santa Clara, California, USA. This method of launching a glider was suggested by Cayley in 1852.
See figure B

JUNE 1905

Lawrence Hargrave's box-kite configuration is first incorporated in two aeroplanes, the Voisin-Archdeacon and Voisin-Blériot float-gliders in France. This is the beginning of the classic type of stable Voisin configuration, with no lateral control.
See figure C

JUNE—OCTOBER 1905

The Wrights have their triumphant season at the Huffman Prairie, near Dayton, with their *Flyer III*. This becomes the first fully practical aeroplane of history, which can bank, turn, circle, and easily fly for half an hour at a time.

18 JULY 1905

Maloney is killed at Santa Clara (California) when flying a Montgomery tandem-wing balloon-launched glider: this is the third aeroplane fatality of history.

OCTOBER 1905

The Fédération Aéronautique Internationale (F.A.I.) is founded in Paris by Count Henry de la Vaulx.

4 OCTOBER 1905

First aeroplane flight of over half an hour: Orville Wright in the Wright *Flyer III*. This flight-duration was not to be exceeded by any pilot other than the Wrights until October 1908.

NOVEMBER 1905

A historic letter is written by the Wrights to Georges Besançon, Secretary General of the Aéro-Club de France, giving a simple and fully circumstantial account of their successful 1905 season of flying with their *Flyer III*. This letter is published in France

A

on 30 November and causes consternation throughout Europe owing to the previous suspicion and disbelief of the Wrights' statement.

1906

Although the Wrights do not fly during the year 1906, it is their unseen presence which pervades the whole European scene in this year, and underlies every move the European pioneers make. The year marks in many respects a curious interregnum in aviation, relieved at the end by the first officially accredited powered hops in Europe by Alberto Santos-Dumont. In January is published for all to see the Wrights' patent (applied for in 1903, and only now granted) which includes both descriptions and drawings of their control linkage. But to the European pioneers, this information falls on deaf ears, and it does not occur to anyone to take a further and searching look at this patent, and then to make more, and more careful, experiments in lateral control.

A   *The first but unsuccessful use of ailerons by Esnault-Pelterie, 1904.*
B   *Maloney flying a Montgomery tandem-wing glider, launched from a balloon, 1905.*
C   *Voisin-Archdeacon float-glider based upon Hargrave's box-kite, 1905.*

B

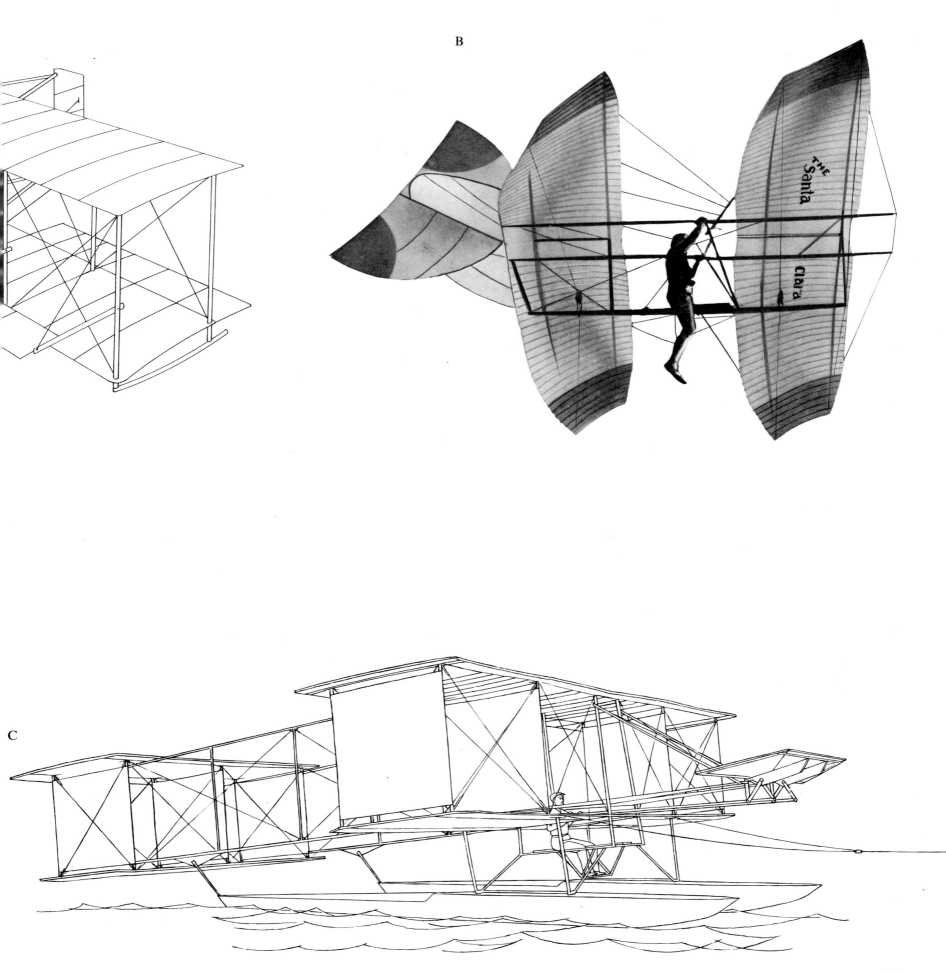

C

A

1906

A. von Parseval tentatively tests his airship in Germany. It is then enlarged to become the semi-rigid *Parseval No. 1*, which also undergoes tests.

JANUARY 1906

L'Aérophile, the official organ of the Aéro-Club de France, reluctantly accepts the Wrights' news as true. This news is corroborated by reliable eye-witnesses. Great bitterness is caused in France.

17 JANUARY 1906

The second Zeppelin (LZ-2) makes its first successful trial over Lake Constance, Germany, reaching a speed of 25 mph (*c.* 40 km/h).

18 MARCH 1906

First full-size tractor monoplane is tested by the Rumanian, Trajan Vuia, at Montesson in France. This machine, although not successful in itself, leads directly to Blériot and the European mono-plane tradition.
See figure C

12 SEPTEMBER 1906

J. C. H. Ellehammer, the Danish inventor, makes a hop-flight of some 140 ft (42 m) on the island of Lindholm, Denmark. But the machine is tethered to a central pole and this cannot rank as even a free hop-flight.
See figure B

30 SEPTEMBER—1 OCTOBER 1906

First Gordon Bennett Balloon race, from the Tuileries, Paris. It is won by the American Frank P. Lahm in his balloon *United States* with a flight of 420 miles (647 km) to Fylingdales, Yorks, in England.
See figure E

23 OCTOBER 1906

Alberto Santos-Dumont makes the first official flight in Europe—in reality only a hop. He flies his *No 14-bis* some 200 ft (60 m) at Bagatelle, France, thus winning the Archdeacon prize for a minimum flight of 25 m (*c.* 80 ft).
See figure D

12 NOVEMBER 1906

With the same aeroplane, Santos-Dumont wins the prize of the Aéro-Club de France for a flight of 100 m (*c.* 330 ft) when he covers some 720 ft (220 m) in 21.5 seconds. The *No 14-bis*, which is totally unpractical, only rises from the ground once more, on 4 April, 1907, when it covers about 160 ft (50 m) at St Cyr in France.

1907

This year witnesses the true, but still tentative, beginnings of practical powered flight in Europe, following the "false dawn" of 1906. Three important configurations, all confirming the European inherent-stability idiom, become well defined during the year; but only one machine achieves significant flights. These configurations are as follows:

(a)   The pusher biplane, Wright-*cum*-Hargrave-derived, with forward elevator, "open" biplane wings, and box-kite tail-unit, but with no lateral control. This type is represented by the first two powered Voisin machines, the *Voisin-Delagrange I* and the *Voisin-Farman I*; the latter, after important modifica-tions by **Henry Farman**, is the first European aeroplane—and the only one in 1907—to achieve productive flying (October onwards), and the first to stay in the air for over a minute.

(b)   The tractor biplane, derived from Ferber, but with no surfaces forward of the propeller. This is first seen in December in the de Pischoff machine which, although itself not successful, is to exert much influence later.

(c)   The tractor monoplane with main wings, fuselage, and tail-unit, devel-oping from the Vuia (which itself makes some hops in 1907), seen in the promising *Blériot VII*, and the diminutive *Santos-Dumont 19*, both of November, but both only tentative.

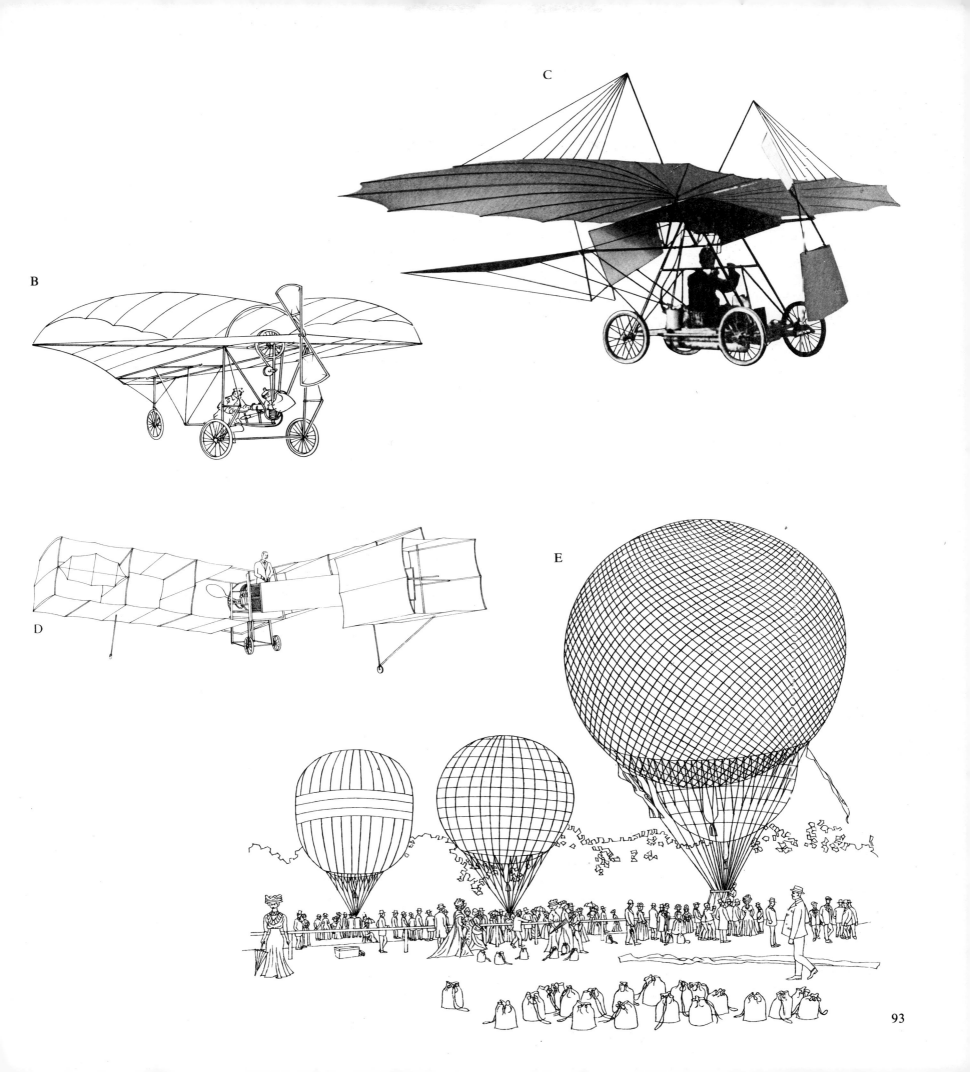

B

C

D

E

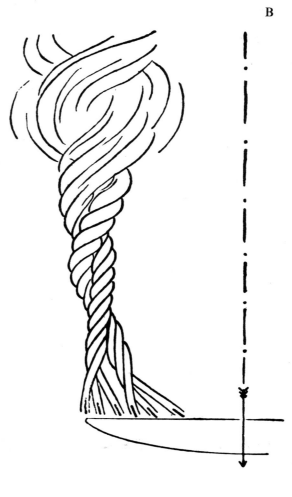

B

A

1907

First full-size triplane is tested by J. C. H. Ellehammer in Denmark. It makes many brief hops, but is unsuccessful.
See figure A

1907

In England, Frederick W. Lanchester publishes his book *Aerodynamics*, which becomes the first generally available account of his vitally important circulation-flow theory.
See figure B

1907

Etrich-Wels glider flies, with swept-back outer portions of the wings, in Austria.

SPRING 1907

First tentative hop-flight in Britain of about 500 ft (*c.* 150 m): Horatio Phillips' multi-slat machine at Streatham near London.

FEBRUARY, MARCH 1907

In France, Voisin crystallises the classic European pusher biplane configuration with Wright-derived forward biplane elevator, and biplane tailplane enclosing rudder. The first such machine tested is the *Voisin-Delagrange I*. The second is the *Voisin-Farman I*.

APRIL 1907

Louis Blériot builds and tests the first cantilever monoplane, the *Blériot V* (Canard), at Bagatelle in France. It is unsuccessful.

SEPTEMBER 1907

Henry Farman—an Englishman who is to live all his life in France—learns to fly in his *Voisin-Farman I* at Issy-les-Moulineaux. He soon becomes the outstanding pilot in Europe.

2 SEPTEMBER 1907

Walter Wellman, the American explorer, makes first trial at Spitzbergen, Norway, with his airship *America*, with a view to flying over the North Pole. Storms force the attempt to be postponed (see 15 October 1909).

19 SEPTEMBER 1907

First piloted helicopter rises—at Douai in France. Built by Louis and Jacques Breguet and Charles Richet, and piloted by Volumard, it rises only about 2 ft (60 cm). It is steadied from the ground and this does not constitute free flight.

29 SEPTEMBER 1907

The same helicopter manages to rise about 5 ft (1.50 m) but is still supported from the ground.

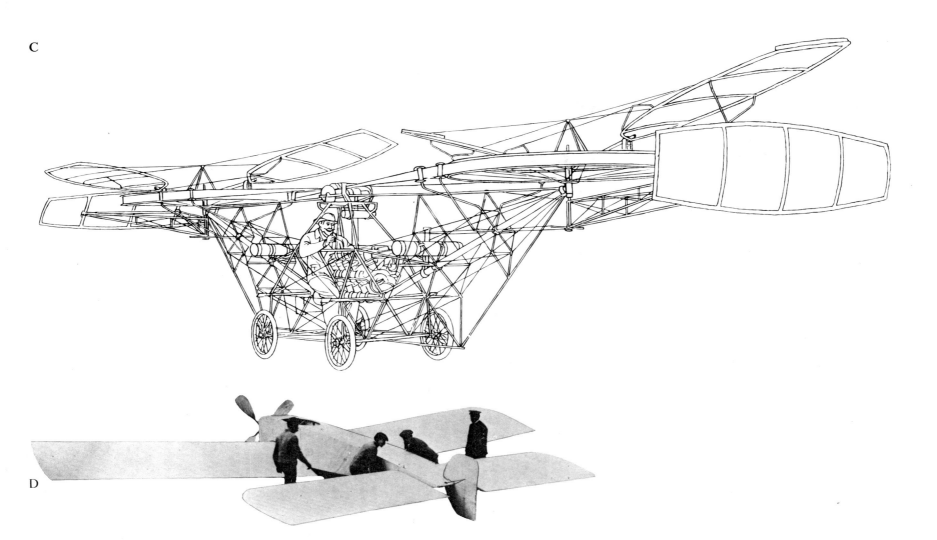

C

D

OCTOBER 1907

The A. E. A. (Aerial Experiment Association) is set up by Dr and Mrs Alexander Graham Bell, and includes Glenn Curtiss, J. A. D. McCurdy and others. It is based at Baddeck Bay, Nova Scotia, and at Hammondsport on Lake Keuka, New York.

5 OCTOBER 1907

First British Government airship, *Nulli Secundus*, flies from Farnborough to the Crystal Palace near London, piloted by Colonel J. E. Capper and S. F. Cody.

10 NOVEMBER 1907

Louis Blériot introduces, at Issy-les-Moulineaux, the modern-configuration tractor monoplane, his *No VII*, with main planes, covered-in fuselage, and tail-unit. It is not successful, but is to have much influence.
See figure D

10 NOVEMBER 1907

First flight in Europe of over one minute: Henry Farman on his *Voisin-Farman I* biplane, at Issy-les-Moulineaux. This is the first European flight to exceed the Wrights' 59 seconds of 17 December 1903.

13 NOVEMBER 1907

First piloted helicopter rises vertically in free flight, at Lisieux, France. Built by Paul Cornu, it is powered by a 24-hp Antoinette engine driving two rotors.
See figure C

30 NOVEMBER 1907

In France, the Lebaudy airship *Patrie* breaks loose, in a high wind, from her ground crew, and flies off with no one on board. She disappears in the direction of the Atlantic Ocean and is never seen again.

A   *Ellehammer's triplane, 1907.*
B   *Diagram of a wing-tip vortex from Lanchester's* Aerodynamics, *1907.*
C   *The first helicopter to rise under its own power with a man, designed by Paul Cornu, 1907.*
D   *Blériot's prophetic monoplane No. VII, 1907.*

SECTION III

FROM THE EARLY PIONEERS TO THE PASSENGER AIRLINER, 1908 TO 1929 A.D.

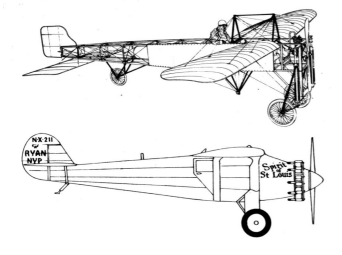

Louis Blériot's frail No. XI *in which he made his epoch-making crossing of the English Channel in 1909 is shown here above another epoch-making aeroplane,* Spirit of St Louis, *which Charles Lindbergh flew solo across the Atlantic in 1927. Both these flights did much to increase public awareness of the possibilities of aviation.*

A

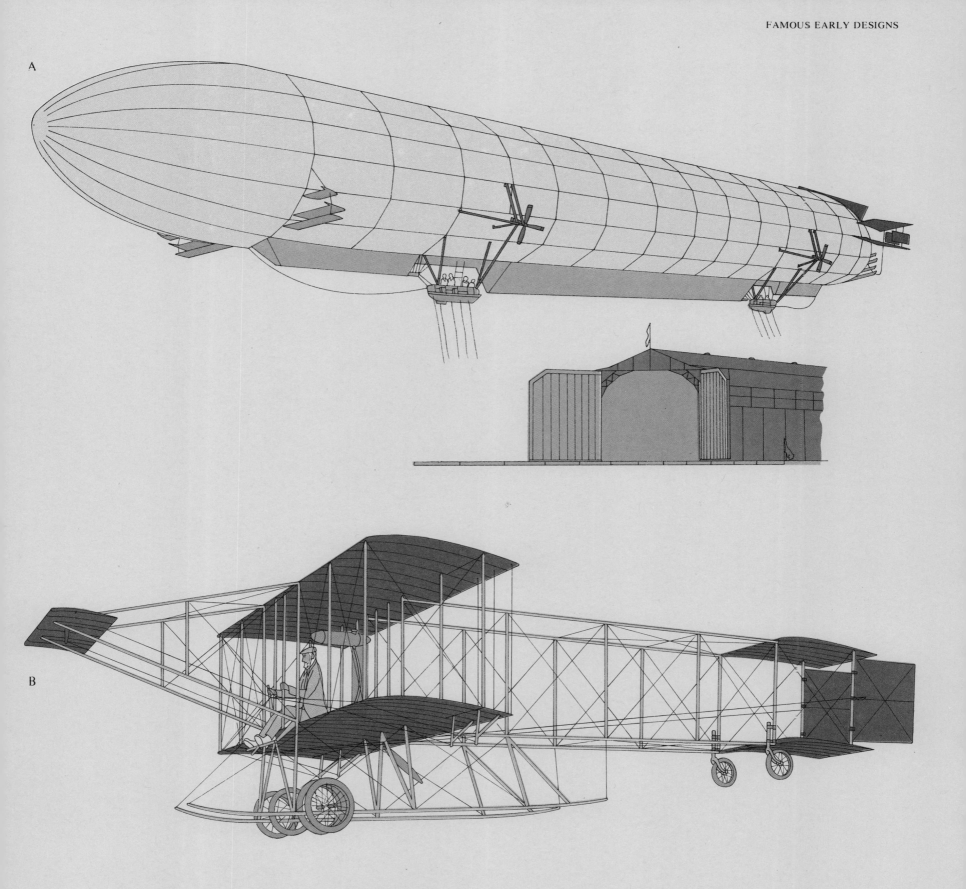

B

A   *Early passenger-carrying Zeppelin
     above its floating hangar, 1909—
     1910.*
B   *Most famous of early European
     biplanes: the* Henry Farman III, *1909.*

On January 13th 1908, Henry Farman made the first circular flight—but only just —in Europe; Farman was English by birth but lived in France, and was later to become a French citizen. But by August, European flying had still only reached a tentative, or hesitant, stage, with Voisin biplanes—which had no control in roll—and Blériot and *Antoinette* monoplanes managing to stay airborne for up to some twenty minutes, with little or no ability to manoeuvre in the air.

Meanwhile, the Wrights in America had been building some fine new aeroplanes and engines; and when at last they reached commercial agreements, both with Europe and the United States Army, they started flying again early in 1908 and took up a passenger for the first time in history. Then Wilbur Wright went to France, and first flew in public in August 1908. He continued to perform brilliantly at Auvours (near Le Mans) throughout the year, making many flights of over an hour, and one of 2 ½ hours: by his flying, he literally "revolutionised the aviators' world", as the French Count de La Vaulx said. This revolution was primarily a revelation of perfect flight-control, with the machine being banked, turned, circled, and flown in figures of eight, all with the greatest of ease; and secondly, a revelation of propulsion technology, as the Wright airscrews were geared down to rotate at optimum speed, producing maximum thrust for minimum power; whereas all the European propellers rotated at engine speed, and thus too fast properly to "grip" the air. Having absorbed these lessons, the Europeans took little more than a year to rival the Wrights, and three years to overtake them.

The first European fully to grasp the Wrights' "message" was Farman; it was he who first fitted large effective flap-type ailerons to his much-modified Voisin machine in the Autumn of 1908. With these in place, he made the world's first cross-country flight, from Bouy to Reims (16 ½ miles) on October 30th. The day after, Blériot made another pioneering cross-country flight. Mention must be made here of the remarkable aeroplanes and engines built by Leon Levavasseur; the latter might almost be said to have made European aviation possible; these aircraft and engines were all named *Antoinette*, after his business chief's daughter.

Meanwhile, the airship had appeared during the years 1900—1908 as the type of aircraft on which hopes—both civil and military—were chiefly focussed; flying, to the Europeans, at first seemed much more within their grasp by means of lighter-than-air craft. The *Lebaudy* airship became the first practical vehicle in 1903—1905; and the great rigid Zeppelins, of which the first had just flown in 1900, had reached a high degree of practicality by 1908. From 1910 to 1914,

five Zeppelins ran a tourist service in Germany during which over 35,000 passengers were carried some 107,000 miles (172,535 km) without a single fatality. Zeppelin was one of the great men of flying, who not only pioneered the large rigid airship, but later helped to pioneer the multi-engine aeroplane.

The year 1909 marked a decisive stage in the history of aviation; for in that year, having learnt the Wrights' prime lesson of flight-control, and having applied it in their machines, the Europeans staged two events of epoch-making importance. One was Louis Blériot's crossing of the English Channel in his frail *No XI* monoplane on July 25th, which the governments of Europe rightly saw as an ominous sign of things to come, especially in the danger of aerial invasion. The other event was the world's first great aviation meeting for the public to attend, held in August near Reims in France. Farman was the popular "hero" of Reims: after using, and constantly modifying, a Voisin biplane since 1907, he designed his own first biplane early this year (1909); it was the *Henry Farman III*, and—with its numerous progeny —this elegant machine became one of the great classic aircraft of history.

Particularly important was the fact that there were six machines at the Reims meeting which were on sale to the public; these were the Wright, Henry Farman, Curtiss, and Voisin biplanes—the last (without any control in roll) being already obsolescent— the Blériot type XI, and the efficient and graceful *Antoinette,* monoplanes. The Goupy and Breguet biplanes, with their tractor-propulsion, long fuselages, and tail-unit control surfaces, were to be practical machines by the end of the year, and were to establish the standard biplane configuration for the next thirty years. Upon these eight aircraft was to be built the entire structure of modern aviation, and every aeroplane flying today is a direct descendant of this first generation of flying-machines. With the Reims meeting, the aeroplane had finally "arrived" in the consciousness of the public; it was now looked upon as the latest of the world's practical vehicles, albeit a somewhat dangerous—but exciting—one.

There were two other items which helped to lead to the Golden Age of Aviation which was now opening: one was the famous Gnome rotary engine, built by the Seguin brothers; the other, the propellers of Lucien Chauvière, which were the first European airscrews to rival the Wrights' screws, and did much to help Europe gain the ascendency in practical flying.

Aviation came to rival the automobile in sport, and the two were closely linked. Automobilism had increased by leaps and bounds during the early 1900s, and the new profession of aviation found a ready-made reservoir of man-power, engineering experience, and know-how, which came to

be of benefit to both the road and the air.

Aviation in the brief period 1910—1914 spread rapidly over the civilised world and the number of different types of aeroplane which appeared was enormous. Women joined men as pilots; passenger-carrying soon became an everyday event and virtually every kind of activity in the air was born during this expansive phase of flying. These activities included: radio communication to and from the ground; night flying; seaplane flying; military flying, including reconnaissance in actual warfare; artillery spotting; practice bombing; shipboard take-offs and landings; long-distance flying; dangerous trans-Alpine and over-water flying; airmail flying; the formation of national air forces; parachuting from aeroplanes; the successful inherently stable aeroplane; and aerobatics. Of particular significance was the successful flying of large multi-engine transports, which were first pioneered by Igor Sikorsky (1913) in Russia; then, inspired by Sikorsky, they were principally promoted in Germany by the far-sighted Count von Zeppelin: from these the airliner of the future was to develop. Of special significance was the first single-seat scout of history, the *B.S.1.,* produced in 1912 by the British Government aircraft factory at Farnborough, which then inspired the Sopwith *Tabloid* in 1913: these two machines were the ancestors of all the fighting scouts and fighters of World War I and of every fighter thereafter.

Meanwhile, two other developments (1910 —1912) were to have a vital and far-reaching influence on the future of aviation. First was the pioneering of the seaplane by Fabre in France, in March of 1910. The seaplane was then siezed upon by Curtiss in America who, in January 1911, flew the first really practical seaplane of history: it was also Curtiss who, next month, created the first amphibian; thereafter, Curtiss led this field for many years. The second vital development was the invention of the "monocoque" method of construction, in which the aircraft's skin bears most of the loads and allows a roomy fuselage for passengers or freight: this was the work of the Swiss inventor Ruchonnet, which the Frenchman Bechereau applied first to the famous Deperdussin monoplane of 1912, named the *Monocoque Deperdussin.* It was this freeing of the interior of the aeroplane fuselage from wires and struts which was to lead directly to the modern transport machines and their cargoes of passengers and freight.

The configurations of the many aircraft being built before World War I divided themselves chiefly into three basic types of machine; (1) the pusher biplane (with forward elevator), (2) the tractor biplane, and (3) the tractor monoplane: all these types had either wing-warping or ailerons, and the last two had their elevators on the tail. As 1914 approached, unfounded fears were fostered

about the structural reliability of the monoplane and designers were reluctantly forced to abandon much of their work with these admirable single-surface aircraft. This meant that by the start of World War I in August 1914, comparatively few monoplane types survived and the biplane had become predominant in all fields of flying.

There were few basic technical advances to be incorporated in successful military aircraft during World War I, although by the end of hostilities some far-reaching developments were just coming into use. When war was declared in 1914 there were only some 200 Allied aircraft and about 180 German machines on the Western front. The aeroplane started the War as a purely reconnaissance machine and this led to highly successful forms of aircraft for gun-spotting, observation of troop movements and other military tasks. When the War ended, the aeroplane had been developed into various specialised

A   *Louis Blériot's No. XI monoplane in which he made the first flight across the English Channel 1909.*
B   *Glenn H. Curtiss built the first flying-boat and tested it in San Diego harbour, 1912.*

forms, from the small fighting scout to the large multi-engine bomber. The War years saw a great increase in engine power; the ability to lift more weight; faster speeds; and better maximum altitudes.

One of the most important of wartime advances was the French invention (in 1915) of a machine-gun firing directly forward through the propeller, the blades being protected by metal deflector plates. As soon as one of these machines was captured by the Germans, they rapidly developed a proper interrupter gear to ensure safe and uninterrupted forward firing between the propeller blades, without hitting them: this in turn was soon copied by the Allies.

Late in the War, some other remarkable technical developments were to be seen, despite previous failure to gain acceptance of them. As early as 1915, Hugo Junkers produced an all-metal, fully cantilever-wing monoplane (the J.1) which evoked scepticism, rather than enthusiasm, from the German High Command. This was neither the first nor the last time that military opinion proved out-of-touch with technical improvements. But by 1917 Junkers had produced one of the most important machines of the whole War period, the J.4; this was an all-metal—chiefly duralumin—sesquiplane for ground attack, heavily armed and armoured. Then came the first low-wing cantilever monoplane fighters from Junkers, which marked a complete innovation. Civil developments of such machines, after the War, were to transform aviation.

In the lighter-than-air field, the Germans at first pinned much faith on their military Zeppelins as terror-weapons for bombing; but they had only limited success. Britain employed to advantage small airships for naval reconnaissance and both sides in the War made considerable use of the tethered observation balloon for gun-spotting, where the French design by Captain Caquot (1916), with its bulbous fins, established itself as the steadiest of these craft, variations of which are still in use.

The aero-engine advanced during the War from small in-line and rotary types of some 80-100 h.p. to large V-motors of 300-400 h.p. Aircraft speeds which, at the start of the War, were between 75 and 100 mph (120-160 km/h) only advanced to some 140-150 mph; but the machines could climb to over 20,000 feet.

During the War, aerial fighting, especially among fighter pilots, created for the first time in history a new and strange kind of life all of its own, and developed an individual character and code of ethics. Such vividly personal combat prompted an almost medieval conception of chivalry; even a new word was coined—the "ace"—for outstanding aerial victors. These men came to experience an intense and romantic relationship with their aircraft, their friends, and their enemies.

With the end of the War there came a great and profound sense of relief and many brave men turned their attention to peaceful adventures involving aeroplanes. In 1919, there occurred a number of spectacular events which focussed attention on the peacetime possibilities of the aeroplane. The Atlantic was flown twice; first across in May but with intermediate landings in the Azores, was the American Lieutenant Commander Read and his crew in a Curtiss NC-4 flying-boat: then in June came the first direct crossing, by the British Captain Alcock and Lieutenant Brown in a converted Vickers Vimy bomber. The airship was not far behind, and in July the British rigid *R.34* made not only the first Atlantic crossing by a lighter-than-air vehicle, but a double crossing.

Air transport, with regular scheduled airlines, got slowly under way, and then progressed somewhat erratically, using at first converted war machines such as Handley Page and Farman bombers, and then specially designed airliners. Germany and Holland were soon far ahead in building transport machines, the Germans using especially the low-wing all-metal Junkers cantilever monoplanes, starting with the small *F.13*; the Dutch kept to the high-wing cantilever monoplanes pioneered by their countryman, Fokker, who had built aircraft for the Germans in the War. For the first years of peace, the Germans were severely handicapped by Peace Treaty prohibitions, which forbade them to build any aircraft except gliders. But when they were allowed to produce civil aircraft, they forged ahead with great energy and ability.

Along with the proliferation of airlines, many long-distance record flights across continents and oceans were carried out by the great nations, often with an eye to pioneering international air-routes. By the end of the 1920s, the Junkers and Fokker firms were flying successful three-engined airliners the world over, and the all-metal—or mostly metal—machine was becoming steadily more popular.

The growth of passenger-carrying led to the full exploitation of the monocoque construction mentioned before; this allowed a large and roomy fuselage for the carriage of passengers or freight. This method was being joined, at the end of the decade, by stressed-skin wings and tail-surfaces, introduced by another German engineer, Adolf Rohrbach, but first brought brilliantly to general attention in the American Lockheed Vega (1927), with a configuration quite new to the aircraft industry. The type represented by the Vega was a single-engine high-wing monoplane, to take five or six passengers at speeds—according to the engine—of some 110-135 mph (175-220 km/h) over distances of 500 -900 miles (800-1400 km). The flying-boat was also gaining in popularity for long overseas routes, with both Britain and Germany in the lead.

A First effective heavy bomber of World War I, the Handley Page 0/100.
B The Farnborough-designed S.E.5 A British fighter of World War I.
C Fokker D.VII, an outstanding German fighter of World War I.

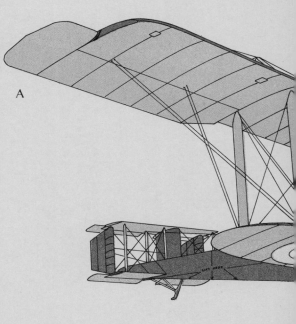

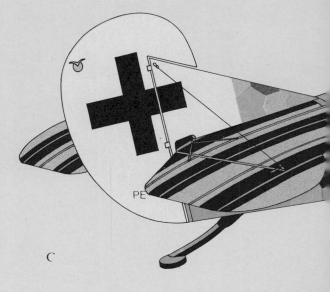

B

Other remarkable features of this decade of the 1920s were the growth of gliding and the high-performance glider—which developed into craft with very high aspect-ratio wings and ultra-light construction— and the spread of light aeroplane clubs. The former was led by Germany, stimulated there by the severe Peace Treaty restrictions on aircraft construction; the latter by Britain, with the de Havilland firm producing in 1925 the ideal machine for club use in their two-seat biplane, the *Moth*.

In military aviation, progress naturally tended to be slow after the War, with a general preference for the biplane still persisting; the chief accent was on manoeuverable fighters. But an event which was to prove of crucial importance took place in the United States in 1921, when Brigadier General "Billy" Mitchell dealt a severe blow to the confidence, pride and out-of-date conceptions of his naval colleagues when he proved his belief in the vulnerability of battleships from the air, by bombing and sinking a so-called "unsinkable" ex-German warship; his action was to change the whole face of warfare at sea within a generation.

One of the best stimulants to producing small fast aeroplanes was the series of races for the Schneider Trophy for seaplanes: although established as far back as 1913, it was in the 1920s that the Schneider Trophy races brought startling innovations in aircraft design, and such winners as the American Curtiss *R3C-2* in 1925 at a speed of 232.5 mph (374.17 km/h) and the British Supermarine *S.5* in 1927 at a speed of 281.65 mph (453.27 km/h) were strongly to influence the design of military fighters in the future.

In 1923, somewhat off the beaten track, there was flown by Juan de la Cierva in Spain—his later work being done in Britain —the first of his Autogiros; although not a helicopter proper, this type of gyroplane was to precipitate the final drive which achieved the practical helicopter in the late 1930s.

In the realm of engines, the outstanding feature of the decade was the rise to eminence of the powerful air-cooled "radials" which, in motors giving some 550 h.p., came to power many of the world's outstanding transports.

In accessories and equipment, great strides were also made in the 1920s, one of the most important being the Handley Page slotted wing, which postponed the onset of stalling, hence lowering the landing speeds of aircraft and making them much safer to operate. By the end of this period, this device was in universal service. The wing-flap also began to come into general use, as did the practical retractable undercarriage; but both were associated with low-wing cantilever monoplanes and it was not until the 1930s that such machines were to become widespread. Metal propellers—but not with variable pitch—came into general use and there was great activity in the field of instruments, the Sperry gyro-horizon and directional gyro being invented during the 1920s.

As thousands of aircraft were now being built the world over, intensive research in aerodynamics was being carried out, particularly as a result of F. W. Lanchester's theory of circulatory flow, which had first been published—but not widely appreciated—in 1907, and was complemented by Ludwig Prandtl in Germany.

The airship in all sizes and forms—rigid, semi-rigid, and non-rigid—had some considerable success in the 1920s, especially when the British rigid *R-34* made a double crossing of the Atlantic in July 1919, and the Italian semi-rigid *Norge* flew over the North Pole in 1926. But there were some major tragedies, and great loss of life, with the larger rigids: the British *R-38* broke up in the air in 1921; the ex-German Zeppelin, handed over to the French (re-named *Dixmude*), mysteriously crashed into the Mediterranean in 1923 with the loss of all on board; and the United States *Shenandoah* broke up in the air in 1925.

In aviation, the United States was surprisingly backward until 1927; she was also slow in opening up passenger routes, and in commercial and private flying generally. The position was dramatically altered—almost overnight—by the sensational impact of Charles Lindbergh's solo flight across the Atlantic in May 1927, in his Ryan monoplane *Spirit of St Louis*. The effect of this fine achievement was immediate and decisive, and American aviation was never again to look back. Lindbergh's flight, and its profound influence on aviation, is one of the great examples in human history where the enterprise and bravery of one individual can influence the fate of nations, and help transform the world we live in.

In June of 1928 a second prophetic event in the field of reaction propulsion took place, when Stamer successfully made a short flight in a glider propelled by rockets, an enterprise which was in the hands of Fritz von Opel, F. W. Sander, and the great aerodynamicist Alexander Lippisch; this work was to continue next year, and it foreshadowed the rocket-powered aircraft of the future.

But this dramatic use of rockets was to hide what was one of the most important events in the history of our world; which led directly to the conquest of space. For in 1927 there was founded in Germany a group which called itself the Society for Space Travel: it was treated with good-humoured derision, but its members were soon to include not only romantic dreamers but down-to-earth practical rocket-engineers. There was also a great rocket-engineer in America, Professor R. H. Goddard, who "flew" the world's first liquid fuel rocket in 1926. But the American was not known to the Germans, and the latter went quietly on with their work.

A

C

HANNIBAL

IMPERIAL AI
LONDO

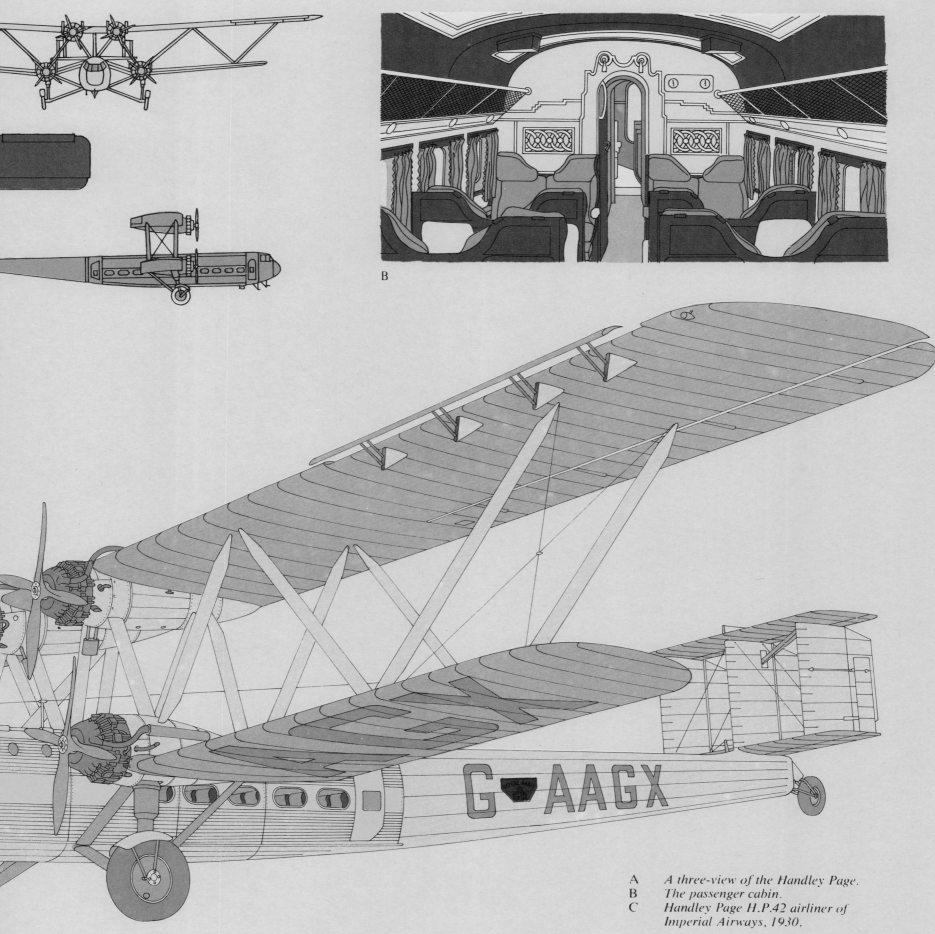

B

A   *A three-view of the Handley Page.*
B   *The passenger cabin.*
C   *Handley Page H.P.42 airliner of*
       Imperial Airways, 1930.

I know of only one bird—the parrot—that talks;
and it can't fly very high.

WILBUR WRIGHT
(IN DECLINING TO MAKE A SPEECH IN 1908)

The ground was very rough and hard, and as we
tore along, at an increasing pace that was very
soon greater than any motor I had yet been in,
I expected to be jerked and jolted. But the motion
was wonderfully smooth—smoother yet—and
then—! Suddenly there had come into it a new,
indescribable quality—a lift—a lightness—a life!
Very many there are now who know that feeling:
that glorious, gliding sense that the sea-bird has
known this million years, and which man so long
and so vainly envied it, and which, even now,
familiarity can never rob of its charm. But picture, if you can, what it meant for the first time;
when all the world of Aviation was young and
fresh and untried; when to rise at all was a glorious
adventure, and to find oneself flying swiftly in
the air, the too-good-to-be-true realisation of a
life-long dream. You wonderful aerial record
breakers of today and of the years to come, whose
exploits I may only marvel at and envy, I have
experienced something that can never be yours
and can never be taken away from me—the
rapture, the glory and the glamour of 'the very
beginning'.

GERTRUDE BACON
(WRITING OF HER FLIGHT WITH R. SOMMER IN AUGUST 1909)

CHAPTER EIGHT

FROM 1908 A.D. TO 1913 A.D.

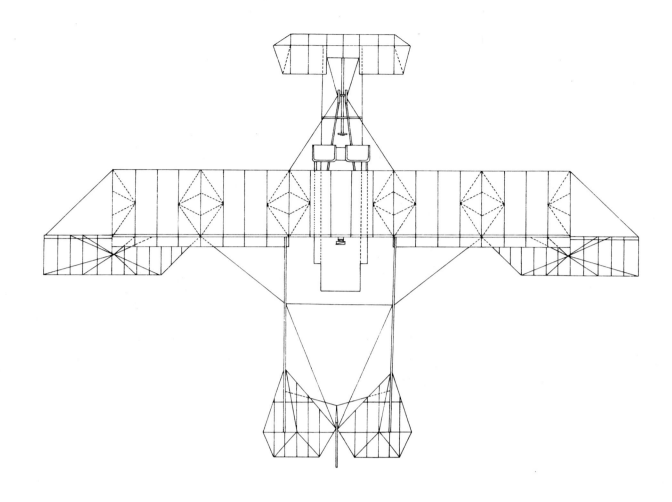

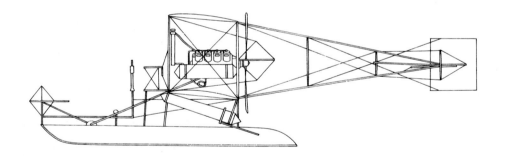

The plans of the Glenn Curtiss A-1 Hydro-
aeroplane which he supplied to the US Navy.

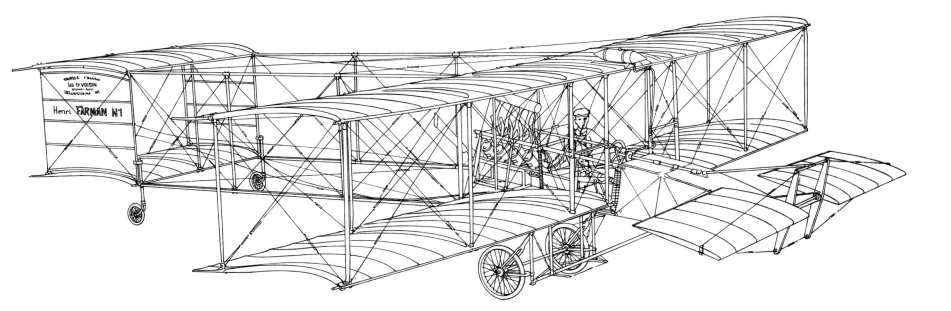

1908

The year 1908 is an *annus mirabilis* in aviation history, for the Wright brothers make their first flight in public during August and September, and thereby transform the whole sphere of practical flying by their demonstration of flight-control, especially lateral control. The Wrights reveal in dramatic fashion the true nature of the aeroplane and its control in the air. They reveal a type of flying-machine whose every part and feature has grown out of masterly design and experi-mentation, a machine inspired by a clear vision of the nature of mechanical flight, and of the proper kind of vehicle to accomplish it. This vision and this experi-mentation are seen to have conditioned and unified the whole aircraft, its aerodynamic qualities, its construction, motor, propellers and—above all—its flight-control system. Where the Europeans chauffeur their machines cautiously and doggedly, as if they were steering fractious winged automobiles through the alien air, the Wrights ride their aircraft as if man and machine are one; ride them with perfect ease and assurance, ride them with the mastery of born airmen. They are, indeed, the mythical "*hommes oiseaux*" come to life.

13 JANUARY 1908

First European kilometre circle flown in 1 minute 28 seconds at Issy-les-Moulineaux, by Henry Farman on his Voisin-Farman, thereby winning the Grand Prix d'Aviation Deutsch-Archdeacon.
See figure A

6 MAY 1908

The Wrights fly for first time since 1905, and first use upright seating. They fly at the Kill Devil Hills, and the machine is their *Flyer III* of 1905, modified to take two people sitting upright. They make flights until 14 May.

14 MAY 1908

First passenger flight in an aeroplane. Wilbur Wright takes up Charles W. Furnas at the Kill Devil Hills, for a flight lasting 28.6 seconds.

23 MAY 1908

First aeroplane flight in Italy is made at Rome by Léon Delagrange.

29 MAY 1908

First passenger flight in Europe: Henry Farman takes up Ernest Archdeacon for a brief hop at Issy-les-Moulineaux.

30 MAY 1908

First European flight of over a quarter of an hour. Léon Delagrange in France on his Voisin-Delagrange. (The Wrights first flew for over a quarter of an hour in September 1905.)

A   *Henry Farman makes the first official circle in Europe; January 13th, 1908.*

A   *Curtiss flying the A. E. A. June Bug,*
    1908.
B   *Standard Wright Flyer A, 1908.*

C   *First effective ailerons are fitted*
    to Henry Farman's Voisin, 1908.
D   *First fatality in an aeroplane crash.*
    Lieutenant Selfridge is killed when
    flying with Orville Wright, 1908.

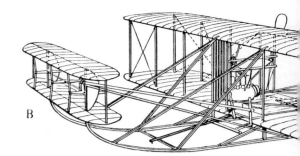

B

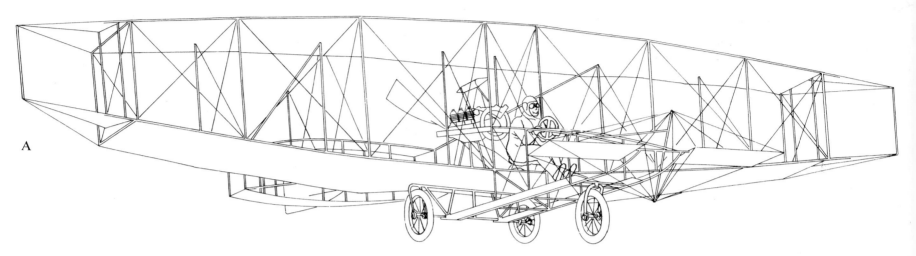

A

JUNE 1908

First American to fly promisingly after the
Wrights is Glenn H. Curtiss who flies his
June Bug 1266 ft (*c.* 386 m) at Hammonds-
port, USA.
See figure A

JUNE 1908

A. V. Roe tests his Wright-derived biplane
on Brooklands motor-racing track in
England. He succeeds in making hops of up
to 150 ft (*c.* 46 m), probably with a downhill
assisted take-off.

28 JUNE 1908

J. C. H. Ellehammer, the Dane, makes the
first hopflights in Germany at Kiel (the best
lasting 11 seconds) on his *No IV*, a tractor
biplane.

4 JULY 1908

Zeppelin LZ-4 makes a 12-hour flight,
during with she covers a distance of 235
miles (*c.* 378 km) and crosses the Alps from
Friedrichshafen to Lucerne and Zürich,
having reached a speed *en route* of 32 mph
(*c.* 51 km/h).

8 JULY 1908

First woman flies as aeroplane passenger:
Mme Peltier with Delagrange at Issy-les-
Moulineaux, France.

4 AUGUST 1908

Zeppelin LZ-4, after high hopes for her,
starts on her government acceptance trials.
But she suffers from engine trouble, lands
for repairs, is torn loose in a violent storm,
and is completely destroyed. This setback
causes immense concern in Germany, and at
last enlists the sympathy of the Emperor
William II.

8 AUGUST 1908

First flight in public by one of the Wright
brothers: Wilbur flies at Hunaudières, near
Le Mans. This starts his brilliant series of
flights in France, first at Hunaudiéres, then
at Auvours, also near Le Mans. Wilbur
revolutionises European aviation by his
mastery of control—especially lateral
control—and Europe at last realises for the
first time the true nature and technique of
flight-control. During his spectacular series
of flights in France, he is in the air for a
total of over 25 hours, which includes
making six flights of over half-an-hour;

six of over one hour; and one of over two
hours. He takes up passengers on more than
60 occasions. His last flight of the year is
on 31 December.
See figure B

SEPTEMBER 1908

René Lorin, a French artillery officer,
publishes the first of his articles suggesting
jet-propulsion by the exhaust from two
petrol engines. He also suggests the jets
should be tiltable down-wards, to aid take-
off.

6 SEPTEMBER 1908

First European flight of about half-an-hour
(29 minutes 53 seconds) by Léon
Delagrange on his Voisin, at Issy-les-
Moulineaux.

9 SEPTEMBER 1908

First flight of over an hour by Orville
Wright at Fort Myer, Virginia, USA.
Orville's flights at Fort Myer cause as great
a sensation as those by Wilbur in France.

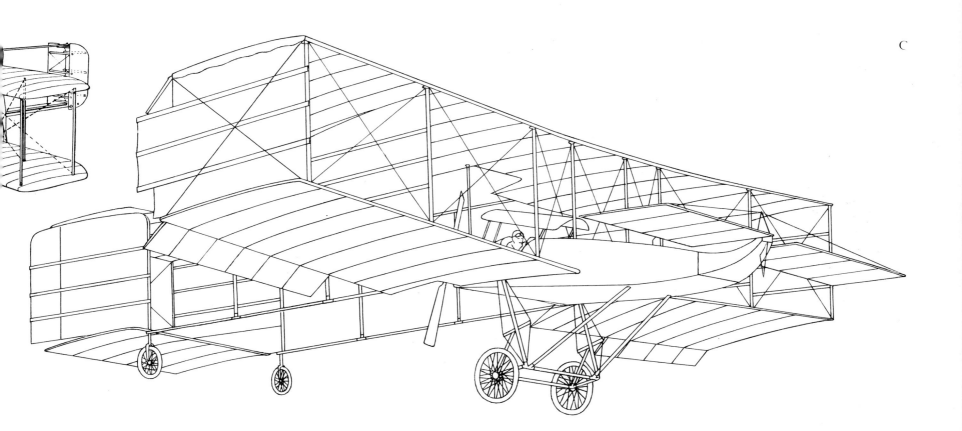

17 SEPTEMBER 1908

First fatality in powered aviation:
Lieutenant Thomas Etholon Selfridge of the
United States Army Signal Corps is killed
when flying with Orville Wright, who is
injured, at Fort Myer. A propeller blade
splits, and this leads to the severing of a
wire, and the collapse of the tail-unit. This is
the fourth aeroplane fatality, and the first
in powered aviation.
See figure D

21 SEPTEMBER 1908

First flight of over 1 ½ hours by Wilbur
Wright at Auvours, France, for 1 hour 31
minutes 25 seconds.

25 SEPTEMBER 1908

The Lebaudy airship *République* bursts in
mid-air after a piece of a propeller pierces
the envelope. It crashes, north of Moulins.

OCTOBER 1908

First near-practical ailerons used on a
biplane: Henry Farman's modified Voisin-
Farman.
See figure C

D

A   *Latham after his first crash into the English Channel, on the* Antoinette IV, *1909.*
B   *The first practical monoplane with ailerons; the* Antoinette IV, *1908—1909.*

C   *A map showing the route Blériot took on his cross-Channel flight, 1909.*

B

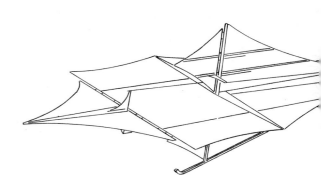

A

OCTOBER 1908

Hans Grade becomes the first native German pilot. He makes tentative flights at Magdeburg on a triplane of his own construction.

OCTOBER 1908

First practical ailerons used on a monoplane: the *Antoinette IV*, in France.
See figure B

6 OCTOBER 1908

First passenger flight of over 1 hour: Wilbur Wright takes Fordyce up at Auvours in France for 1 hour 4 minutes 26 seconds.

7 OCTOBER 1908

Wilbur Wright takes up his first woman passenger, Mrs Hart O. Berg, at Auvours.

16 OCTOBER 1908

First powered flight in Britain: by S. F. Cody, who is still an American citizen,

at Farnborough in his *British Army Aeroplane No. 1 (Cody 1b)*, when he covers 1 390 ft (*c.* 424 m) in 27 seconds.

30 OCTOBER 1908

First cross-country flight: Henry Farman flies from Bouy to Reims, France, about 16 ½ miles (27 km) in 20 minutes. His modified Voisin-Farman biplane is fitted with four large ailerons.

31 OCTOBER 1908

In France, Louis Blériot flies, in his *VIII-ter* from Toury, round Artenay, and back, with two landings *en route* some 17 miles (28 km) in 22 minutes flying time.

DECEMBER 1908

A. E. A. *Silver Dart* is first tested by McCurdy, a Canadian.

31 DECEMBER 1908

First flight of over 2 hours: Wilbur Wright flies for 2 hours 20 minutes 23 seconds,

covering some 77 miles (124 km), at Auvours, France, thus winning the Michelin prize.

1909

In this year powered aviation comes of age. The aeroplane becomes technically mature and established in the public mind. It is looked upon, of course, not as a form of general transport but as a new species of mechanical steed, for sport and spectacle. Then, after Blériot flies the Channel in July, the resulting huzzas are tempered with suspicion, and with the fear that this novel "toy" might one day become a menace to civilisation. But it is the Reims aviation meeting in August that brings home, to governments and public alike, the technical maturity and practicality of the aeroplane.

JANUARY 1909

First flying school is opened; the Wright school at Pau (Pont-Long), France.

FEBRUARY 1909

First aerodrome in Britain is established at Shellbeach (Leysdown) on the Isle of

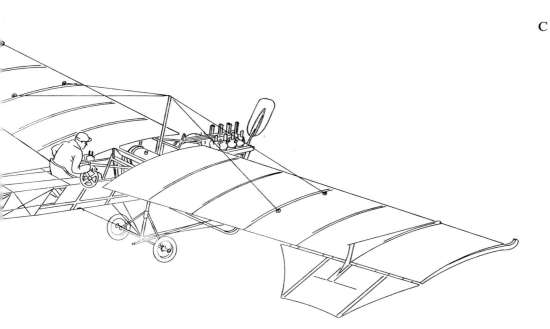

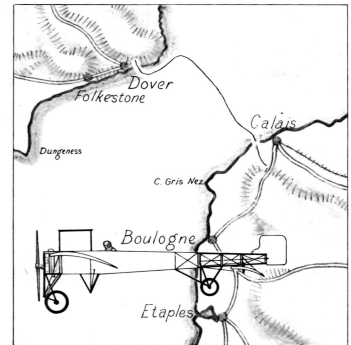

Sheppey in the Thames estuary, by the Aero Club of Great Britain and Short Brothers Ltd.

APRIL 1909

Henry Farman first flies *Henry Farman III*. This is the first machine wholly designed by him, and becomes one of the classic aircraft of history. It is also the first practical aileroned biplane.

15 APRIL 1909

Wilbur Wright begins flying at Centocelle near Rome and starts to train the first Italian to fly, Lieutenant Calderera.

23 APRIL 1909

First aeroplane flight in Austria: by the Frenchman, Georges Legagneux, on his Voisin at Vienna.

MAY 1909

Opening of Port-Aviation (Juvisy), France, as an aerodrome: it is the first to be deliberately prepared for aerial displays.

JUNE 1909

In France, the Gnome rotary engine made by the Seguin brothers, Louis and Laurent, goes into service, the first machine powered by it being Louis Paulhan's Voisin.

JUNE 1909

The Lebaudy airship *Russie*, having been commissioned by Russia, successfully passes trials in France and is then shipped to Russia. This is the first airship built by one nation for another.

5 JUNE 1909

First monoplane flight of over 1 hour; the Englishman, Hubert Latham, on the *Antoinette IV*, for 1 hour 7 minutes 37 seconds.

19 JULY 1909

First attempt to fly the English Channel: Hubert Latham on the *Antoinette IV*, attempts to fly from near Calais, France, and crashes into the sea. He is rescued unhurt.
See figure A

25 JULY 1909

First flight in Russia by Van den Schkrouff on a Voisin at Odessa.

25 JULY 1909

FIRST AEROPLANE CROSSING OF THE ENGLISH CHANNEL

Louis Blériot flies his Blériot XI from Les Baraques near Calais to Dover in 37 minutes. This event causes deep and universal concern about the possible military future of the aeroplane.
See figure C

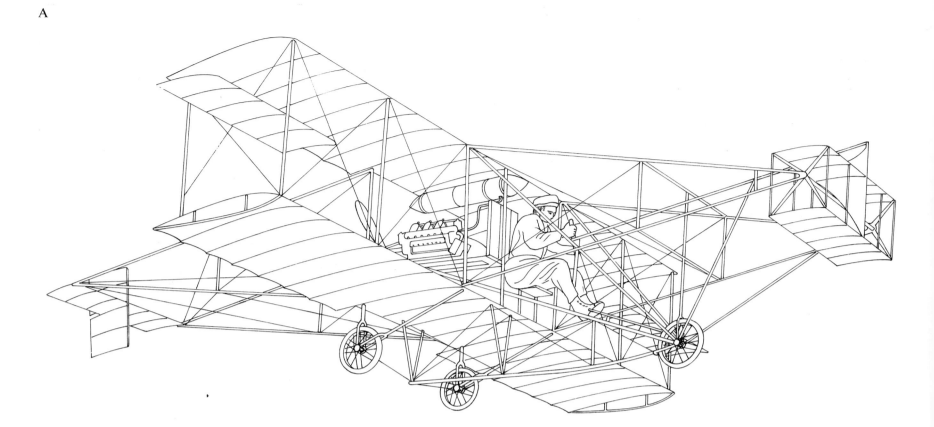

29 JULY 1909

First aeroplane flight in Sweden; by Georges Legagneux on his Voisin at Stockholm.

22—29 AUGUST 1909

The first great aviation meeting, at Bétheny, north of Reims in France: its full title is "La Grande Semaine d'Aviation de la Champagne", and it is to become known as the "Reims" meeting. It is largely financed—and generous prizes are given—by the Champagne industry. This meeting has as profound an effect on the technical and military world as the Channel crossing had on the world at large. Twenty-three machines are airborne and over 120 take-offs are made, eighty-seven of them resulting in flights of over three miles (c. 5 km). The record distance flight is made by Henry Farman on his *Henry Farman III*, when he covers some 112 miles (180 km) in 3 hours 4 minutes and 56.4 seconds. There are six practical types of machines at Reims, four biplanes (Wright, Farman, Curtiss and Voisin) and two monoplanes (Blériot and Antoinette).

28 AUGUST 1909

Two speed records are set up at the Reims meeting: over 20 km at 75.7 km/h (roughly 12 1/2 miles at 47 mph) by Glenn H. Curtiss on his *Golden Flyer*; and over 10 km at 76.95 km/h (roughly 6 miles at 48 mph) by Louis Blériot on his *No XII*. *See figure A*

15 OCTOBER 1909

Walter Wellman sets out from Spitzbergen, Norway, with three companions in his airship *America* in an attempt to fly over the North Pole. The flight is abandoned after 12 miles (c. 19 km), owing to the trail-rope breaking, and they return to base. Wellman abandons the project altogether after Peary reaches the North Pole. Wellman now changes his plans.
(See 15 October 1910)

18 OCTOBER 1909

The Comte de Lambert flies around the Eiffel Tower on Brancsy's Wright, taking off from and returning to Port-Aviation. He is Wilbur Wright's first pupil.

30 OCTOBER 1909

First circular mile flown in Britain on an all-British aeroplane by J. T. C. Moore-Brabazon on a Wright-derived Short machine, at Shellbeach.

NOVEMBER 1909

In Austria, Igo Etrich's *Taube* flies for the first time. It is derived from the Etrich-Wels glider of 1907.

1910

This year sees the wide popularisation of flying, with exploits, meeting, races, competitions and demonstrations staged to meet the new public demand to see aeroplanes, and even to fly in them. This great popular interest leads to a rapid expansion of aviation, and to a proliferation of aeroplane types. But, despite a growing reliability of aircraft and engines, basic technical progress is slow. The increase in joy-riding directs attention to the aeroplane as a possible passenger vehicle, and its ability thus to carry "cargo" also draws attention to its potential uses in war.

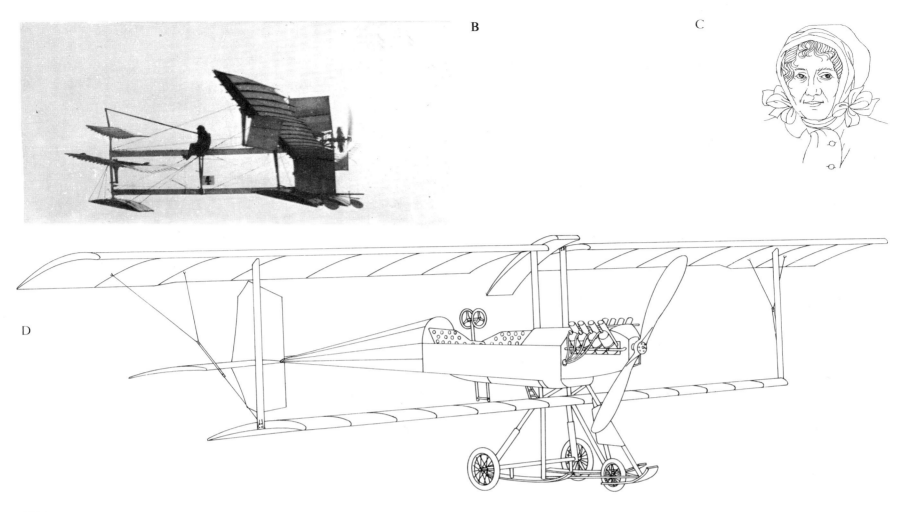

B

C

D

1910

In France, Louis Breguet and Ambroise Goupy tractor biplanes fly successfully and are very influential in establishing the tractor biplane tradition. The Goupy has staggered wings.
See figure D

10—20 JANUARY 1910

The Los Angeles aviation meeting is held, the first in the United States.

FEBRUARY 1910

A patent is granted to Professor Hugo Junkers for a cantilever "flying-wing" aeroplane, which would enclose all components. Junkers later founds the famous German aircraft company of the same name.

8 MARCH 1910

First woman becomes a qualified pilot: the Baroness de Laroche in France.
See figure C

10 MARCH 1910

First flights at night: by the Frenchman, Emile Aubrun, on a Blériot near Buenos Aires in the Argentine.

13 MARCH 1910

First flight in Switzerland; by Captain P. Engelhardt on his Wright at St Moritz.

28 MARCH 1910

First flight by a seaplane; by Henri Fabre on his canard float-plane, at Martigues, near Marseilles, France.
See figure B

27 APRIL 1910

The first aeroplane flight takes place in Portugal, by Mamet at Belem.

A   *Curtiss'* Golden Flyer, *1909*.
B   *The world's first seaplane, by Henri Fabre, 1910*.
C   *Baroness de Laroche*.
D   *The first successful Ereguet biplane, 1910*.

A

27, 28 APRIL 1910

London to Manchester air race and *Daily Mail* prize are won by Louis Paulhan against Claude Grahame-White; both fly Henry Farman biplanes.

22 JUNE 1910

First regular passenger-carrying airship service inaugurated: the firm DELAG operates an inter-urban service in Germany with five Zeppelins, and their record is magnificent. In their three years of operation they carry 34,228 passengers some 107,213 miles (172,535 km) in 1587 flights, and are airborne for 3167 hours without a single injury to any passenger or crew-member.
See figure B

30 JUNE 1910

First aeroplane bombing tests are made with dummy bombs on the shape of a battleship marked by buoys on Lake Keuka, New York State, USA, by Glenn H. Curtiss.
See figure A

17 AUGUST 1910

First Channel crossing with a passenger (Calais to Dover), by Franco-American J. B. Moisant who took a passenger and his mascot, a tabbycat named "Miss Paris" —the first animal to cross the Channel in an aeroplane.

27 AUGUST 1910

Radio is first used to send messages to and from an aeroplane in flight; by J. A. D. McCurdy on a Curtiss at Sheepshead Bay, New York State, using an H. M. Horton set.

28 AUGUST 1910

Armand Dufaux, the first native Swiss pilot, flies across Lake Geneva in his biplane.

3—7 SEPTEMBER 1910

The Harvard aviation meeting is held at Boston, Massachusetts, USA.

23 SEPTEMBER 1910

First aeroplane flight over the Alps, from near Brig to Domodossola (through the Simplon Pass) by the Peruvian Georges Chavez on a Blériot. He is fatally injured when landing and dies four days later.
See figure D

2 OCTOBER 1910

First mid-air collision: at the Milan meeting, between M. Thomas on an Antoinette and Captain Bertram Dickson on a Henry Farman. Dickson is seriously injured.
See figure C

15 OCTOBER 1910

Walter Wellman enlarges his airship *America* and sets off to fly the Atlantic with three companions, from Atlantic City, USA. She develops engine and other troubles, which force her to radio for help—the first airship-to-surface use of radio—and the crew are taken off, 400 miles (*c.* 644 km) out to sea, by the steamer *Trent* on October 18. The *America* drifts away and is never seen again.

17 OCTOBER 1910

A. R. Hawlsy and Augustus Post fly 1173 miles (*c.* 1890 km) in a balloon from St Louis, to North Lake Chilogoma, Canada. This is the longest balloon voyage in America.

22—31 OCTOBER 1910

Belmont Park, Long Island, International Aviation Meeting is held, (comparable to the Reims meeting of 1909), in which some forty planes are shown, and there is a race to the Statue of Liberty.

NOVEMBER 1910

Publication of the official report on Ader's trials with his *Avion III* on 12 and 14 October 1897, which shows clearly that he never left the ground on either occasion. (see 12, 14 October 1897)

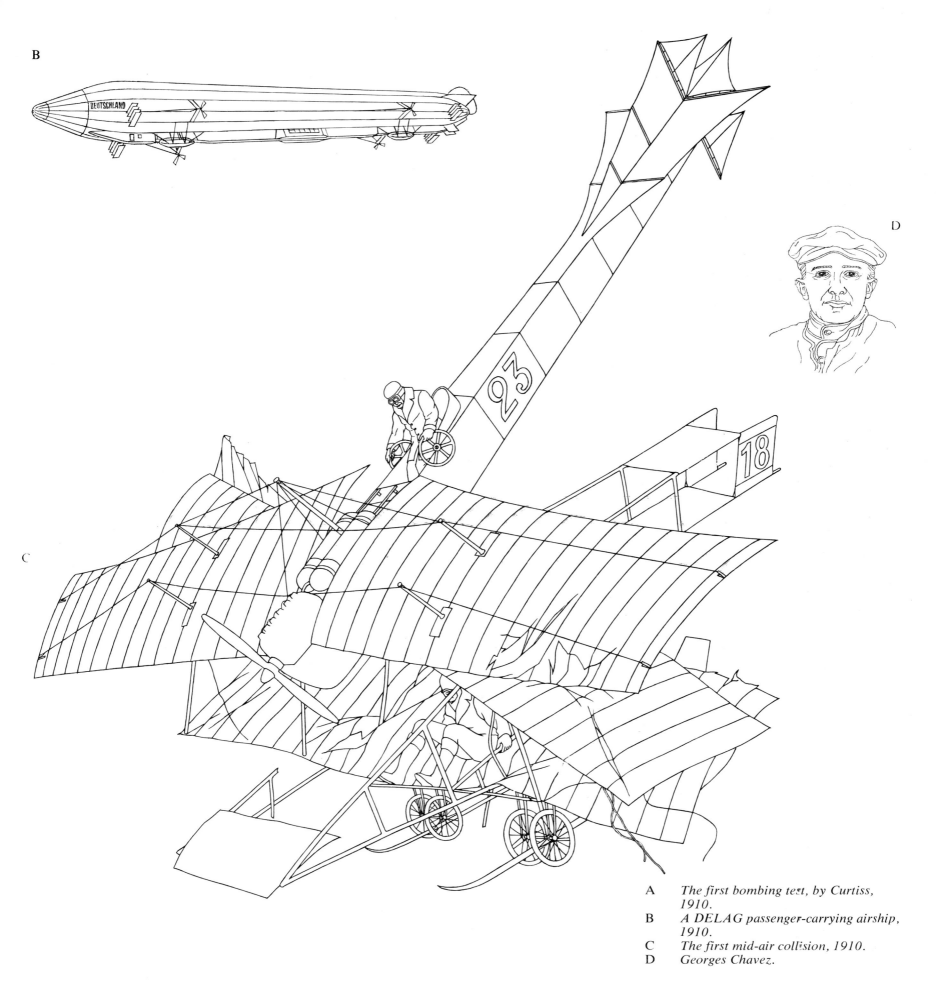

A *The first bombing test, by Curtiss, 1910.*
B *A DELAG passenger-carrying airship, 1910.*
C *The first mid-air collision, 1910.*
D *Georges Chavez.*

A

A   *Glenn H. Curtiss.*
B   *Ely takes off from the* USS
     Birmingham, 1910.
C   *The Farnborough B. S. 1 biplane*
     scout, the ancestor of all modern
     fighters, 1912.

D   *The Curtiss' single-float seaplane,*
     1911.
E   *The first use of the acroplane for*
     reconnaissance in warfare, 1911.

B

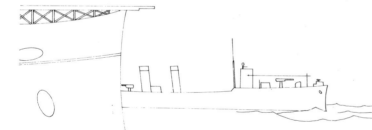

14 NOVEMBER 1910

Birth of the aircraft-carrier when Eugene B.
Ely takes off from the USS *Birmingham*
in Hampton Roads, Virginia, USA, on a
Curtiss biplane (see also 18 January 1911).
See figure B

1911

Basic progress is again slow in this year
which sees, however, the first long-distance
flights, the growing popularity of joy-riding,
an added apprehension and concern about
aerial warfare, the first actual use of the
aeroplane in war and a number of innovations in practical flying.

1911

First oleo-undercarriage is produced by
Robert Esnault-Pelterie, in France.

1911

Also in France, a Nieuport two-seat monoplane (derived from a Blériot by E. Nieuport)
is one of the earliest—if not the earliest
—aeroplane to be equipped with a machine-
gun.

EARLY 1911

First bomb-sight made; by US Lieutenant
Riley Scott.

18 JANUARY 1911

Eugene B. Ely, on a Curtiss biplane, flies
out to sea from San Francisco and lands on
the cruiser USS *Pennsylvania*. He then
takes off again and returns.

26 JANUARY 1911

First practical seaplane flies: the Curtiss
single-float plane, which is strongly influenced
by a tentative development by Fabre of his
1910 float-plane. Glenn H. Curtiss is the
pilot and he takes off from and lands in San
Diego Harbour, California, USA.
See figure D

MAY 1911

The Paris-Rome race is won by Lieutenant
de Vaisseau Conneau on a Blériot. He uses
the pseudonym André Charles Beaumont.

18 JUNE—19 JULY 1911

The International Circuit Race (Paris—
Brussels—London—Amiens—Paris) is won
by Lieutenant de Vaisseau Conneau
(Beaumont) on a Blériot.

C

E

D

21 JULY 1911

First woman to be killed in an aeroplane: Madame Denise Moore, when learning to fly a Henry Farman at the Camp de Châlons, France. She is flying solo at the time.

AUGUST 1911

First amphibian flies: a Voisin canard fitted with Fabre floats, in France.

AUGUST 1911

First air-sea rescue operation carried out: Hugh Robinson, on a Curtiss seaplane, rescues a pilot who has crashed in Lake Michigan, USA.

15 SEPTEMBER—5 NOVEMBER 1911

Calbraith P. Rodgers, on a Wright, flies across the United States from Long Island to Long Beach, California, *via* Chicago and San Antonio, Texas, 4000 miles (*c.* 6400 km) in 68 stages during 82 hours over 49 days. The machine is constantly damaged and repaired from spares carried—with Rodgers' wife—in a following train.

22 OCTOBER 1911

First use of the aeroplane in warfare: the Italian Captain Piazza on a Blériot, makes reconnaissance flight from Tripoli to Azizia, over Turkish positions.
See figure E

OCTOBER—NOVEMBER 1911

First "Concours Militaire" is held at Reims, France, and arouses widespread interest.

1912

This year was marked by a large-scale and official concern with the aeroplane's role in warfare; and by several important technical advances, including the introduction of monocoque construction, the first flying-boat, the first flight of over 100 mph (*c.* 161 km/h), and the extended use of metal in aircraft structures.

1912

The first single-seater scout flies: the British Farnborough BS1 biplane. This machine is the direct ancestor of every subsequent fighter. The chief designer is Geoffrey de Havilland.
See figure C

A   B

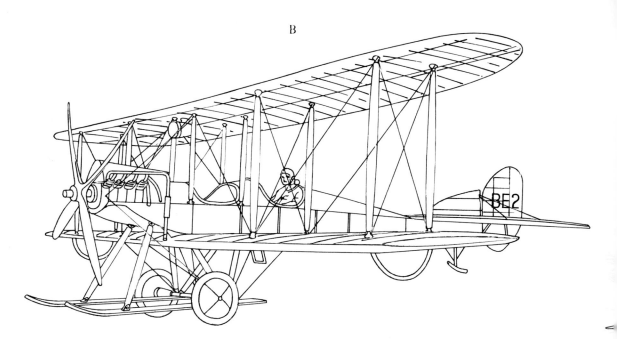

A   *Petr N. Nesterov.*
B   *The Farnborough B. E. 2
       aeroplane, 1913.*
C   *The Avro enclosed cabin biplane.*
D   *Igor Sikorsky's four-engined* Bolshoi,
       1913.

1912

The first successful flying-boats; by Curtiss in the United States and Denhaut in France: the latter adapts the Curtiss idea on his *Donnet-Lévêque* and then Curtiss copies Denhaut.

1912

Introduction of the monocoque fuselage at La Vidamée in France by Ruchonnet and Béchereau for the Deperdussin monoplane called "*Monocoque Deperdussin*".

1912

In Germany, Professor H. Reissner adopts aluminium wings, without fabric covering, in his canard-type monoplane.

MARCH 1912

The first seaplane meeting is held at Monaco. Seven pilots attend and it is won by Fischer, flying a Henry Farman float-plane.

16 APRIL 1912

First cross-Channel flight by a woman; the American Miss Harriet Quimby, on a Blériot monoplane, from Deal to Cap Gris-Nez.

1 JULY 1912

First woman pilot to be killed: Miss Quimby at Boston, in the United States.

2 JULY 1912

Melville Vaniman—one of Wellman's airship crew—builds his own airship *Akron* with the intention of flying the Atlantic, but it mysteriously bursts into flames on a test over Absecon Inlet. It crashes into the sea killing Vaniman and his four companions.

AUGUST 1912

The first enclosed cabin aeroplanes fly at the Military Trials in Great Britain: the Avro cabin monoplane and Avro cabin biplane, the pilot also sitting inside. *See figure C*

9 SEPTEMBER 1912

Jules Védrines, the French pilot, wins the Gordon Bennett Cup at Chicago on the *Monocoque Deperdussin* with a speed of 108.2 mph (*c.* 174 km/h).

27—29 OCTOBER 1912

Maurice Bienaimé and Rumpelmayer win the Gordon Bennett balloon race with a

flight of about 1360 miles (2191 km) from Stuttgart, Germany, to Ribnoyé, Russia.

NOVEMBER 1912

First successful catapult launch of a flying-boat at the Washington Navy Yard, from an anchored barge. The flying-boat is a Curtiss A-1 and the pilot is Lieutenant T. Ellyson.

31 DECEMBER 1912

A temporary ban of one year on monoplanes in Britain and France because of supposed structural weaknesses is lifted.

1913

French historians refer to this year as *La Glorieuse Année*, and indeed it was a memorable year in various departments of aviation. Most spectacular perhaps were the first intentional aerobatics—including loops and upside-down flying—by the Frenchman Adolphe Pégoud on his Blériot in September, which formed an unconscious prelude to the necessary maneouvres of wartime flying.

1913

In England, the Sopwith *Tabloid* biplane, owing much to the Farnborough B. S.-1, first

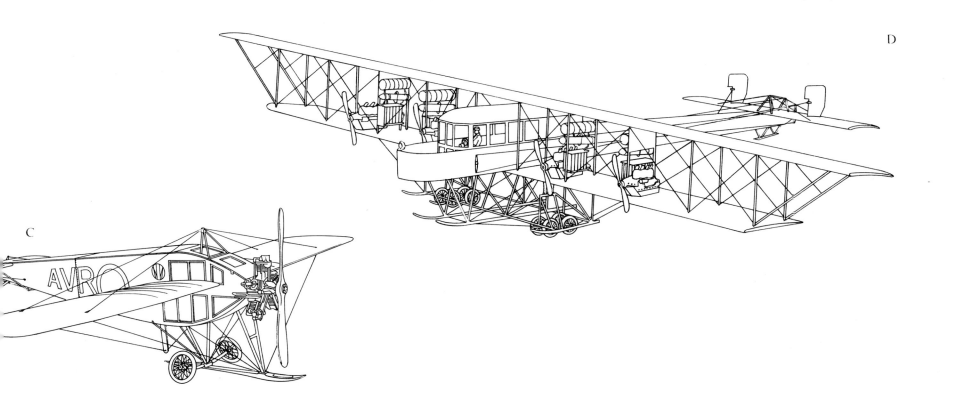

flies, and does much to condition the future scout and fighter. The designers are Harry Hawker and F. Sigrist.

1913

First practical stable aeroplane flies: the Farnborough B. E.-2c, as a result of the work of E. T. Busk, in England.

1913

The improved French monoplane, *Monocoque Deperdussin*, first flies and becomes outstandingly successful, breaking the world's speed record three times during this year, the best being 126.67 mph (203.86 km/h).

1913

The Avro 504 two-seater biplane first flies in England, and is to become one of the world's outstanding trainers, over 10,000 being built.

1913

First large multi-engined aeroplane flies: Igor Sikorsky's four-engined biplane *Bolshoi* (The Great) at St Petersburg in Russia. *See figure D*

1913

First Schneider Trophy race for seaplanes, at the second Monaco meeting: it is won by Maurice Prévost on a Deperdussin float-plane at an average speed of 45.75 mph (*c.* 74 km/h).

19—21 MARCH 1913

Rumpelmayer of France, and Mme Goldschmidt, in the balloon *Stella* make a flight of about 1504 miles (2420 km) from Paris to Kharkov, Russia.

19 AUGUST 1913

First parachute descent from an aeroplane in Europe; by the Frenchman, Adolphe Pégoud, from a Blériot.

27 AUGUST 1913

First loop-the-loop is performed by Lieutenant Petr Nikolaevich Nesterov of the Imperial Russian Army on a Nieuport Type IV monoplane at Kiev in Russia. *See figure A*

SEPTEMBER 1913

In France, Adolphe Pégoud becomes the first true exponent of aerobatics, including loops and upside-down flying. He is not the first to make a loop (see previous entry).

20 NOVEMBER—29 DECEMBER 1913

Jules Védrines, on a Blériot, flies from Nancy, France to Cairo (*via* Sofia and Constantinople), 2500 miles (*c.* 4000 km).

10 NOVEMBER 1913—1 JANUARY 1914

Marc Bonnier and N. N. Barnier fly a Nieuport from Paris to Cairo, *via* Bucharest and Constantinople.

31 DECEMBER 1913

By the end of the year, records stand at:
SPEED: 126.67 mph (203.86 km/h) by Maurice Prévost of France on a Deperdussin at Reims;
DISTANCE: (over a closed circuit): 634.54 miles (1021.19 km) by A. Séguin of France on a Henry Farman at Buc;
HEIGHT: 20,079 ft (6120.08 m) by Georges Legagneux of France on a Nieuport at St Raphael.

First Europe, and then the globe, will be linked by flight, and nations so knit together that they will grow to be next-door neighbours. This conquest of the air will prove, ultimately, to be man's greatest and most glorious triumph. What railways have done for nations, airways will do for the world.

CLAUDE GRAHAME-WHITE AND HARRY HARPER (1914)

When my brother and I built and flew the first man-carrying flying machine, we thought that we were introducing into the world an invention which would make further wars practically impossible.

ORVILLE WRIGHT (1917)

In 1492 Christopher Columbus sailed across the Atlantic and discovered America. I cannot help feeling that this afternoon we are to some extent in contact with that event, and that when we welcome our guests, the heroes of today, who have come back from the other side, come to us from America in something less than 16 hours—we are in the presence of another event of something like the same order as that stupendous event which revealed to Europe and Asia the boundless glories and possibilities of the new world across the Atlantic Ocean.

WINSTON S. CHURCHILL
(SPEAKING AT A LUNCHEON IN 1919 TO HONOUR ALCOCK AND BROWN)

This is earth again, the earth where I've lived and now will live once more . . . I've been to eternity and back. I know how the dead would feel to live again.

CHARLES A. LINDBERGH
(ON SIGHTING IRELAND AFTER HIS SOLO ATLANTIC CROSSING IN 1927)

CHAPTER NINE

FROM 1914 A.D. TO 1929 A.D.

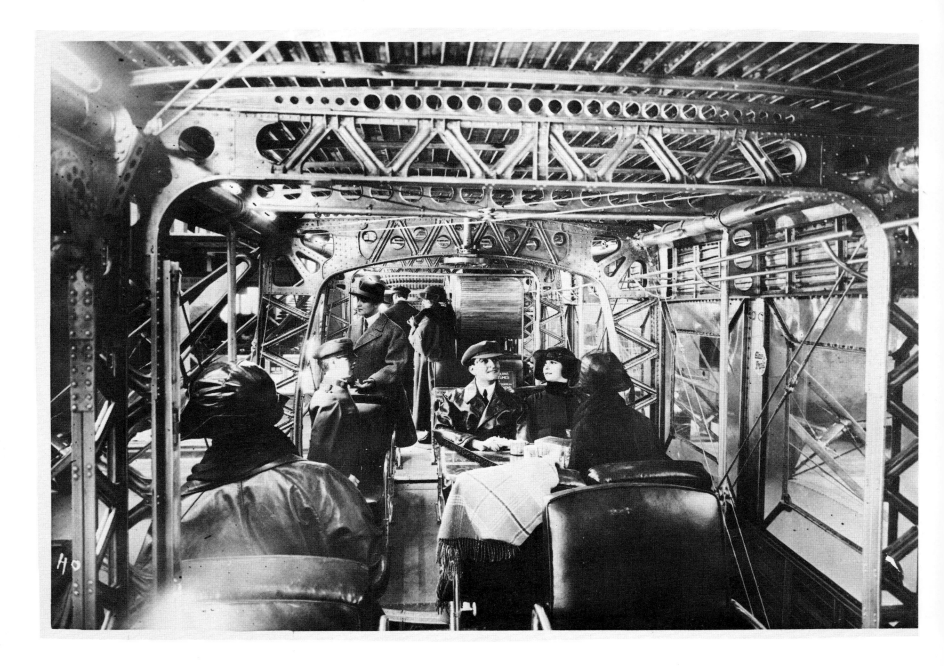

In 1921, Breguet experimented with the Le-
viathan, one of the first specially built
transports. Passenger accommodation was
advanced, as this cross-section photograph of
the fuselage shows. In fact, the aircraft was
far ahead of its time and was never mass-
produced.

A   Ilya Mouriametz: *Sikorsky's 1913 aeroplane had an open promenade deck where passengers could walk in flight.*

A

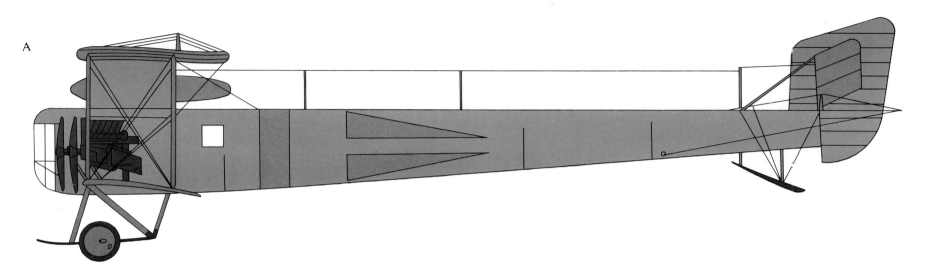

1914

Lawrence B. Sperry demonstrates his new automatic gyroscopic stabiliser, which is installed in a Curtiss F. flying-boat. He wins the Concours de la Sécurité en Aéroplane, at Buc, France.

1914

First use of flaps: they are fitted to a Farnborough S. E.-4, in England.

JANUARY 1914

Igor Sikorsky's four-engined biplane *Ilya Mouriametz* first flies in Russia. It is an improved version of the *Bolshoi*, and the type is to make about 400 bombing sorties during World War I.
See figure A

1 JANUARY 1914

P. E. Fansler opens the first scheduled air-line—between St Petersburg and Tampa, Florida, 22 miles (*c.* 35 km)—with a Benoist flying-boat piloted by A. Jannus. It carries one passenger.

11—13 FEBRUARY 1914

Overland distance record for balloons is set up by H. Berliner, who flies 1890 miles (*c.* 3040 km) from Bitterfeldt, Germany to Kirgischano, Russia.

4 AUGUST 1914

At the start of the First World War, the following approximate numbers of aero-planes are at the disposal of the powers:

Britain	48
France	136
Belgium	24
Germany	180

30 AUGUST 1914

Paris becomes the first capital to be bombed by an aeroplane: Lieutenant Ferdinand von Hidessen in a German Rumpler Taube.

5 OCTOBER 1914

First aircraft in the world to be shot down by another: a German two-seater Aviatik

over Jonchery, Reims by Sergeant Joseph Frantz and Corporal Quénault in a Voisin Escadrille VB 24 using a Hotchkiss machine-gun.

NOVEMBER 1914

Three British Avro 504s raid the Zeppelin works at Friedrichshafen, Germany.

1914—1918

Count Zeppelin comes to play a vital part, not only in the production of rigid airships, but also of all-metal aeroplanes, many of which are built at the Zeppelin factory at Seemoos, Constance, Germany, during the War. The Dornier Company, which is later to produce many all-metal aeroplanes, also derives from this Zeppelin activity. Zeppelin is therefore the father of the large modern all-metal aeroplane.

1915

Solution of recovery from a spin is first achieved (by centralising the controls) at Farnborough, England.

A

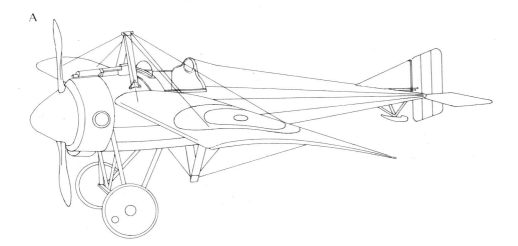

B

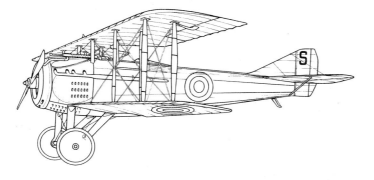

C

19 JANUARY 1915

First Zeppelin raid on Britain, by three German Navy Zeppelins, in which only 25 bombs are dropped on four cities. Zeppelins are to make 53 raids—at night— on Britain, in which 556 people are to be killed, but with little other effect. Black-outs of cities, anti-aircraft guns and the attacks by aircraft provide terrible hazards for the Zeppelins (see later).

1 APRIL 1915

Era of the true fighter aeroplane is opened; when Roland Garros shoots down a German machine by firing through the propeller of his Morane-Saulnier, using metal deflector plates, made by Raymond Saulnier, on the blades.
See figure A

19 APRIL 1915

Roland Garros is shot down and captured, and his deflector-plate method is discovered. Three German designers examine it, and

they soon devise a proper synchronised gun to fire through the propeller, when no blade is in front of the muzzle. Anthony Fokker did not invent this device, as so often asserted.

31 MAY 1915

First Zeppelin raid on London, by LZ38, at night.

7 JUNE 1915

First Zeppelin is destroyed in the air: LZ37 is bombed over Ghent, Belgium by Flight-Lieutenant R. A. J. Warneford of the Royal Navy flying a Morane-Saulnier Parasol.

1 AUGUST 1915

First allied machine is shot down over Douai in France by Lieutenant Max Immelman flying a German Fokker E. 1 using a synchronised gun and propeller. This marks the start of the "Fokker Scourge".

DECEMBER 1915

Hugo Junkers introduces the first successful all-metal fully cantilever-wing aeroplane, the J-1 monoplane, at Dessau, Germany.
See figure D

During the following four years, Junkers produces:
(a) the first practical cantilever-wing aeroplanes,
(b) the first practical all-metal aeroplanes, and
(c) the first low-wing monoplanes. All of these are to continue to be developed successfully over the years.

1916

The supercharger is successfully adapted to aero-engines at the Royal Aircraft Factory at Farnborough, England.

APRIL 1916

The Fokker scourge is finally neutralised by the effectiveness of the British pusher-engined D. H. 2 and the F.E.-2b.

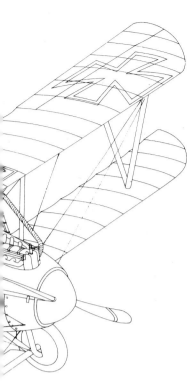

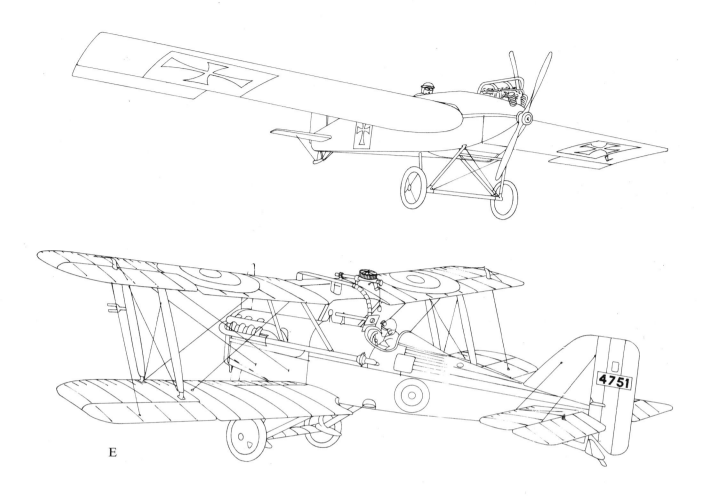

D

E

12 SEPTEMBER 1916

First radio-controlled aerial bomb (in fact a small aeroplane) is tested. Built in the United States by Glenn H. Curtiss and designed by Lawrence B. Sperry, it can fly 50 miles (*c.* 80 km) with 308 lbs (*c.* 140 kg) of bombs.

1917

Heavy bombers are in action on both sides: the British Handley Page 0/400, and the German *Gotha*, both with two engines.

13 JUNE 1917

First heavy daylight raid on London by 14 German *Gotha* aeroplanes, none of which are shot down.

12—16 NOVEMBER 1917

Zeppelin L-59 makes a remarkable flight from Jambol, Bulgaria, in an effort to take ammunition and medical supplies to the beleaguered troops in German East Africa. Near Khartoum she hears the troops have surrendered, and returns to Jambol. She covers 4225 miles (*c.* 6800 km) without trouble.

EARLY 1918

First use of a parachute from an aeroplane in warfare, by Captain Sarrat of the French Air Force.

19 MARCH 1918

First operational flights are made by United States aeroplanes in France.

DECEMBER 1918

By the end of the war, Germany has dropped a total of 275 tons of bombs on Britain by Zeppelin and aeroplane, whereas Britain drops 5000 tons of bombs on Germany during the one year 1918.

13 DECEMBER 1918—16 JANUARY 1919

First flight from England to India: Mac-Laren, Halley and McEwen in a Handley Page V-1500 four-engined bomber.

A *Morane Saulnier fighter which was equipped with deflector plates to enable a machine-gun to be fired through the blades, 1915.*
B *The French Spad 13 was one of the most popular Allied fighters on the 1918 front.*
C *The Albatros fighter was much used by German aces during the First World War.*
D *Junkers J-1: the first all-metal cantilever monoplane, 1915.*
E *The Farnborough S.E.5a, First World War.*

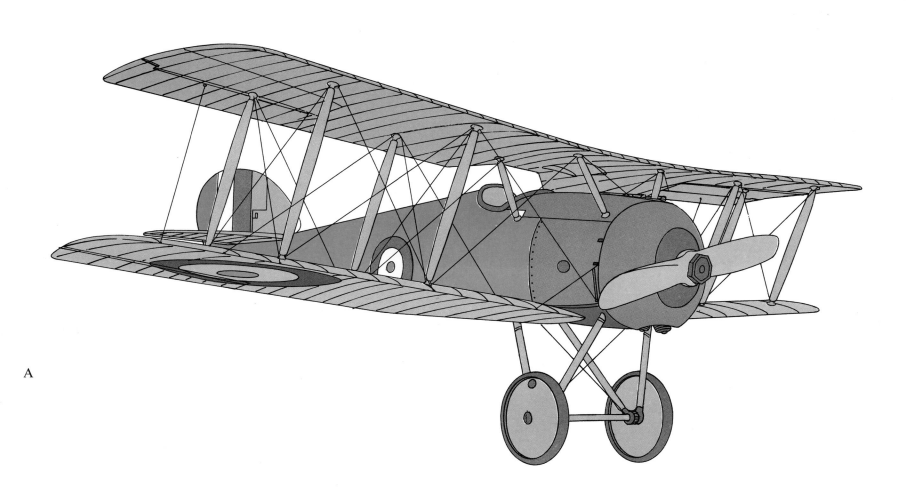

A

1919

In the United States, Professor R. H. Goddard publishes his "A Method of Reaching Extreme Altitudes", marking the origins of practical rocket flight.

1919

Hugo Junkers invents auxiliary aerofoil wing-flaps. Slotted flaps are developed by Handley Page soon afterwards. Flaps of this type come into use in the late 1930s.

5 FEBRUARY 1919

First sustained scheduled daily passenger air service starts: Deutsche Luftreederei on the route Berlin—Leipzig—Weimar.

8 FEBRUARY 1919

Lignes Aériennes Farman fly eleven passengers from Paris to London in a Farman Goliath. This is the first international passenger flight.

1 MARCH 1919

The RAF starts an air-mail service from Folkestone to Cologne for the Forces of Occupation in the Rhineland.

6 MARCH 1919

First flight of *R-33*, the rigid airship built by Armstrong Whitworth. *R-33* was of the same class as *R-34* built by Beardmore, first flown eight days later. *R-33* and *R-34* were the two most successful British rigids.

15 MAY 1919

Start of the United States Aerial Mail Service at first between Chicago and Cleveland, later extended to New York and San Francisco. This service was operated with de Havilland D. H. 4s and initially carried only mail.

16—17 MAY 1919

First transatlantic flight, made in stages by

the US Navy's Curtiss NC-4 flying-boat flown by Lieutenant-Commander A. C. Read and crew, from Rockaway, New York to Plymouth, England.

14—15 JUNE 1919

First direct non-stop crossing by aeroplane of the Atlantic is made. Captain John Alcock and Lieutenant Arthur Whitten Brown fly a Vickers Vimy from St Johns, Newfoundland to Clifden, Ireland. *See figure B*

25 JUNE 1919

First flight of the first production all-metal transport aeroplane, the Junkers F-13 single-engined monoplane, in Germany.

2—13 JULY 1919

First crossing of the Atlantic by airship, and the first double crossing, by the rigid *R34* (flown by Scott and crew).

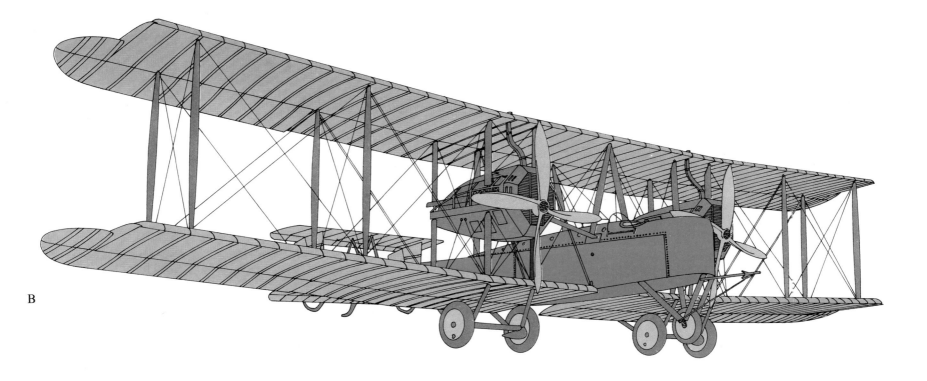

B

20 AUGUST 1919

First flight of the Zeppelin LX 120 *Bodensee*, a small rigid built by the Germans after the First World War for commercial use. *Bodensee* ran the first regular scheduled passenger service by airship. This was between Friedrichshafen and Berlin from August to November 1919.

25 AUGUST 1919

First sustained scheduled daily international air service starts between London and Paris: de Havilland D. H.-16 of Aircraft Transport and Travel Ltd flown by Cyril Patteson.

28 AUGUST 1919

International Air Traffic Association (IATA) is formed at The Hague, Holland.

13 OCTOBER 1919

International Convention for the Regulation of Air Navigation—I.C.A.N.— is signed in Paris.

OCTOBER 1919

In Holland, the first flight of the first Fokker F-II single-engined high-wing mono-plane transport, the first of a long line of successful Fokker airliners.

7 OCTOBER 1919

The Dutch airline K. L. M.—Koninklijke Luftvaart Maatschappij— is formed by Albert Plesman.

A   *Sopwith Snipe: an effective British fighter in World War I.*
B   *The Vickers Vimy converted bomber which made the first non-stop Atlantic crossing, 1919.*

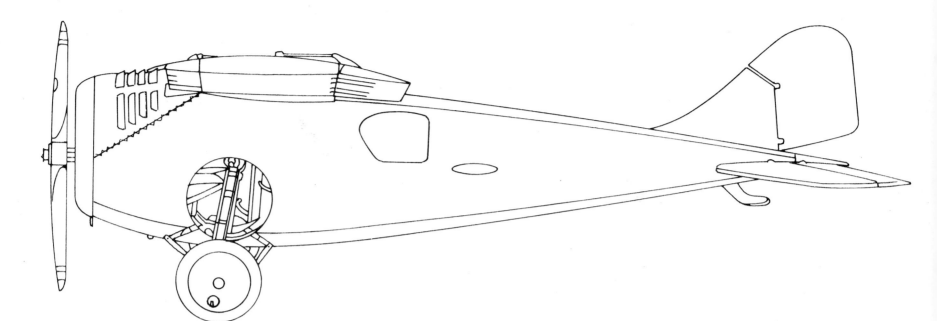

First flight from England to Australia: Ross and Keith Smith plus crew in a Vickers Vimy, 4 weeks and 2 days.

16 NOVEMBER—
12 DECEMBER 1919

First trans-Australian flight from Point Cook, Victoria to Darwin: Wrigley and Murphy.

1920

First aeroplane with a retractable under-carriage flies: the American Dayton-Wright RB high-wing racing monoplane.
See figure A

1920

Split wing-flaps are invented by Orville Wright and Jacobs in the United States.

These flaps come into widespread use from the mid-1930s.

1920

Handley Page in England announces the invention of the wing leading-edge slot. This device had been previously proposed by Lachmann in Germany who later joined Handley Page. Wing slots added greatly to the safety of aircraft.

4 FEBRUARY—
20 MARCH 1920

First flight from England to Cape Town: a Vickers Vimy and a de Havilland D. H.-9 are flown by Lieutenant-Colonel Pierre Van Ryneveld and Squadron Leader Christopher Q. Brand.

14 FEBRUARY—31 MAY 1920

First flight from Rome, Italy, to Tokyo, Japan, 12,000 miles (c. 19,300 km) by two

Italian airmen, Ferrarin and Masiero, in two aeroplanes.

5 JULY 1920

First RAF Pageant is held at Hendon in England. This becomes an annual display which continues until shortly before the Second World War.

19 JULY 1920

First flight of the Vickers *R-80*, a British rigid airship which marked an important advance in aerodynamic design of airships when started in 1917.
See figure C

15 AUGUST 1920

First sustained soaring flight over closed circuit in slope lift: a Wenk Weltensegler sailplane over the Feldberg near Fribourg, Germany (flown by Peschke).

30 SEPTEMBER 1920

Zeppelin-Staaken E-4/20 four-engined all-metal 18-passenger transport monoplane prototype is completed in Germany. Flown successfully soon afterwards, this aircraft was the forerunner of the modern large all-metal airliner.

7—17 OCTOBER 1920

First trans-Canada flight from Halifax to Vancouver: Leckie and others in various aircraft.

22—23 FEBRUARY 1921

First coast-to-coast air-mail flight from San Francisco to Mineola, Long Island, New York in 33 hours 20 minutes by Jack Knight and Allison in a de Havilland D. H. 4.

21 JULY 1921

First battleship sunk by bombs in a test on an ex-German battleship *Ostfriesland* by Brigadier General William Mitchell of the US Army with Martin MB-2 bombers. *See figure B*

10 AUGUST 1921

US Navy Bureau of Aeronautics is formed under Rear-Admiral Moffett.

14 AUGUST 1921

In Germany, the first soaring flight in which a transfer from slope lift to thermals is made: by a Wenk Weltensegler sailplane over the Wasserkuppe in the Rhön (flown by Leusch). A fatal accident results from structural failure during this flight.

A *The Dayton-Wright R.B. racing monoplane, built for the 1920 Gordon Bennet Aviation Trophy Race, was the first aeroplane with a retractable undercarriage to fly.*
B *The 22,800-ton Ostfriesland being bombed by US Army MB-2 bombers during a bombing demonstration, 1921.*
C *The Vickers R-80 rigid airship, 1920.*

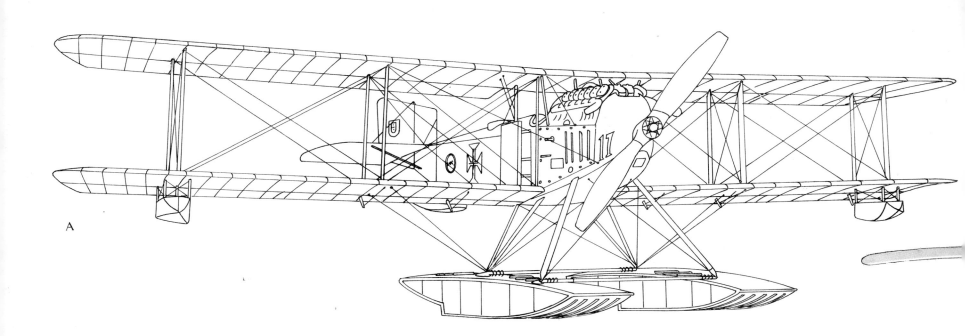

A

24 AUGUST 1921

Loss over the Humber, England, from structural failure in flight, of the Royal Airship Works rigid airship *R-38*, which was to have been supplied to the U. S. Navy as the *ZR-2*.
See figure B

13 SEPTEMBER 1921

Harth, on a sailplane of his own design, breaks the soaring endurance record established by Orville Wright in 1911 with a sustained flight of 21 minutes near Hildenstein, Germany.

4 DECEMBER 1921

Western Australian Airways begins to operate first regular air service in Australia: between Derby and Geraldton. The aeroplanes are Bristol Tourer Coupés.

29—30 DECEMBER 1921

World endurance record established at Roosevelt Field, New York: Stimson and Bertraud fly for 26 hours 19 mins 33 secs.

1922

First airship to be filled with non-inflammable helium gas: US Army *C-7* non-rigid.

13 MARCH 1922

First flight across the South Atlantic (in stages): a Fairey III seaplane, *Lusitania*, flown from Portugal to Brazil by Captain Sacadura Cabral and Vice Admiral Gago Continho.
See figure A

11 JULY 1922

International Convention for the Regulation of Air Navigation becomes operative on ratification by the following states: British Empire, Belgium, Bolivia, France, Greece, Japan, Portugal, Kingdom of Serbs, Croats and Slovenes, Siam.

18 AUGUST 1922

First soaring flight of one hour in slope lift: by Martens in a Wampyr sailplane at the Wasserkuppe, Rhön, Germany.

19 AUGUST 1922

The first thermal soaring flight in which height was gained by circling in lift: Henry Farman sailplane flown by Bossoutrot at Combegrasse, France.

4 SEPTEMBER 1922

First coast-to-coast crossing of the United States in one day: Lieutenant James H.

Doolittle in de Havilland D. H. 4B flies 2163 miles (*c.* 3480 km) in 21 hours 20 minutes flying time from Pablo Beach, Florida to San Diego, California.

1 OCTOBER 1922

The RAF takes over military control of Iraq: the first Air Force to assume complete control of a military command.

24 NOVEMBER 1922

First flight of the prototype of the Vickers Virginia twin-engined night-bomber, which remains the main heavy bomber of the RAF throughout the 1920s.

1923

In Canada, the Turnbull variable-pitch propeller is demonstrated. This propeller is later developed and put into production by Curtiss in the mid-1930s.

9 JANUARY 1923

First flight of a practical gyroplane: Juan de la Cierva's C-3 Autogiro flown by Spenser Gomes at Cuatro Vientos, Madrid, Spain.
See figure C

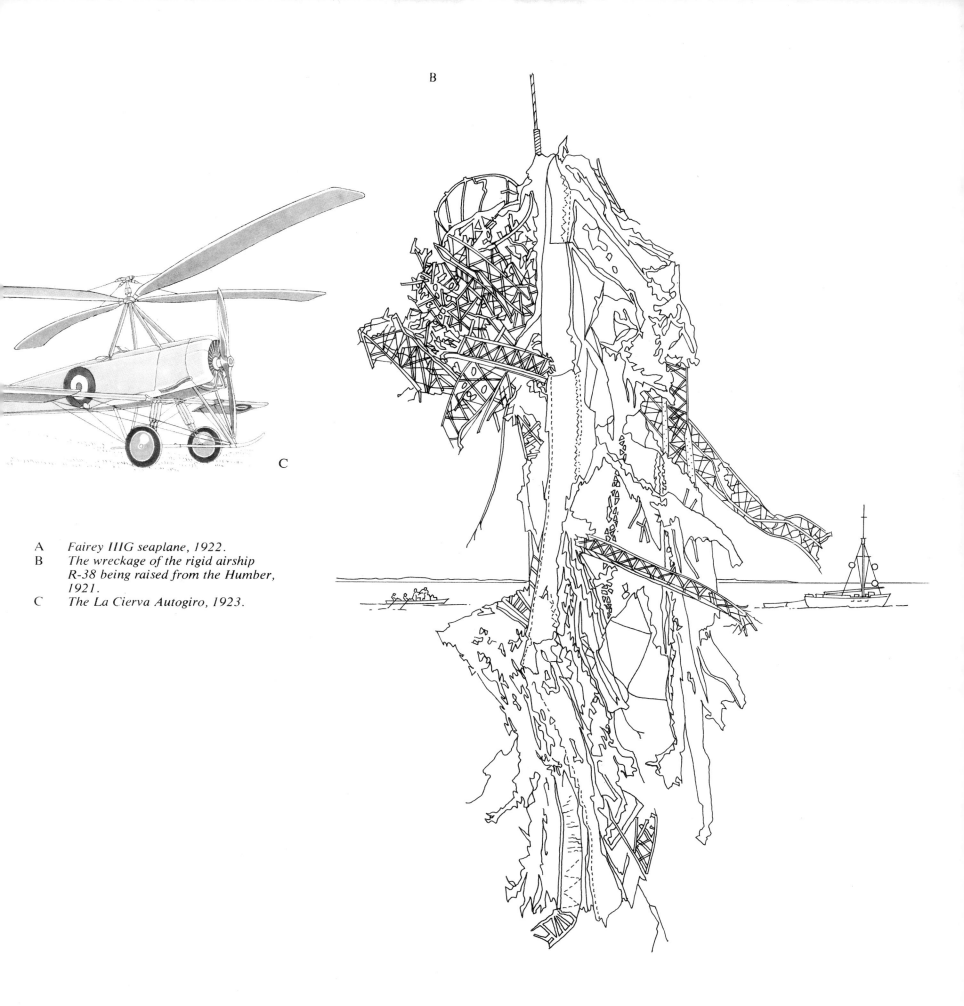

B

A   *Fairey IIIG seaplane, 1922.*
B   *The wreckage of the rigid airship*
     R-38 being raised from the Humber,
     1921.
C   *The La Cierva Autogiro, 1923.*

3 JANUARY 1923

First soaring flight of more than five hours: a Hanriot HD-14 biplane flies with engine stopped in slope lift at Biskra, France (flown by Lieutenant Thoret).

2—3 MAY 1923

First non-stop coast-to-coast crossing of the United States: Lieutenant O. G. Kelly and Lieutenant J. A. Macready of the US Air Service in a Fokker T-2, 2520 miles (*c.* 4055 km) from New York to San Diego in 26 hours and 50 minutes.

27 JUNE 1923

First complete pipeline refuelling in flight of one aeroplane by another: a de Havilland D. H.-4B from another similar aircraft over San Diego (flown by Captain L. H. Smith and Lieutenant J. P. Richter).

1 SEPTEMBER 1923

The Royal Australian Air Force is formed.

1924

The Hele-Shaw/Beacham variable-pitch constant-speed propeller is demonstrated in England. This design is later developed and

put into production by Rotol in the late 1930s.

1924

In the United States, Fowler area-increasing wing-flaps are invented. This design is to be widely used from the late 1930s.

1 APRIL 1924

The Royal Canadian Air Force is formed.

1 APRIL 1924

The British national "chosen-instrument" airline, Imperial Airways, is formed by the amalgamation of Handley Page Transport, Aircraft Transport and Travel, the Instone Airline and the British Marine Air Navigation Co.

7 APRIL—28 SEPTEMBER 1924

First flight round the World by two Douglas World Cruisers in 174 days (flown by Captain L. H. Smith and Lieutenant Erik Nelson and crews).
See figure A

14 APRIL 1924

Etienne Oehmichen's helicopter No. 2 establishes the World's first helicopter record, in France, recognised by the Fédération Aéronautique Internationale, of 1182 ft (*c.* 360 m) distance. This helicopter later makes a flight of 14 minutes and covers 5550 ft (*c.* 1690 m).

18 APRIL 1924

The Marquis de Pescara's helicopter establishes in France a record of 2550 ft (*c.* 777 m) in 4 minutes 11 seconds.

1 JULY 1924

Start of transcontinental air-mail service across the United States.

27 AUGUST 1924

First flight of the Zeppelin LZ-126 rigid airship supplied to the US Navy as the *Los Angeles*. This very successful ship remains in service until 1932 and is not broken up until 1939.

LATE 1924

First flight of the Junkers G-23 three-engined all-metal monoplane airliner. This

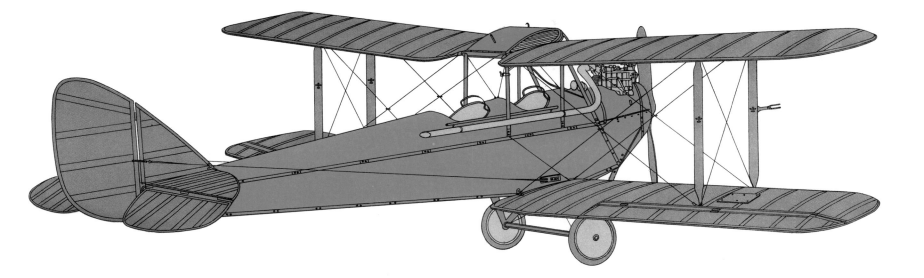

aircraft starts the trimotor era which lasts for many years.

1925

H. A. Wagner, in Germany, evolves the Tension Field Beam Theory which is to make an important contribution to the design of all-metal stressed-skin aircraft.

1925

First flight of the first Daimler Klemm L-20 wooden low-wing light monoplane. This clean two-seater German design marks an important step in light aeroplane development.

15 FEBRUARY 1925

First hook-on of an aeroplane to an airship in flight: Sperry Messenger onto US Army non-rigid over Scott Field, Illinois, USA.

22 FEBRUARY 1925

First flight of the de Havilland D. H. 60 Moth, the first widely-used light aeroplane, with which the Government-sponsored British Flying Club Movement is started and later spreads to other countries.
See figure B

13 APRIL 1925

The first regular air-freight service, between Detroit and Chicago, is started by Henry Ford.

21 APRIL—9 NOVEMBER 1925

Flight from Rome to Japan, Australia and return to Italy, 34,000 miles (*c.* 54,720 km) flown by Commandant de Pinedo, with Campanelli as mechanic, on a Savoia S.16*ter* flying-boat.

15 MAY 1925

The Junkers G-23, the first three-engined all-metal monoplane airliner goes into commercial service between Malmö in Sweden, Hamburg in Germany, and Amsterdam in Holland.

21 MAY—17 JUNE 1925

First attempt to reach the North Pole by aeroplane: Roald Amundsen (Norway) and C. W. Ellsworth (United States) plus crews in two Dornier Wal flying-boats. Landings are made 140 miles (*c.* 225 km) from the Pole.

26 JULY 1925

First soaring flight of ten hours (by Belgian Massaux in a Poncelet sailplane) at Vauville, near Cherbourg, France.

3 SEPTEMBER 1925

Loss at Marietta, Ohio, from structural failure in flight of the US Naval Aircraft Factory rigid airship *ZR-1, Shenandoah*. Like *R-38*, *ZR-1* is based on a German wartime design of lightened, and therefore structurally weak, high-altitude bomber airship.

A   *Douglas World Cruiser, 1924*
B   *De Havilland Moth, 1925.*

A

4 SEPTEMBER 1925

First flight of the Fokker F-VII/3m trimotor airliner which is widely used by operators in Europe and North America. The prototype wins the Ford Reliability Trial in the United States.
See figure A

16 NOVEMBER 1925— 13 MARCH 1926

First flight from England to Cape Town, South Africa, and back: de Havilland D. H.-50 flown by Alan Cobham and crew.

17 DECEMBER 1925

General William Mitchell of the US Army found guilty by a court-martial of bringing discredit on the military service by criticising the unsatisfactory state of US military aviation.

1926

First proposals for gas-turbine propeller propulsion by A. A. Griffith. These lead to a gas-turbine development programme at the Royal Aircraft Establishment at Farnborough, England.

22 JANUARY—10 FEBRUARY 1926

Flight from Spain to Rio de Janeiro in stages: Commandante Ramón Franco in a Dornier Wal flying-boat, *Plus Ultra*.

16 MARCH 1926

First flight of a liquid-fuel rocket, designed by and launched by R. H. Goddard at Auburn, Massachusetts, USA.
See figure B

9 MAY 1926

First successful flight over the North Pole: Commander Richard Byrd and Floyd Bennet in a Fokker F-VII/3 m *Josephine Ford* from Spitzbergen, Norway.

11—14 MAY 1926

First airship flight over the North Pole and first crossing of the Arctic Ocean: Umberto Nobile, Roald Amundsen, Lincoln Ellsworth and crew in Italian semi-rigid airship, N-1, *Norge,* from Spitzbergen to Alaska.
See figures D and E

11 JUNE 1926

First flight of the first Ford 4-AT trimotor, corrugated metal-skin, three-engined, high-wing, monoplane airliner which pioneered many of the early American airlines. It is known affectionately as the "Tin Goose".
See figure C

30 JUNE—1 OCTOBER 1926

First flight from England to Australia and back: Alan Cobham in de Havilland D. H.-50 floatplane, 5 weeks outbound, 3 weeks 6 days homeward.

1 JULY 1926

The Royal Swedish Air Force is formed.

2 JULY 1926

The US Army Air Corps is formed out of the former Air Service.

C

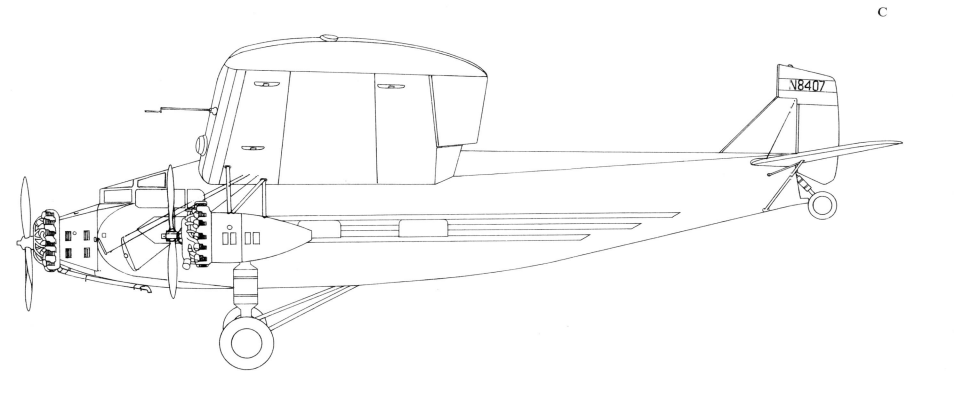

B

D

E

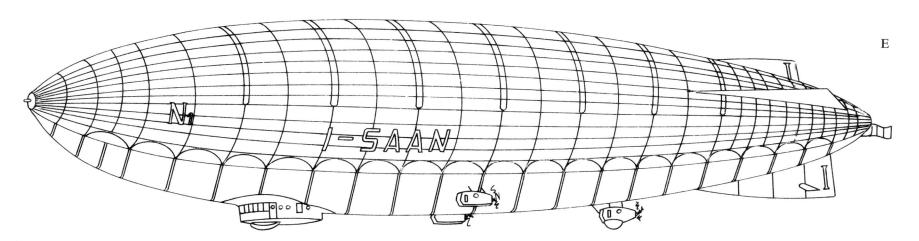

A *The arrival of Charles Lindbergh on the* Spirit of St Louis *at Paris, 1927.*
B *The Lockheed Vega transport, 1927.*

B

16 JULY 1926

Armstrong Whitworth Argosy three-engined biplane airliner enters service with Imperial Airways on the London—Paris route. This is the first aircraft developed to Imperial's specific requirements.

1927

George A. Townend at the National Physical Laboratory invents in England the ring engine-cowling for radial engines.

7 JANUARY 1927

Regular air service between Cairo and Basra started by Imperial Airways using de Havilland Hercules three-engined airliners.

20—21 MAY 1927

First solo transatlantic crossing, non-stop from Long Island, New York to Paris: by Captain Charles Lindbergh in a single-engined Ryan monoplane *Spirit of St Louis*. *See figure A*

4 JULY 1927

First flight of the first Lockheed Vega, a single-engined, high-wing, monoplane transport which marks an important step towards the low-drag monoplanes with which the Americans are to revolutionise airliner design in the 1930s. *See figure B*

14 OCTOBER 1927

First non-stop crossing of the South Atlantic: Dieudonné Costes and Joseph Le Brix in a Breguet XIX from Senegal to Brazil.

19 OCTOBER 1927

First regular service by Pan American Airways starts, between Key West, Florida and Havana, Cuba.

1928

Fred Weick, of the National Advisory Committee for Aeronautics in the United States, invents the long-chord cowling for radial engines.

1928

In the United States, C. S. Caldwell demonstrates his variable-pitch propeller. This design is later developed and put into service by Hamilton Standard and is the most popular of the first variable-pitch propellers.

7—22 FEBRUARY 1928

First solo flight from England to Australia by the Australian, Squadron Leader H. J. L. ("Bert") Hinkler, in an Avro 581 Avian light aeroplane in 15 1/2 days.

12—13 APRIL 1928

First east-to-west crossing of the Atlantic by aeroplane by a Junkers W-33L, *Bremen*, flown by Hermann Koehl and crew from Dublin, Ireland to Labrador.

21—22 APRIL 1928

First crossing of the Arctic Ocean by aeroplane: Sir Hubert Wilkins, the Australian explorer, and Carl B. Eielson in a Lockheed Vega from Point Barrow, Alaska to Spitzbergen, Norway.

31 MAY—10 JUNE 1928

First flight across the Pacific from San Francisco to Australia by a Fokker F-VIIB/3m (flown by Captain Charles Kingsford-Smith and crew).

JUNE 1928

First flight of the prototype of the Hawker Hart two-seater biplane light bomber which, in many different versions, is to become the most numerous type in the RAF and other air forces for many years.

A   *The Graf Zeppelin airship, 1929.*
B   *Count Ferdinand von Zeppelin.*
C   *Dornier DoX flying-boat, 1929.*
D   *First rocket aeroplane: Friedrich*
     Stamer, 1928.

A

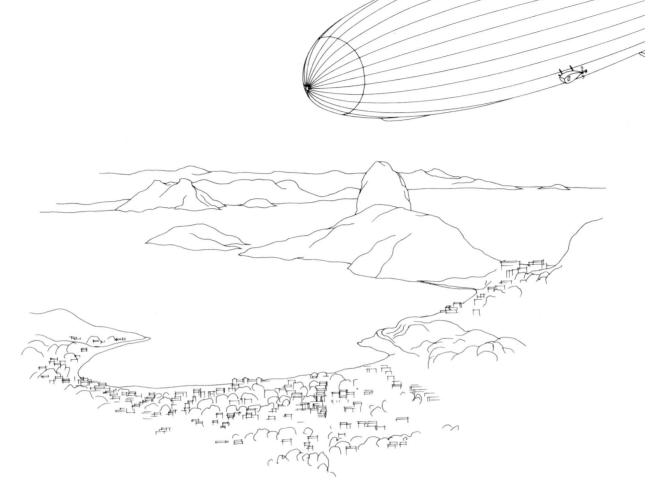

B

11 JUNE 1928

Friedrich Stamer pilots a canard-type glider propelled by rockets made by F.W. Sander. The experiments are directed by A. Lippisch and financed by Fritz von Opel.
See figure D

3—5 JULY 1928

Non-stop flight from Rome to Point Genipabu, Brazil, 4466 miles (*c.* 7188 km) by Arturo Ferrarin and Carlo Del Prete in a Savoia S.64.

11 SEPTEMBER 1928

First flight from Australia to New Zealand: Fokker F-VII/3m *Southern Cross* (flown by Charles Kingsford-Smith and C.T.P. Ulm).

18 SEPTEMBER 1928

First flight by Autogiro from London to Paris: Cierva C-8L (flown by Juan de la Cierva).

18 SEPTEMBER 1928

First flight of the Zeppelin LZ-127 *Graf Zeppelin*, which is the most successful rigid ever built. Is operated commercially by the Zeppelin Company, particularly on a regular service from Europe to South America. Broken up in 1940.
See figure A

**23 DECEMBER 1928—
25 FEBRUARY 1929**

RAF evacuates by air 586 people from Kabul in Afghanistan, the first emergency aircraft.

1929

First flight of giant Dornier Do-X flying-boat from Lake Constance, Germany. This aircraft had a loaded weight of 115,000 lbs (*c.* 52,000 kg) and carried 169 people on one flight.
See figure C

1929

Melville Jones publishes his influential paper on The Streamlined Aeroplane.

24—26 APRIL 1929

First non-stop flight is made from England to India: by Squadron Leader A.G. Jones-Williams and Flight-Lieutenant N. H. Jenkins flying a Fairey Long Range Monoplane.

C

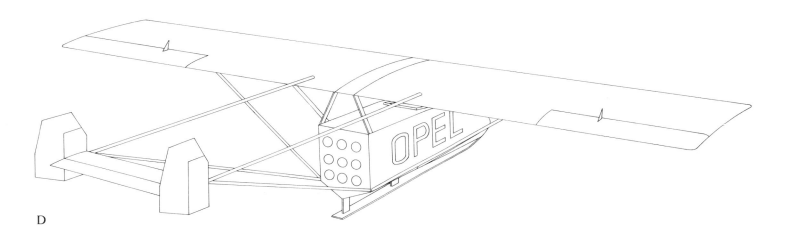

D

8—29 AUGUST 1929

First flight round the world by an airship made by the Zeppelin LZ-127 *Graf Zeppelin*: in 21 days, 7 hours, 34 minutes. Dr Hugo Eckener captains the airship, which leaves from and returns to Lakehurst, New Jersey, USA.

19 SEPTEMBER 1929

First flight of the metal-skinned airship ZMC-2 built the Metalclad Airship Corporation in Detroit. This airship is the only one of its type ever built but is operated by the US Navy until 1941.

24 SEPTEMBER 1929

First complete flight on instruments takes place as the culmination of the work on all-weather flying by the Guggenheim Full Flight Laboratory: Lieutenant J.H. Doolittle on a Consolidated NY-2 biplane at Mitchell Field, near New York.

30 SEPTEMBER 1929

First successful rocket-propelled aeroplane flight is made by Fritz von Opel at Rebstock, near Frankfurt, Germany. Propulsion is by solid-fuel rockets and the flight covers a distance of about 2000 yds (1830 m) at up to 100 mph (161 km/h).

14 OCTOBER 1929

First flight of the Royal Airship Works rigid *R-101*, which is the first ship of a new British programme of civil airship development. This ship is later lengthened some time before her disastrous loss.

28—29 NOVEMBER 1929

First flight over the South Pole is made by a Ford 4AT Tri-Motor monoplane from the American base at Little America on the Ross ice-shelf, (flown by Richard Byrd, Bernt Balchen and crew).

16 DECEMBER 1929

First flight of the Airship Guarantee Company's *R-100* rigid airship which is the second ship in the British commercial airship programme. *R-100* makes a flight across the Atlantic to Canada and back. She is broken up in 1931.

SECTION IV

FROM THE INVENTION OF THE JET ENGINE TO THE JET AIRLINER, 1930 TO 1956 A.D.

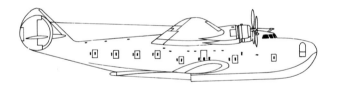

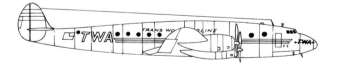

The giant Boeing Model 314 "Clipper" flying boat was built for Pan Am's services across the Atlantic and Pacific in 1938 and it is illustrated here above the Lockheed Constellation which was an important airliner in the years following the Second World War.

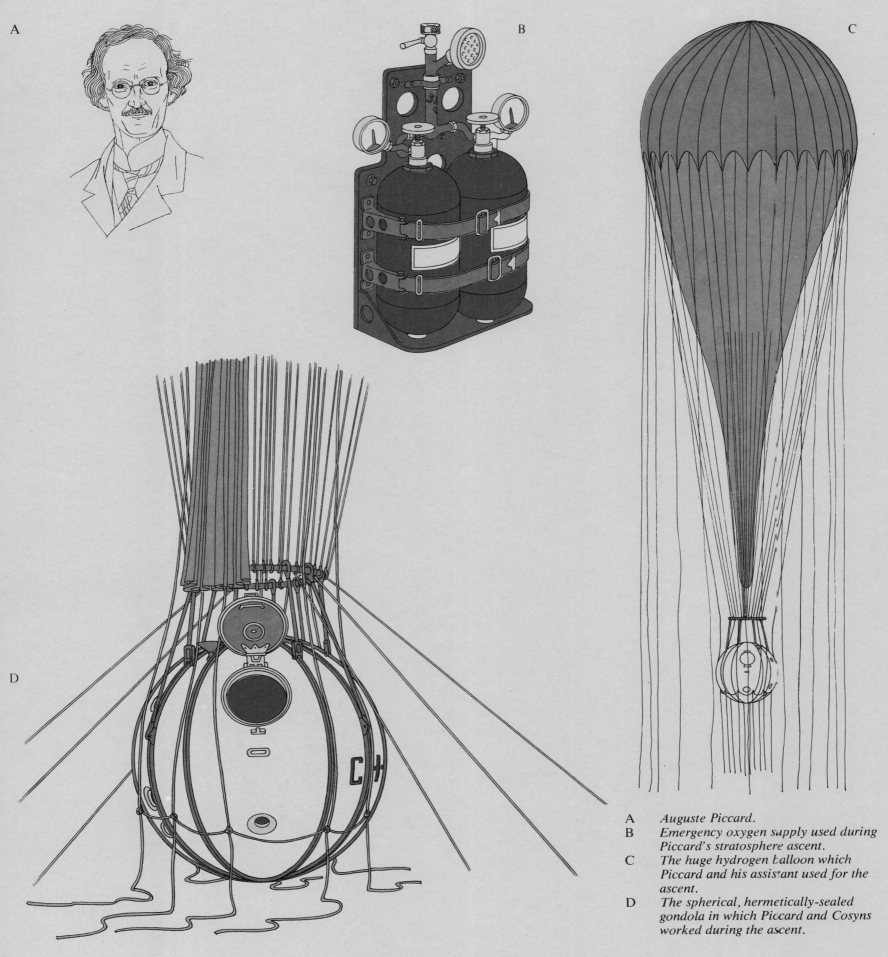

A   *Auguste Piccard.*
B   *Emergency oxygen supply used during Piccard's stratosphere ascent.*
C   *The huge hydrogen balloon which Piccard and his assistant used for the ascent.*
D   *The spherical, hermetically-sealed gondola in which Piccard and Cosyns worked during the ascent.*

At the end of the 1920s and in the early 1930s the airship saw its greatest triumphs, its greatest tragedies, and its eclipse. In September 1928, the Zeppelin named *Graf Zeppelin* was launched: it was the greatest airship of history. Paid for by public subscription, this 776 ft (236.5 m) long monster carried some 20 passengers and over 26,000 lb (*c.* 11,800 kg) of mail and freight for over 6000 miles (9656 km) at 70 mph (112 km/h). From 1928 to 1937—when she was honorably "retired"—this remarkable vessel carried 13,100 passengers, flew over 1,060,000 miles (1,705,911 km) and was 16,000 hours in the air; this record included 140 crossings of the South Atlantic, and a triumphant round-the-world voyage (1929). In 1930, the British *R-100* made a double crossing of the Atlantic, this airship being the best rigid ever built in Great Britain. But apart from the *Graf Zeppelin,* it was a tale of bad fortune and disaster with a tragic loss of life: the British *R-101* crashed and burnt at Beauvais in 1930; the American *Akron* smashed into the Atlantic Ocean during a storm; the American *Macon* came down on the sea and sank, without serious loss of life, in 1935; and the Zeppelin *Hindenburg* crashed in flames spectacularly at Lakehurst in 1937. Her successor, the *Graf Zeppelin II,* had made only some 20 flights when World War II broke out, and she was scrapped. Although a few small pressure airships continued in service the Airship Age had come to a tragic end.

In aviation, this immediate pre-World War II decade of the 1930s saw the steady growth of civil aviation and a sharp upsurge in military flying. What may be termed the first modern-type airliner appeared in the United States in the twin-engine Boeing 247 (in service in 1934), carrying 10 passengers at some 150 mph (*c.* 240 km/h). By the time the Douglas DC-3 came into service in 1936, the form and nature of the modern airliner was standardised, with the following features: (a) low-wing, all metal, stressed-skin monoplane construction; (b) two—later four—powerful supercharged air-cooled radial engines, on one of which the machine could still maintain level flight; (c) variable pitch propellers; (d) retractable undercarriage; and (e) flaps to allow for increased wing-loading, with a slow stalling speed. Cabin pressurisation in airliners was to wait until 1940. The DC-3 was by far the most famous and successful airliner in history, and was sold to nearly every nation; it was powered by two 1000-1200 h.p. engines, carried 21 passengers at a speed of some 170 mph (273 km/h) over a stage length of 500 miles (800 km); by the time production ceased in 1945, some 13,000 of this remarkable machine had been built, and some are still flying today. By 1940, there had appeared the first of the pressurised four-engined airliners, the American Boeing 307, which thereafter helped to inaugurate a new epoch of great transport aircraft.

The flying-boats continued to be minor rivals of the 1928—1939 generation of transports, for over-water travel, of which the American Martin 130 (1934) and Sikorsky S-42 (1934), the British Short Empire class (1936), and the American Boeing 314 Clipper (1938—1939), were typical. Small float-planes were also produced in large numbers both for civil and military use, being ideal—as they still are—for operating in areas of lakes and forests such as abound in Canada and Scandinavia.

The coming to power of Adolf Hitler (1933), with his warlike intentions, was to transform the whole of aviation. In both Europe and America, new bombers, and airliners which could be modified to become bombers, were designed and built. There was soon a wholesale rush to produce fighters and other military machines of various types, both by Germany and by her enemies-to-be: thus were created many famous machines.

High-speed flying, again in races for the Schneider Trophy, encouraged manufacturers to pursue aerodynamic research which was to be invaluable for war-time purposes: in 1931, Britain won the Trophy outright with the Supermarine S.6B with a speed of 340.6 mph (548.15 km/h).

The helicopter, recently re-stimulated by Cierva's Autogiros, finally arrived in practical form with the twin-rotor German Focke-Achgelis of 1936; but this valuable kind of aircraft was not to attract world-wide attention until Sikorsky produced the first fully practical single-rotor machine in 1942. Thereafter, the helicopter rapidly established itself as indispensable in an ever-widening number of spheres.

The balloon had been usefully employed for scientific observation since the eighteenth century; and the *ballon sonde*—for meteorological work—had proved a most valuable scientific tool since the end of the last century, and will always continue to play an important part in meteorology. Now, in 1931, the Swiss Professor, Auguste Piccard, was the first man to reach the stratosphere; and he did it in a balloon (from Augsburg) when it rose to 9.8 miles (15.78 km) above the earth. This feat was eclipsed when the American Captains Stevens and Anderson reached an altitude of 13.7 miles (22.05 km) over South Dakota in 1935. With the advent of suitable plastics after World War II, vast balloons of over 3 million cubic feet (85,000 cubic metres) capacity were to ascend to more than 20 miles (32 km) and play an important part in scientific research.

The dream of the jet-propelled aircraft, first envisaged for balloons by Joseph Montgolfier in 1783 and for aeroplanes by De Louvrié in 1865, was finally realised in practice with the German turbojet aeroplane,

A

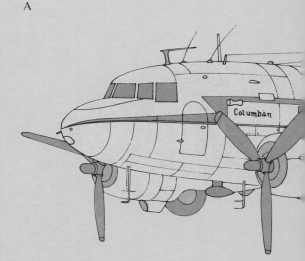

B

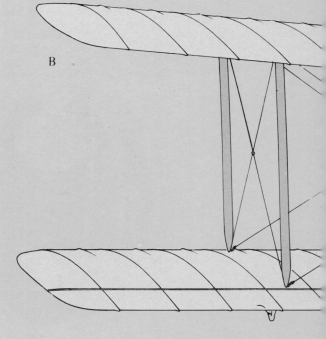

A Douglas DC-3 airliner, 1936.
B De Havilland Moth, first cheap light
aeroplane for the mass market, was a
popular club aeroplane in the 1930s.

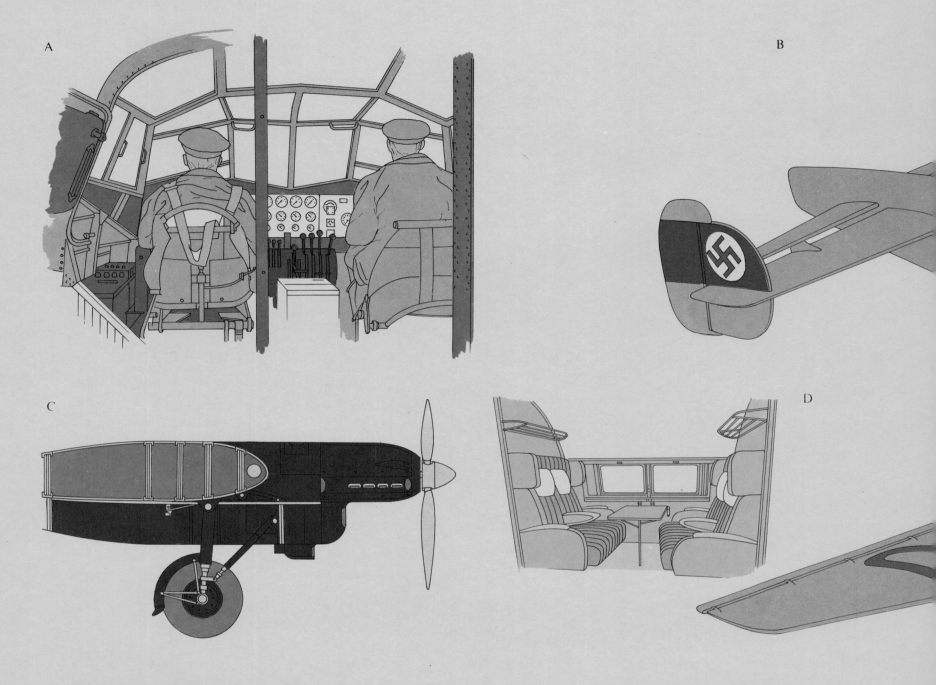

the Heinkel He 178 in 1939. The German engineers had been working on parallel lines to that of the British Royal Air Force officer Frank (later Sir Frank) Whittle, from 1930 onwards. The Heinkel He 178 was itself not a practical aeroplane; and the equivalent British Gloster E.28/39, when first flown in 1941, was merely a test-bed for the Whittle engine. But the jet-age had been born, although it was to progress very slowly despite the pressures of war.

In 1939, the conflict, which Hitler had planned, broke out and the aeroplane went to war for the second time in a generation. But this time it became the decisive weapon of the conflict both over land and water; and it emerged in such a wide variety of forms that it has dominated the world transport scene ever since.

Although jet aeroplanes were developed rapidly and remarkably during the War, they did not influence the course of hostilities, except in the form of the German V-1 "Flying Bomb". The contestants fought it out with growingly sophisticated varieties of the airscrew-engine combination. There were fighters (which were also built as light bombers), night fighters, fighter-bombers (including ground attack), heavy bombers, medium bombers, transports, liaison aircraft, reconnaissance and photo-reconnaissance machines, light observation machines, primary trainers, basic trainers, advanced trainers, training gliders, towed gliders (for airborne invasion), seaplanes of all kinds, target-towers, and helicopters. In addition there were—on the German side—winged and wingless pilotless jet and rocket missiles,

long-range rocket missiles, and—on both sides—smaller artillery rocket missiles of all kinds. The approximate total of Allied aircraft alone built during the War amounted to over 380,000. By the end of the War, conventional fighters could make over 450 mph (725 km/h) and climb to 40,000 feet (21,450 m), armed with two 20 mm cannon and four machine-guns. The heavy long-range night bombers carried 12,750 lbs (5787 kg) of bombs at 160 mph (257.5 km/h) for 1200 miles (c. 1930 km) and returned home; or 22,000 lbs (c. 1000 kg) of bombs for shorter distances; while the heavy day bombers carried 12,800 lbs (c. 5800 kg) at 250-300 mph (400-485 km/h) for medium sorties.

Then, standing alone and isolated in the history of civilisation, came the dropping, by United States bombers, of the world's first

D-AALU DER GROSSE DESSAUER

D-A[...]

A   *Ju 90 flight deck.*
B   *Junkers Ju 90 four-engined 40-passenger transport aircraft, 1937.*
C   *One of the 1 050 h.p. Daimler-Benz DB 600A engines of the prototype Ju90.*
D   *Part of the Ju 90's passenger cabin.*

atomic bombs on Japan in 1945, the first on August 6th, the second (and final one) on August 9th. It was the end of an epoch in warfare; and the beginning of a new and ominous age. Despite the appalling havoc these bombs created, they may have been a strange blessing in disguise; for no nation has ever dared to drop one on another nation since.

The expendable glider, towed by a high-powered aircraft, and carrying troops and weapons, also came into its own on both sides of the conflict. Further, the helicopter also reached final maturity as a unique vehicle, and was produced in practical man-carrying form.

Where jet propulsion was concerned, the Germans—haunted by the mass of Allied bombers—led the way throughout the War,

although it did not materially aid them. But if the War had continued much longer, the German ascendancy in jet planes would have presented a severe threat to the Allies. The most outstanding turbojet aeroplane of the period—and one of the classic aeroplanes of history—was the German Messerschmitt Me 262 fighter, which first flew in 1942 and was in action in 1944, with a maximum speed of 525 mph (845 km/h).

Of vital future importance were the large transport aircraft, mostly developed during the War by America. The backbone of the Allied transport service was the ubiquitous Douglas DC-3; but the machine which was to set the standard for a whole generation of four-engine airliners was the Douglas DC-4, which went into service in 1943, and carried a crew of 6, and over 40 passengers,

at 200 mph (c. 320 km/h) non-stop for 1500 miles (c. 2400 km).

Here, we must take another look at the subject of jet propulsion. The United States, with her great record of energy and enterprise in aircraft design and production, was inexplicably slow in this all-important new field: she had taken little interest in jet propulsion before 1941. In that year a British Whittle engine had been shipped from England to the United States; and in 1943 a de Havilland jet engine was also sent over. From these two British engines alone, the great turbojet industry of the United States was developed.

Of even more vital significance for the future of civilisation had been the first successful launch, in 1942, of the V-2 (A.4) rocket missile by the Germans. It was this vehicle which was to make possible the rapid strides in space rocketry in the postwar years and it was the ancestor of all space vehicles of today, itself being the direct outcome of that enthusiastic band of romantics and scientists which had forged ahead with their studies and experiments in the between-war period. On the outbreak of War the German authorities had the imagination and confidence to take them quietly and secretly into service, and put them to work on the so-called "revenge weapons". Many experts, both in Germany and among the Allies, had no faith in the future of the rocket; but it only took a few years to confound them. The V-2 weighed about 12 ½ tons at take-off; reached a height of 60 miles (96.5 km), after attaining an upward speed of some 3600 mph (*c.* 5800 km/h); and, slowing down in its descent, landed at about 2000 mph (*c.* 3200 km/h) anywhere up to 220 miles (354 km) from the firing point: it first went into action in 1944. In action earlier the same year (1944) but of less long-term importance, was the notorious German pilotless flying bomb (FZG-76); powered by a pulse-duct jet motor, it had a range of about 150 miles (*c.* 240 km) at 390-410 mph (*c.* 630-660 km/h) and created much havoc. It was at last beaten by rapidly traversing guns firing shells with "proximity" fuses, which only had to come near their targets in order to explode and destroy them.

We ought, I feel, to turn finally to the human side of World War II in the air. It is so easy to forget that these vastly complicated pieces of airborne machinery were not only designed and built by human beings, but flown and fought by them in conditions of stress and danger which beggar description. As Lord David Cecil wrote, "However we may try to analyse it, their superhuman heroism is an elemental attitude of human nature;... It is better to accept it as a fact of existence, happily not so infrequent as might be expected; and to offer it, in humility, our tribute of admiration."

In the late 1940s and early 1950s, jet propulsion made giant strides, spurred on both by the demands for combat aircraft and by the rapidly increasing needs of the airlines for large and fast jet transport machines. The first aeroplane to fly faster than sound in level flight (about 670 mph or 1078 km/h at sea level) was the American Bell X-1 in 1947; the first to exceed twice the speed of sound (Mach 2) was the American Douglas Skyrocket in 1953, a machine which also—in the same year—climbed to an altitude of over 15 miles (*c.* 24 km).

Along with the need for high cruising speeds came another demand, for slow take-off and landing speeds; and, where the air forces were concerned, there was also a need for aeroplanes which combined all these virtues. The first machine other than a helicopter to take off vertically was the wing-

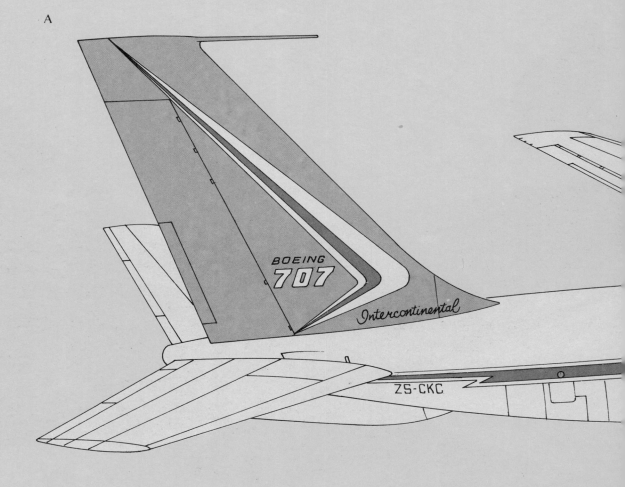

A

less Rolls-Royce *Flying Bedstead* rig, which was flown in 1953. Then, in 1954, the first winged VTOL (vertical-take-off-and-landing) aeroplane, the American Convair ZFY-1, completed its full flying sequence; and in 1957, the first jet-propelled VTOL (the American Ryan X-13) completed its first full flying sequence.

A year back (1956), the Bell X-2 had climbed to over 23 miles (126,000 ft or 38,405 m); on another occasion in the same year, it flew at over three times the speed of sound (Mach 3, which equalled over 2000 mph or 3200 km/h). Men were now nearing the day when they could at last venture into space.

Of far greater social importance was the growing production of airliners, which flooded from the world's factories after the War was over, making air-travel across oceans and continents as practical and commonplace as journeying by rail or boat. Pressurised cabins soon became the rule, allowing both airscrew and jet machines to fly at optimum speeds at heights where ordinary breathing would be impossible.

By 1945—1946, regular airlines were in operation across the North Atlantic, which gives a good indication of the range and reliability of the new machines. It was Britain who pioneered the jet-propelled passenger transport, with the de Havilland Comet being the first to enter airline service in 1952. It was also Britain who pioneered the airliner with turbo-prop propulsion (i.e. a jet engine driving a propeller), and achieved world-wide success with the Vickers Viscount, which first went into service in 1953. Then arrived the two main types of giant jet airliners, the American Boeing 707 and the Douglas DC-8, the former entering airline service in 1958. These great four-engine aircraft carry over 170 passengers at speeds of over 500 mph (800 km/h) non-stop over distances of some 4000 miles (*c.* 6400 km), flying at 30,000 feet (9144 m). This vast extension of the world's passenger-carrying facilities also reached down to the medium and light transport jet-machines for inter-urban and feeder-line transport. By the end of the 1950s, air travel had revolutionised transport, and had also revolutionised the holiday habits of the world. Countries quite inaccessible—in the time available for holidays by those who work—were now brought within one or two days flying.

A   The Boeing 707-320 Intercontinental
     airliner, the first jet transport to have
     a true non-stop transatlantic range.
B   Cross-section through passenger cabin.

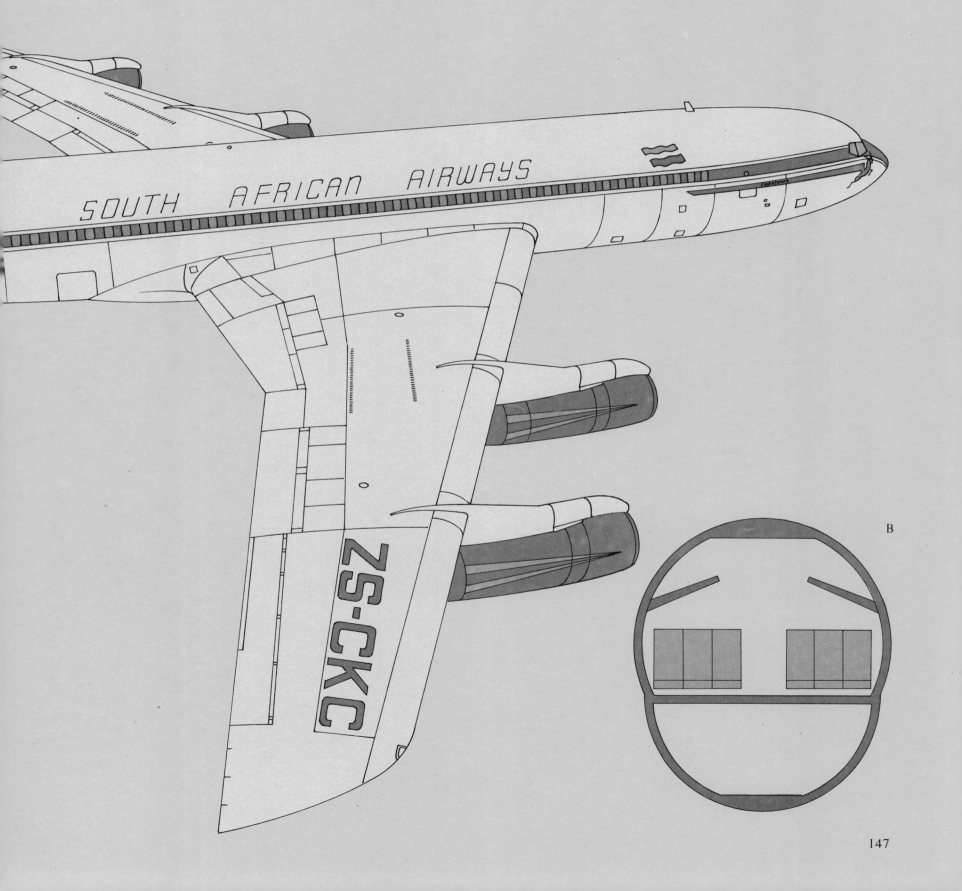

B

The more man can enlarge the frontiers of mystery, the better for his health of mind. Storm and lightning cater generously for our sense of wonder, and those who travel from one city to another by the Valkyrie's route find still subtler, yet more awe-inspiring Valhallas opening up to the imagination.

JEAN COCTEAU

Our descendants will certainly attempt journeys to other members of the Solar system . . . By 2030 the first preparations for the first attempts to reach Mars may perhaps be under consideration. The hardy individuals who form the personnel of the expedition will be sent forth in a machine propelled like a rocket.

LORD BIRKENHEAD (1930)

Scientific investigation into the possibilities [of jet propulsion] has given no indication that this method can be a serious competitor to the air-screw-engine combination.

The British Under-Secretary of State for Air (1934)

The lines of my policy have not been to create an offensive air arm which might constitute a threat to other nations, but to provide Germany with a military air force strong enough to defend her at any time against aerial attack.

HERMAN GOERING, 8TH MARCH 1935

I wish for many reasons flying had never been invented . . . somehow we have got to Christianise it.

Stanley Baldwin (1935)

CHAPTER TEN

FROM 1930 A.D. TO 1938 A.D.

Passenger traffic in the early 1930s. Lufthansa operated its internal services with transports such as this Focke-Wulf A29 which carried eight passengers and was powered by one BMV-VI engine.

A *First successful delta-wing aeroplane: Lippisch, 1931.*

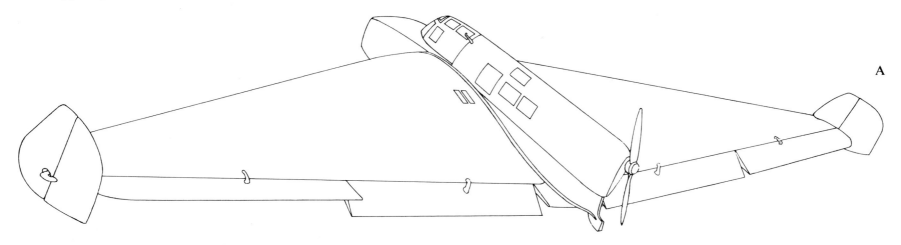

A

1930

In England, Frank Whittle takes out his first jet-engine patents. These are published in 1932.

5—24 MAY 1930

First solo flight from England to Australia by a woman: Amy Johnson in a de Havilland D.H. 60G Moth *Jason*, 19 days.

22 MAY 1930

First flight of the Boeing Monomail takes place in the United States, a clean, single-engined, all-metal cantilever monoplane with retractable undercarriage which marks an important step in airframe development.

21 JULY—17 AUGUST 1930

World flight-refuelled endurance record is established in the United States: Jackson and O'Brien fly for 3 weeks 5 days 23 hours 28 minutes.

20—26 AUGUST 1930

First crossing of the Atlantic by flying-boat: Wolfgang von Gronau and crew in a Dornier Wal from Germany to New York.

1—2 SEPTEMBER 1930

First non-stop flight from Paris to New York: Dieudonné Costes and Maurice Bellonte in a Breguet XIX in 37 hours 18 minutes.

10 SEPTEMBER 1930

First flight of the first Taylor E-2 Cub two-seater light monoplane. This American design develops into the Piper Cub which is to become one of the world's most popular light aircraft.

5 OCTOBER 1930

Loss at Beauvais, France, from collision with high ground, of the Royal Airship Works *R-101* rigid airship. The British Air Minister and Director of Civil Aviation are amongst the 48 people who lose their lives. This accident ends British airship development.

8 OCTOBER 1930

In Italy, the D'Ascanio helicopter establishes a helicopter record of 8 minutes 45 seconds. Flies 3540 ft (*c.* 1078 m) on 10 October flown by Marienello Nelli.

25 OCTOBER 1930

First coast-to-coast through air service across the United States is started by Transcontinental and Western Air between New York and Los Angeles.

1931

First flight by a delta-wing aeroplane. It was designed in Germany by Professor Alexander Lippisch.
See figure A

1931

First application of jet-propulsion (compressed air) to a full-size aircraft, the Italian airship, *Omniadir*.

29 APRIL 1931

In the United States, the first flight of the Boeing B-9 bomber. This aircraft marked the next step in airframe development from the Monomail to the Boeing 247, the first modern-type airliner.

27 MAY 1931

Balloon height record of 51,775 ft (*c.* 15,780 m) by Auguste Piccard and his assistant, Paul Kipfer, at Augsburg, Germany.

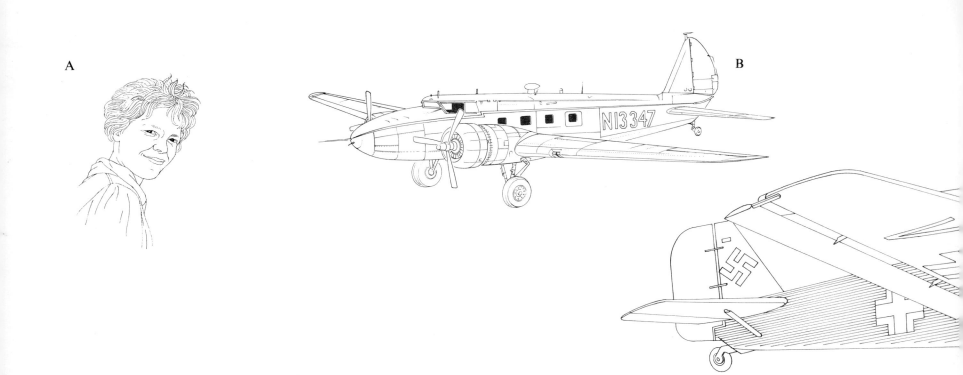

A   B

11 JUNE 1931

Handley Page HP-42 four-engined airliner enters service with the British airline, Imperial Airways, and sets new standards of passenger service and comfort.

23 JUNE—1 JULY 1931

Record round-the-world flight: Wiley Post and Harold Gatty in a Lockheed Vega, 15,474 miles (*c.* 24,900 km) in 8 days 15 hours 51 minutes.

23 JULY 1931

First non-stop flight from New York to Istanbul! Russel Boardman and John Polando in a Bellanca monoplane.

25 SEPTEMBER 1931

First flight of the Goodyear-Zeppelin XR-4. *Akron*, rigid airship which is the first ship of the US Navy's last rigid airship programme. *Akron* is lost in an accident in 1933 and her sister-ship *Macon* in another in 1935, thus ending American rigid airship development.

4—5 OCTOBER 1931

First non-stop flight across the Pacific: Hugh Herndon and Clyde Pangborn fly from Tokyo to Wenatchee, Washington, 4558 miles (*c.* 7330 km) in 41 hours 13 minutes in a Bellanca Pacemaker.

26 NOVEMBER 1931

First solo crossing of the South Atlantic and first direct west-to-east crossing: de Havilland Puss Moth, flown by Squadron Leader "Bert" Hinkler.

21—22 MAY 1932

First solo transatlantic flight by a woman, in a Lockheed Vega, Amelia Earhart, from Harbour Grace, Newfoundland to Derry, Northern Ireland.
See figure A

JUNE 1932

Introduction of R/T (radio telephone) on the United States airlines, on Stimson T trimotors.

21 JULY—9 NOVEMBER 1932

First flight round the world by a flying-boat: von Gronau and crew in a Dornier Wal in 111 days.

18 AUGUST 1932

Balloon height record of 53,153 ft (*c.* 16,200 m): Auguste Piccard and Max Cosyns over Switzerland, having ascended from Dubendorf.

18 AUGUST 1932

First solo east-to-west flight across the Atlantic by a de Havilland Puss Moth light aeroplane flown by J. A. Mollison from Portmarnock Strand, Dublin, Ireland, to Pennfield Ridge, New Brunswick, Canada.

14—18 NOVEMBER 1932

Amy Johnson flies solo from England to Cape Town, South Africa, in 4 days 54 minutes.

JANUARY 1933

First fatal accident in a Cierva Autogiro occurs at Villacoublay, France, ten years after the first flight by an Autogiro. During this time some 120 Autogiros had been built and over 30,000 hours flown.

MARCH 1933

The Boeing 247 twin-engined airliner enters service in the United States with United Airlines, thus setting new standards with its

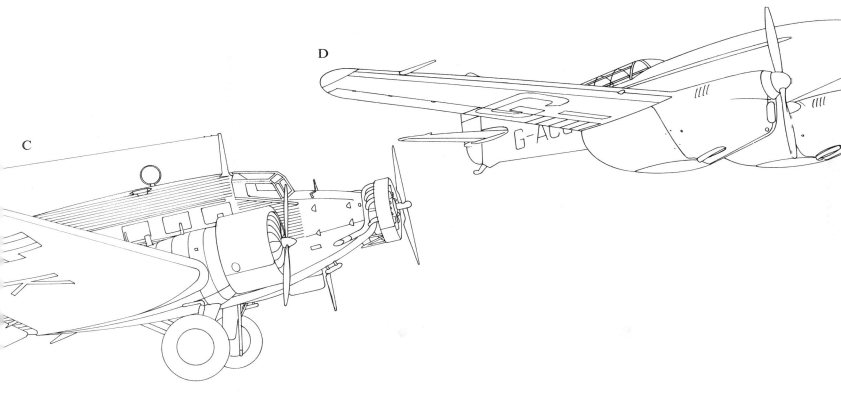

aerodynamically-clean all-metal monoplane structure and retractable undercarriage.
See figure B

29 MARCH 1933

First flight of the first Miles Hawk wooden light monoplane at Reading, England, which marks an important step in light aircraft development.

1 APRIL 1933

The Indian Air Force is formed.

MAY 1933

The Junkers Ju-52/3m three-engined air-liner enters service with Lufthansa. This aircraft is widely used by the Germans as a military transport during the Second World War.
See figure C

10—11 JUNE 1933

First non-stop flight from Spain to Cuba: Joaquin Collart and Mariano Barberan in a Breguet XIX.

15—22 JULY 1933

First solo flight round the world: by a Lockheed Vega *Winnie Mae* in 7 days, 18 hours, 49 minutes, flown by Wiley Post from the Floyd Bennet Field, New York.

22—24 JULY 1933

First direct flight from Britain to the United States: Jim and Amy Mollison in a de Havilland Dragon from Pendine Sands in Wales to Bridgeport, Connecticut.

AUGUST 1933

First practical variable-pitch two-position propeller is introduced into airline service: Hamilton Standard in Curtiss Condor biplanes.

30 AUGUST 1933

The French flag airline, Air France, is formed.

1934

Constant-speed variable-pitch propellers are introduced into airline service: Boeing 247D twin-engined airliners with United Air Lines in the United States.

19 FEBRUARY—1 JUNE 1934

US Army Air Corps fly internal air-mail services in the United States.

28 JULY 1934

Balloon height record of 60,613 ft (c. 18,475 m): William E. Kepner, Albert W. Stevens and Orville A. Anderson from Rapid City, South Dakota, USA in *Explorer I*.

20—22 OCTOBER 1934

The Mac Robertson Race from England to Australia. It is won by Charles W. Scott and Tom Campbell Black in a de Havilland D. H.-88 Comet in 71 hours.
See figure D

A *Amelia Earhart.*
B *Boeing 247 twin-engined monoplane airliner, 1933.*
C *Junkers Ju-52/3m airliner, 1933.*
D *De Havilland D. H. 88 Comet, 1934.*

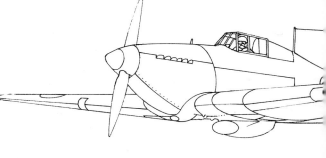

A

B

C

22 OCTOBER—4 NOVEMBER 1934

First flight from Australia to North America: in a Lockheed Altair from Brisbane to Oakland, California, flown by Charles Kingsford-Smith and P. G. Taylor.

1935

In the United States, exhaust-driven turbo-superchargers are brought into service on aero-engines.

1935

Adolf Busemann, a German scientist, at the Volta Conference in Rome suggests the use of swept wings and tails to delay and reduce the sharp increase in drag which occurs as the speed of sound is approached and exceeded.

1935

Meredith, of the Royal Aircraft Establishment in England, invents the ducted radiator for use in high-speed aircraft fitted with liquid-cooled engines. This greatly reduced cooling drag. Meredith was also responsible for ejector exhausts some time later.

9 MARCH 1935

Formation of the Luftwaffe, the German Air Force, is announced.

24 MARCH 1935

First flight of the prototype of the British Avro Anson twin-engined reconnaissance monoplane, which is widely used during the Second World War, particularly for training in the Empire Air Training Scheme.

26 JUNE 1935

The first practical helicopter flies successfully after a long period of development: the Breguet Dorand 314 with twin co-axial rotors, flown by Maurice Claisse in France.

28 JULY 1935

First flight of the Boeing 299 four-engined bomber prototype of the B-17 Flying Fortress, in the United States, which becomes one of the most successful bombers of the Second World War.
See figure A

1 OCTOBER 1935

British Airways is formed out of an amalgamation of a number of smaller private airlines.

6 NOVEMBER 1935

First flight of the prototype of the Hawker Hurricane single-seater fighter which plays the major part in winning the Battle of Britain in 1940.
See figure B

11 NOVEMBER 1935

World height record for balloons of 72,395

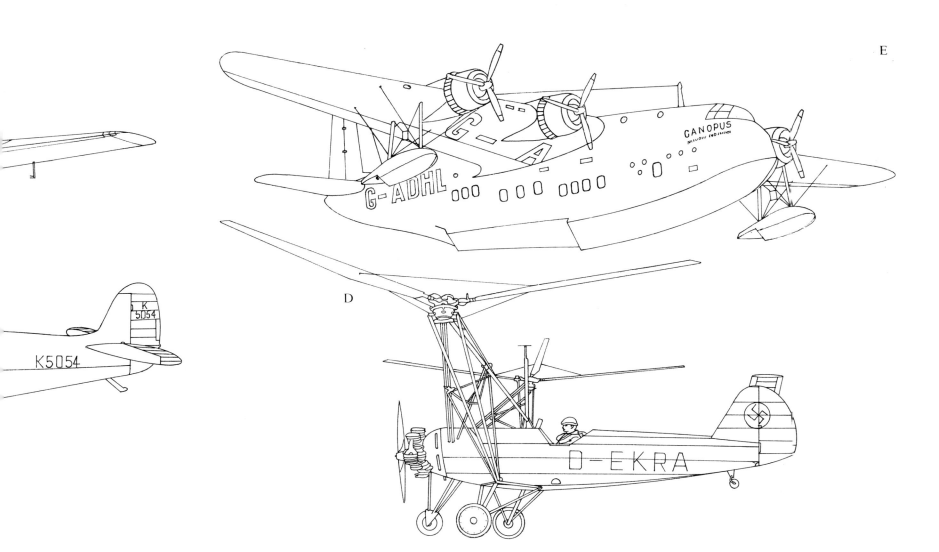

ft (*c.* 22,066 m) is established in the United States by Orville A. Anderson and Albert W. Stevens in *Explorer II*.

22 NOVEMBER 1935

First scheduled air-mail flight across the Pacific from San Francisco to the Philippines: Edwin C. Musick in a Pan American Martin Clipper.

4 MARCH 1936

First flight of the Zeppelin LZ-129 *Hindenburg*, in Germany. She and her sister-ship LZ-130 *Graf Zeppelin II*, are the last rigid airships built.

5 MARCH 1936

First flight of the prototype of the British Supermarine Spitfire single-seater, monoplane fighter, perhaps the most famous aircraft of the Second World War.
See figure C

13 MAY 1936

The Australian National Airways is formed.

15 JUNE 1936

First flight of the prototype of the Vickers-Armstrong Wellington twin-engined, medium bomber of geodetic construction, which is to become the most important RAF bomber at the start of the Second World War.

26 JUNE 1936

First flight of the first practical helicopter with side-by-side rotors: Focke-Achgelis Fa-61, designed by Professor H. K. J. Focke and flown by Ewald Rohlfs, in Germany.
See figure D

4 JULY 1936

First flight of the Short C-Type Empire four-engined metal monoplane flying-boat. This aircraft is supplied in quantity to Imperial

Airways and is also the basis of the military Sunderland which is the last flying-boat to serve with the RAF.
See figure E

26 JULY 1936

The Japanese Military Air Force is formed as a separate service.

A   *Boeing 299 four-engined bomber, 1935.*
B   *Prototype of the Hawker Hurricane single-seater fighter, 1935.*
C   *Prototype of the Supermarine Spitfire, 1936.*
D   *Focke-Achgelis Fa-61 helicopter, 1936.*
E   *Short C-Type Empire flying-boat, 1936.*

30 JULY 1936

The RAF Volunteer Reserve is formed.

1937

First flight of the Ju-87 single-engined dive-bomber, prototype of the Stuka which was widely used by the Germans in support of their armies during the Second World War.

1937

First flight of over an hour by a helicopter: the Focke-Achgelis Fa-61, in Germany.

20 JANUARY 1937

Maybury Committee on British Civil Aviation reports.

26 APRIL 1937

The bombing of Guernica during the Spanish Civil War by German aircraft supporting General Franco's Nationalists. *See figure B*

28 APRIL 1937

First commercial flight across the Pacific: Pan-American Clipper arrives in Hong Kong.

6 MAY 1937

Loss in an accident at Lakehurst, New Jersey, of Zeppelin LZ 129, *Hindenburg*, at the end of a scheduled passenger service from Europe. This accident leads to the ending of rigid airship development. *See figure A*

7 MAY 1937

First flight of the first fully-pressurised aeroplane: the Lockheed XC-35, in the United States.

16 JUNE 1937

Air services are started between New York and Bermuda by Imperial Airways and Pan American.

12—14 JULY 1937

First non-stop flight from Moscow to California over Arctic regions 6750 miles

(c. 10,860 km) by Gromov, Yumasheff and Danilin in an Antonov ANT 25.

30 JULY 1937

The British Fleet Air Arm is brought under the control of the Admiralty.

SEPTEMBER 1937

Feathering propellers are brought into service on Lockheed 14 transport aircraft, in the United States. These cut the drag of a failed engine on multi-engined aircraft.

31 DECEMBER 1937

During 1937 2 ½ million passengers are carried on the world's scheduled airlines in a year for the first time.

23 FEBRUARY 1938

First separation in flight of the British Short-Mayo composite aeroplane, two seaplanes (the Short S.21 *Maia* flying-boat and the Short S.20 *Mercury* seaplane) which can take off together so that the over-loaded upper component can fly great distances.

A

A   *The airship* Hindenburg *crashes in flames at Lakehurst, New Jersey, 1937.*

B   *A German Stuka of the Spanish Nationalist forces during the Spanish Civil War, 1937.*

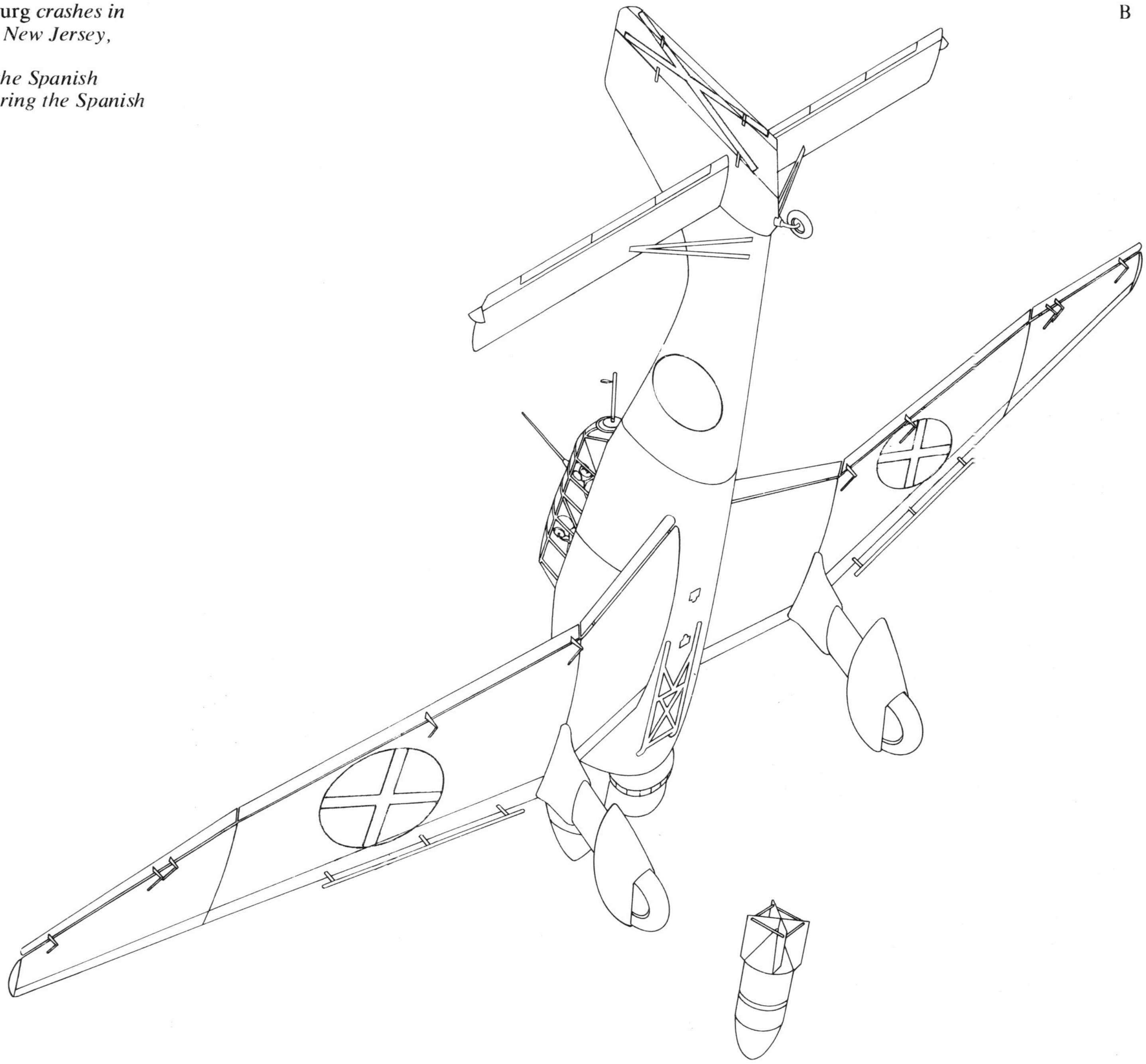

This aircraft establishes a world seaplane distance record 6—8 October 1938, but is not developed further.

8 MARCH 1938

Cadman Committee on British Civil Aviation reports. It recommends two "chosen instrument" airlines: Imperial and British Airways.

11—14 AUGUST 1938

First return flight Berlin—New York—

Berlin: the four-engined Focke-Wulf Condor in 24 hours 56 minutes outbound and 19 hours 55 minutes return.

17 OCTOBER 1938

Trans-Canada Air Lines (later Air Canada) starts operating.

5—7 NOVEMBER 1938.

First non-stop flight from Egypt to Australia: two Vickers Wellesleys cover 7162 miles (c. 11,520 km).

The Battle of France is over. I expect that the Battle of Britain is about to begin. Upon this battle depends the survival of Christian civilisation. Let us therefore brace ourselves to our duties, and so bear ourselves that, if the British Empire and its Commonwealth last for a thousand years, men will still say "This was their finest hour".

WINSTON CHURCHILL (18TH JUNE 1940)

I've tried to think back to that first flight past Mach 1, but it doesn't seem any more important than any of the others. I was at about 37,000, straight, level, and it was just a matter of flying the airplane. It flew very nicely and got up to 0.97 on the Mach indicator, and then the meter jumped to about 1.05 as I accelerated past the shock wave that was on the nose of the airplane. I was kind of disappointed that it wasn't more of a big charge than it was.

Captain CHARLES YEAGER
(SPEAKING OF HIS FIRST SUPERSONIC FLIGHT IN THE BELL X-1 ON
14TH OCTOBER 1947)

It is one thing to have an idea. It is another to have the technical and executive ability to give it flesh. It is another to have the tenacity of purpose to drive through to success unshaken in confidence, in the face of discouraging opposition. Whittle, whose name in the annals of engineering comes after those of Watt, Stephenson, and Parsons only for reasons of chronology or alphabetical order, had these things.

LORD KINGS NORTON (1947)

We are buying airplanes that haven't yet been fully designed, with millions of dollars we don't have, and are going to operate them off airports that are too small, in an air traffic control system that is too slow, and we must fill them with more passengers than we have ever carried before.

A US AIRLINE PRESIDENT (1956)

CHAPTER ELEVEN

FROM 1939 A.D. TO 1956 A.D.

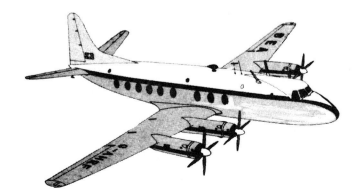

After World War II BOAC operated passenger services from London to South Africa with aircraft such as this Avro York which could carry a crew of 5 and 24 passengers. Here we see a BOAC traffic-clerk conducting a party of passengers aboard.

A

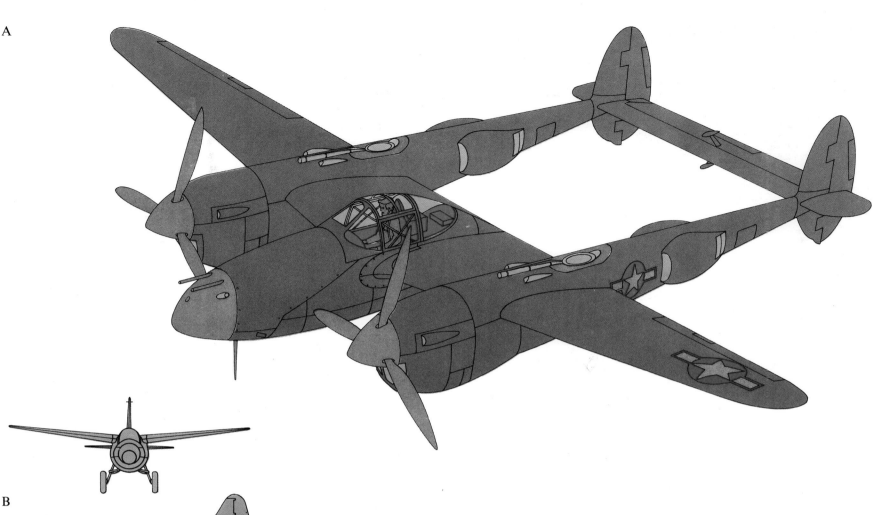

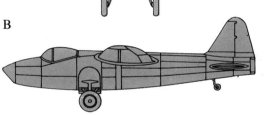

B

A *Lockheed P-38 Lightning, Second World War.*
B *First turbo-jet aeroplane to fly: the Heinkel He-178, 1939.*

1939

In England, gear-driven multi-speed superchargers are brought into use on aero-engines. These increase the efficiency of aero-engines when operating at different heights.

27 JANUARY 1939

First flight of the prototype of the American Lockheed P-38 Lightning twin-engined single-seater fighter of the Second World War.
See figure A

18 JUNE 1939

First direct transatlantic flying-boat service from New York to Southampton, England, by way of Botwood, New Foundland, and Foynes, Ireland, by Pan American Airways.

5—7 AUGUST 1939

First British transatlantic air-mail service from Southampton to Montreal by way of Foynes and Botwood: by Imperial Airways Short Empire flying-boat, flight-refuelled.

27 AUGUST 1939

First flight of the first turbojet aeroplane: the Heinkel He-178 at Marienehe, Germany, flown by Captain Erich Warsitz.
See figure B

26 NOVEMBER 1939

BOAC (British Overseas Airways Corporation) is established by the amalgamation of Imperial and British Airways with Reith as chairman and Pearson as deputy chairman.

A

D

C

B

29 DECEMBER 1939

First flight of the prototype of the Consolidated B-24 Liberator four-engined heavy bomber, one of the two types of American heavy bomber which play a major part in Europe and North Africa in the Second World War.
See figure C

1940

In England, gear-driven multi-stage superchargers are brought into use on aero-engines. These were also sometimes multispeed and incorporated intercoolers or aftercoolers. These developments increased still further the powers of aero-engines and the heights to which these powers were developed.

13 MAY 1940

First free flight by the Sikorsky VS-300

single main-rotor plus tail-rotor helicopter, flown by Igor Sikorsky, the Russian engineer now living in the United States.

Mid-1940

Boeing 307 four-engined airliner enters service in the United States with TWA. This is the first pressurised transport aeroplane.

8 AUGUST—31 OCTOBER 1940

The Battle of Britain is fought over South East England between the Luftwaffe and RAF Fighter Command.

19 AUGUST 1940

First flight of the prototype of the North American B-25 Mitchell, perhaps the most successful Allied medium bomber of the Second World War.

27 AUGUST 1940

First flight of the experimental Caproni-Campini N-1 piston-engine-driven compressor jet aeroplane at Tatiedo near Milan, Italy.
See figure D

26 OCTOBER 1940

First flight of the first prototype of the North American P-51 Mustang fighter, which plays an important part in the Second World War, particularly on long-range bomber escort work.

25 NOVEMBER 1940

First flight of the first prototype of the de Havilland Mosquito twin-engined all-wood high-speed light bomber, which is one of the most successful aircraft of the Second World War.

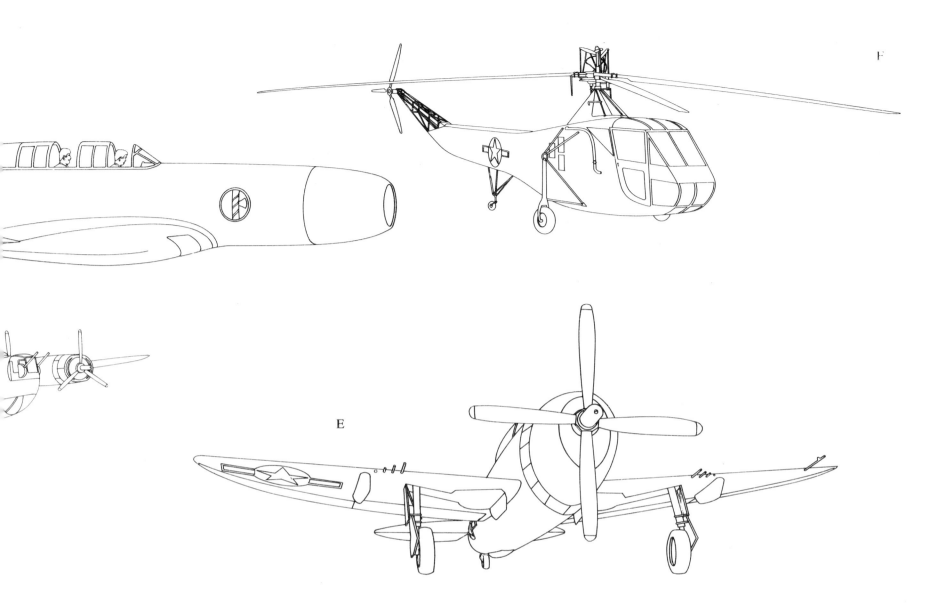

E

9 JANUARY 1941

First flight of the prototype Avro Lancaster four-engined heavy bomber, which becomes the most successful British bomber of the Second World War.

10—11 FEBRUARY 1941

First British four-engined bomber to be used operationally enters service: Short Stirling with No. 7 Squadron, RAF at Oakington.

15 MAY 1941

First flight of the first British jet-aeroplane: Gloster E-28/39 at Cranwell, England, flown by Flight Lieutenant P. E. G. Sayer.

14 AUGUST 1941

First flights of the finally satisfactory form of

the first practical single-main-rotor helicopter: the Sikorsky VS-300 flown by Igor Sikorsky.

6 MAY 1941

First flight of the prototype of the Republic R-47 Thunderbolt, one of the two most successful American fighters of the Second World War.
See figure E

SEPTEMBER 1941

The Whittle jet-engine is flown from Britain to the United States and provides the model for the first practical American jet-engines.

14 JANUARY 1942

First flight of the Sikorsky R-4 helicopter, the first production helicopter with single

main-rotor, in the United States.
See figure F

14 FEBRUARY 1942

First flight of the first production-type Douglas DC-4 four-engined airliner — in the United States: this is the first modern-type long-range airliner and sets the fashion for a whole post-war generation of piston-engined transports.

A   *Heinkel He-111 bomber, Second World War.*
B   *Vickers Supermarine Spitfire fighter, Second World War.*
C   *Consolidated Liberator bomber, 1939.*
D   *Caproni-Campini quasi-jet, 1940.*
E   *Republic Thunderbolt fighter, Second World War.*
F   *Sikorsky R-4b helicopter, 1942.*

A

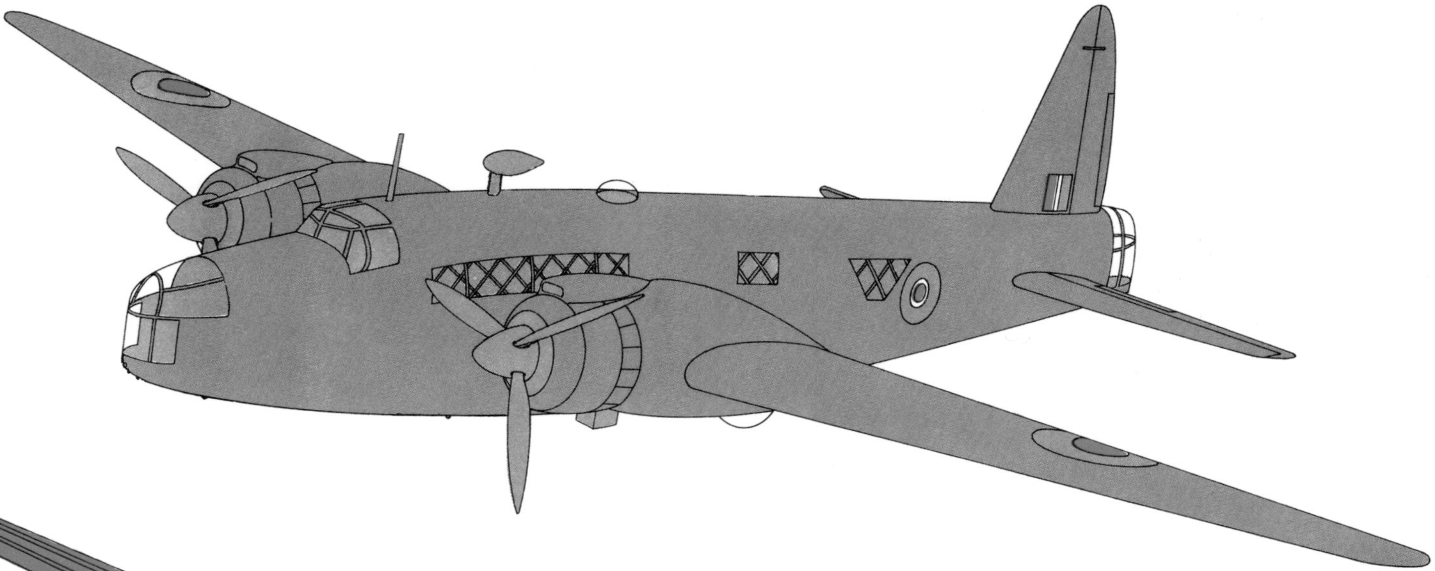

C

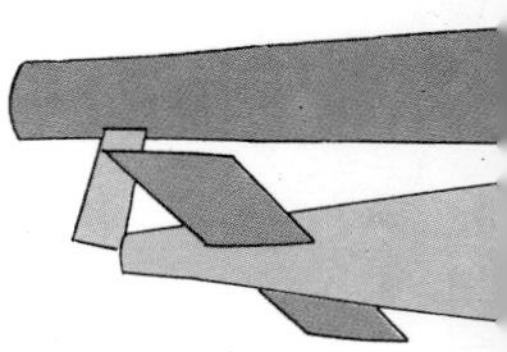

B

A *Vickers-Armstrong Wellington bomber, Second World War.*
B *The first operational jet-propelled combat aeroplane, the Messerschmitt Me-262: 1942.*
C *V-1 Flying Bomb, 1944.*
D *Lockheed Constellation airliner, 1944.*
E *Focke-Wulf Fw 190 fighter, Second World War.*

3 MARCH 1942

Avro Lancaster four-engined bomber enters service, with No. 44 Squadron RAF at Waddington. This is the most successful British heavy bomber of the Second World War.

21 SEPTEMBER 1942

First flight of the first prototype of the Boeing B-29 heavy bomber, in the United States. This is to play a major part in the strategic bombing and defeat of Japan in the Second World War.

1 OCTOBER 1942

First flight of the first American jet-aeroplane: the Bell XP-59A *Airacomet* powered by two General Electric engines based on the British Whittle design, at Lake Muroc (now the Edwards Air Force Base).

1943

First flight of the first practical helicopter with a torqueless, jet-propelled rotor: the Doblhoff WNF-342 in Germany.

1943

In England, De Bruyne invents Redux metal adhesive, which is to be widely used thereafter in aircraft construction.

5 MARCH 1943

First flight of the prototype of the Gloster Meteor, the first Allied jet-fighter to enter service.

15 JUNE 1943

First flight of the first jet-bomber: the Arado Ar-234B *Blitz* for the German Luftwaffe.

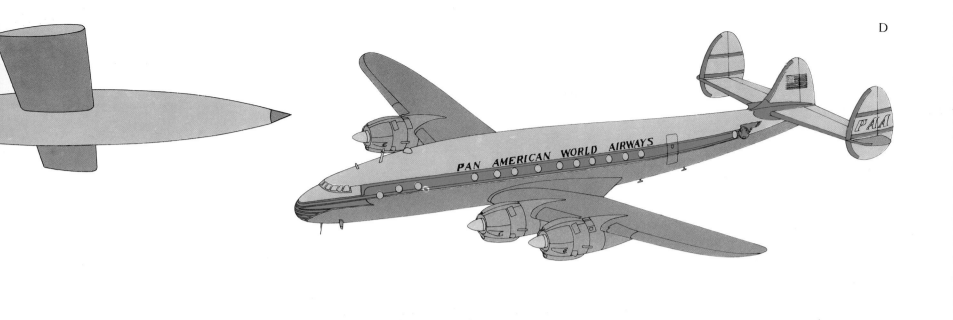

1944

First long-range surface-to-surface aerodynamic missile becomes operational: Fieseler Fi-103, FZG-76, "Flying Bomb" (V-1) used by the Germans against England. *See figure C*

9 JANUARY 1944

In the United States, the first flight of the first prototype of the Lockheed P-80 Shooting Star jet-fighter, which is to be widely used by numerous Western air forces for many years.

MID-1944

Lockheed Constellation four-engined pressurised transport aeroplanes enter service with the US Army Air Forces. After the war, in airline service, this aircraft is for a number of years the world's leading long-range airliner. *See figure D*

8 SEPTEMBER 1944

First long-range ballistic rocket missile becomes operational. A-4 (V-2) rocket used by the Germans, and two are fired at Paris and London on the same day. This rocket is

the ancestor of all subsequent ballistic missiles and space launchers.

LATE 1944

First production rocket-powered aeroplane enters service with the Luftwaffe: the Messerschmitt Me-163.

19 APRIL 1945

International Air Transport Association (IATA) is inaugurated at Havana, Cuba: it succeeds the International Air Traffic Association formed in 1919 at The Hague, Holland.

A

B

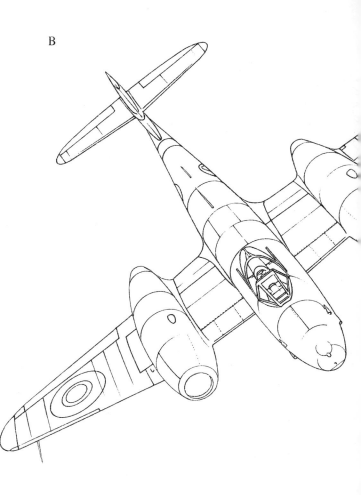

16 JULY 1945

First atom-bomb experimentally exploded at Alamogardo, New Mexico, USA.

6—9 AUGUST 1945

First atomic fission bombs used operationally, dropped by the Americans from Boeing B-29s on Hiroshima and Nagasaki in Japan, thus ending the Second World War. Japan surrenders on 14—15 August. *See figure A*

20 SEPTEMBER 1945

First flight of the first experimental turboprop aeroplane: the Gloster Meteor with Rolls-Royce Trent engines (flown by Eric Greenwood).

23 OCTOBER 1945

American Overseas Airlines inaugurates a scheduled passenger service across the North Atlantic with Douglas DC-4s.

7 NOVEMBER 1945

First speed record of over 600 mph established: Hugh J. Wilson in a Gloster Meteor jet-fighter at 606 mph (*c*. 975 km/h). *See figure B*

18—20 NOVEMBER 1945

Non-stop flight from Guam in the Pacific to Washington, D. C., 7882 miles (*c*. 12,680 km), establishing a world distance record: Irvine and crew in a Boeing B-29 bomber.

1 JANUARY 1946

Wartime restrictions on civil flying are revoked in Britain.

1 AUGUST 1946

British European Airways and British South American Airways are established.

8 AUGUST 1946

First flight of the Convair B-36 heavy bomber, which becomes the main equipment of the USAAF Strategic Air Command through the 1950s. *See figure C*

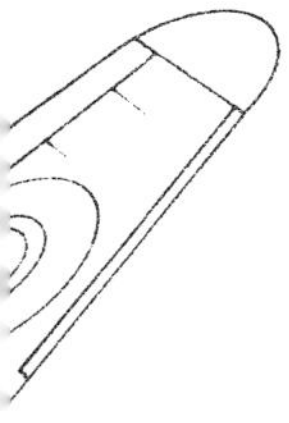

13 AUGUST 1946

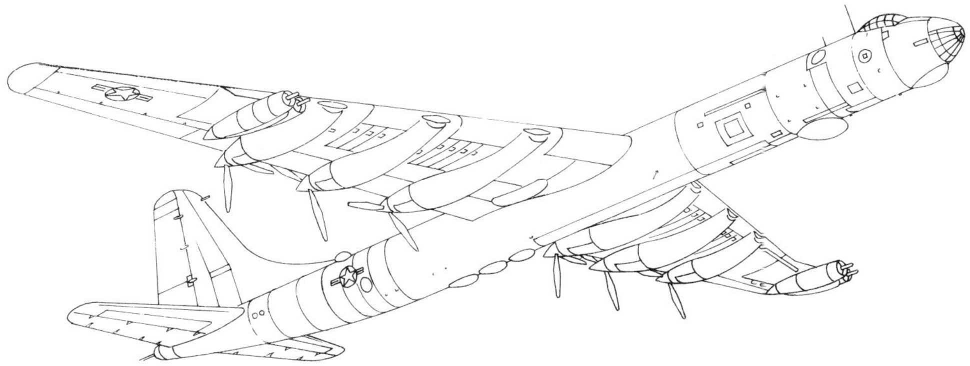

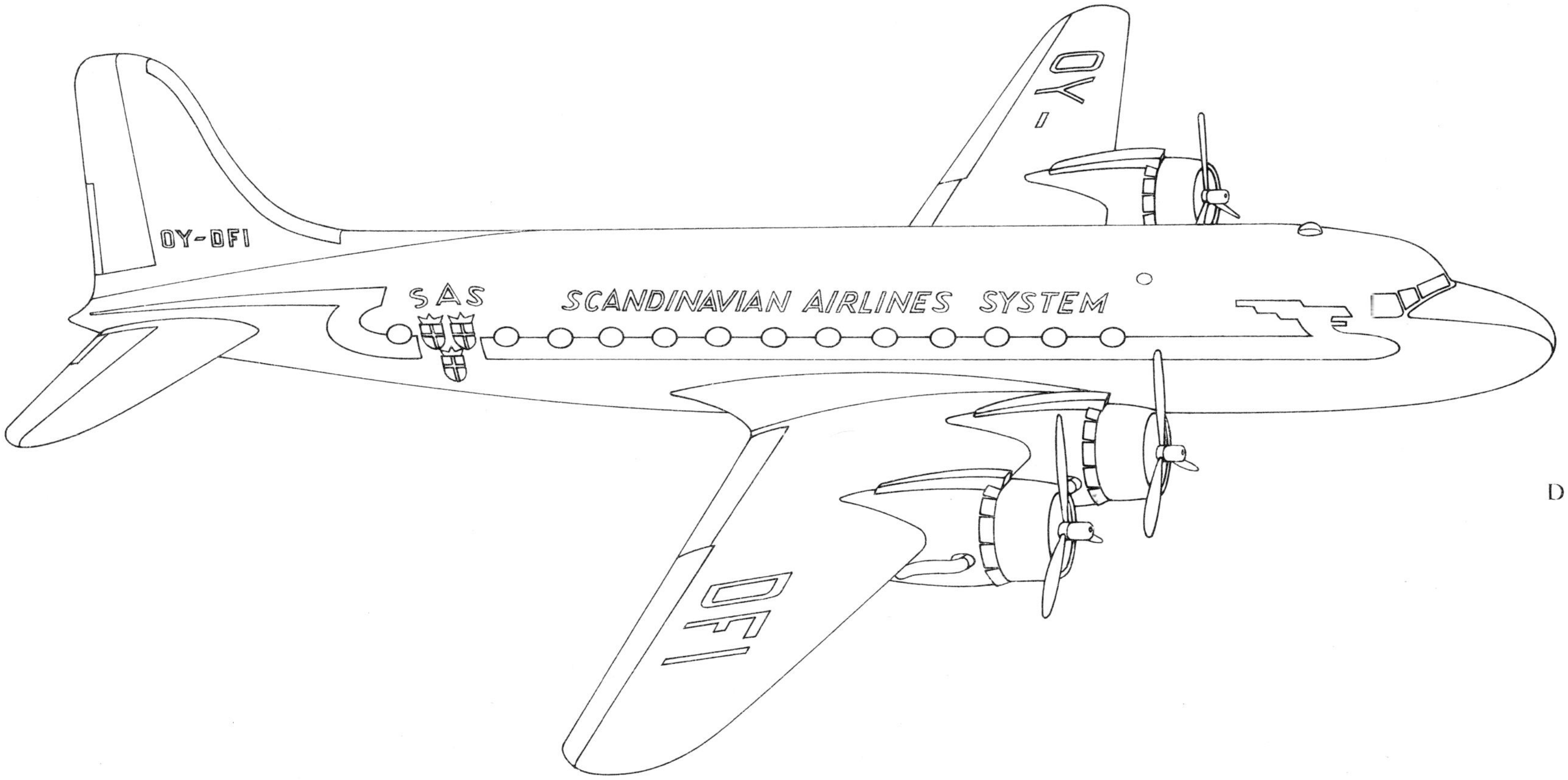

Agreement is reached to form the consortium airline, Scandinavian Airlines System, as the joint Swedish, Norwegian and Danish flag airline.
See figure D

21—23 AUGUST 1946

Flight from London to Darwin, Australia in 45 hours 35 minutes: D'Aeth and crew in Avro Lancaster *Aries*.

1 SEPTEMBER 1946

Vickers Viking airliner enters service with BEA (British European Airways).

15 SEPTEMBER 1946

First regular air service inaugurated between Sydney, Australia and Vancouver, Canada across the Pacific: Australian National Airways with Douglas DC-4s.

24 SEPTEMBER—1 OCTOBER 1946

First non-stop flight from Perth, Australia to Columbus, Ohio, of 11,236 miles (*c.* 18,080 km) establishes a world distance record: Thomas D. Davies and crew in a Lockheed P-2V-1, *Neptune*.

A *The first atomic bombs destroy Nagasaki and Hiroshima, 1945.*
B *Gloster Meteor turbo-prop jet-fighter, 1945.*
C *Convair B-36 heavy bomber for the USAAF Strategic Air Command, 1946.*
D *Scandinavian Airlines System Douglas DC-4 passenger airliner, 1946.*

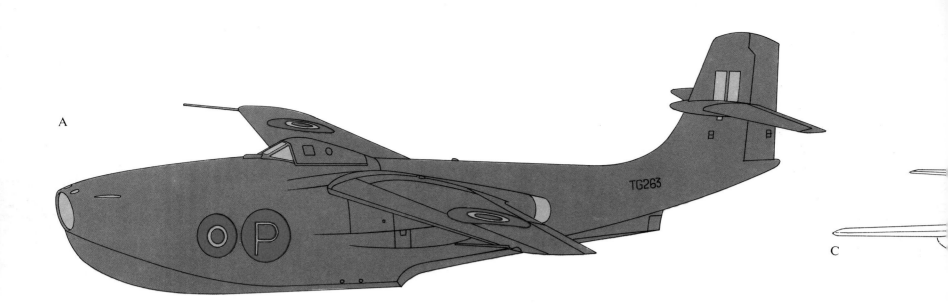

A

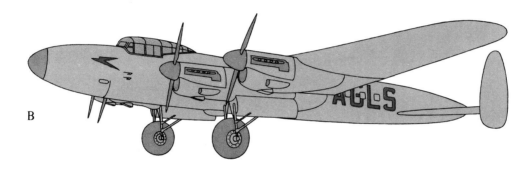

B

C

| 6 OCTOBER 1946 | 2 JULY 1947 | 18 SEPTEMBER 1947 |

First non-stop flight from Hawaii to Egypt over the North Pole: Irvine and crew in a Boeing B-29, 9442 nautical miles (*c.* 17,500 km).

4 APRIL 1947

The International Civil Aviation Organisation (ICAO) comes into being on ratification by 26 States of the Convention drawn up at Chicago in 1944.

11 JUNE 1947

The British Air Transport Advisory Council is set up to make recommendations on applications to operate scheduled air services.

2 JULY 1947

The first production swept-wing jet-fighter flies: the Russian MiG-15, which is to distinguish itself on the North Korean side during the Korean War.
See figure C

16 JULY 1947

First flight of the world's first jet-powered flying-boat: Saunders-Roe S. R. A. 1. This aircraft does not go into production and the flying-boat as a type is decreasingly used from about this time.
See figure A

4 AUGUST 1947

British Commonwealth Pacific Airlines set up by the United Kingdom, Australian and New Zealand Governments.

18 SEPTEMBER 1947

The United States Air Force becomes an independent service within the new unified US armed forces.

1 OCTOBER 1947

First flight of the North American F-86 Sabre swept-wing jet-fighter which is to distinguish itself with the United Nations forces in the Korean War and remains in service with numerous air forces for many years.

14 OCTOBER 1947

First piloted aeroplane exceeds the speed of sound in level flight: the Bell XS-1, flown by Captain Charles Yeager, USAF, at a speed of 670 mph (*c.* 1078 km/h).
See figure D

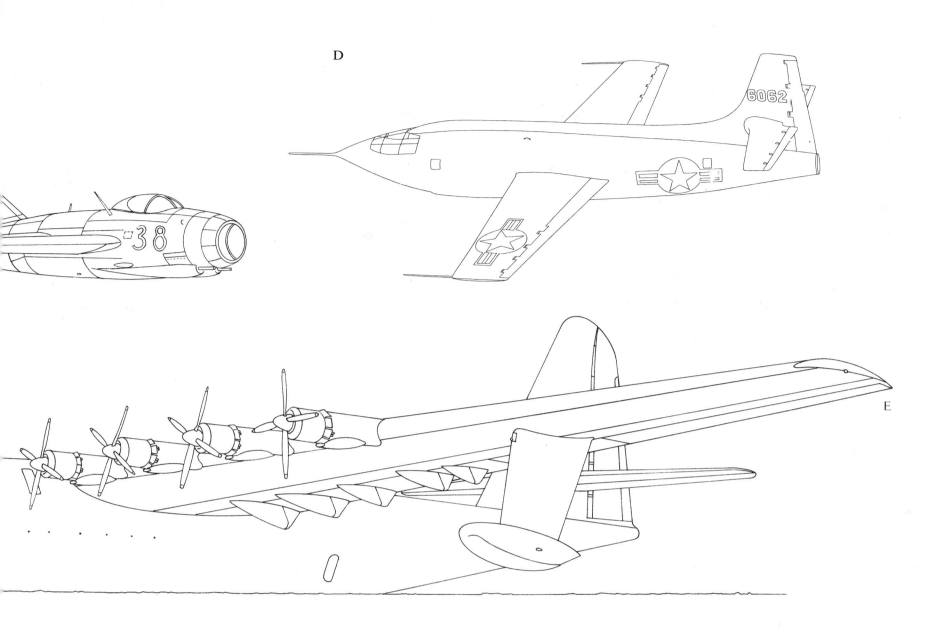

D

17 DECEMBER 1947

First flight of the Boeing B-47 swept-wing jet-bomber which inaugurates the configuration of engines in wing-pods which is subsequently widely adopted for large American jet aircraft. The B-47 is used by the USAF in large numbers for many years.

1948

First experimental jet-transport flies: the Vickers New-Viking, in England.

4 FEBRUARY 1948

The US Military Air Transport Service (M. A. T. S.) is established, as a joint-services organisation. It was originally formed during the War as the Air Transport Command of the US Army Air Forces.

23 MARCH 1948

Height record of 59,446 ft (18,119 m) is established by John Cunningham in a de Havilland Vampire jet-fighter, in England.

26 JUNE 1948

The Berlin airlift starts to a blockaded Berlin.

12—14 JULY 1948

First Atlantic crossing by jet-aircraft: six de Havilland Vampires of No. 54 Squadron, RAF.

16 JULY 1948

First flight of the first turbo-prop transport: Vickers V-630 Viscount prototype.

A   *First turbo-jet seaplane; Saunders-Roe, 1947.*
B   *After the war, BOAC begin trans-atlantic flights with Lancastrians, converted Lancaster bombers.*
C   *Mikoyan-Gurevich MiG-15 swept-wing jet-fighter, 1947.*
D   *The Bell X-1, launched from a B-52 mother plane, at a height of 30,000 ft. (9144 m), breaks the sound barrier, 1947.*
E   *Hughes Hercules flying-boat, 1947.*

A

B

23 AUGUST 1948

Experimental parasite fighter first successfully launched from its parent bomber: the Mc-Donnell XF-85 from a Boeing B-29, in the United States.

18 SEPTEMBER 1948

First delta-wing jet-aeroplane flies: the Convair XF-92A.

25 FEBRUARY 1949

Record height of 250 miles (c. 400 km) is reached by a two-stage rocket fired from White Sands, New Mexico, USA. It consists of a V-2 and a *WAC* Corporal.

26 FEBRUARY—2 MARCH 1949

First non-stop flight-refuelled flight round the world: James Gallagher and crew in a Boeing B-50

4 MARCH 1949

A Martin Mars flying-boat carries 269 people from San Diego to San Fransisco, in the United States.

7—8 MARCH 1949

William P. Odom flies a Beech Bonanza light aeroplane non-stop 4957 miles (c. 7978 km) from Hawaii to Teterboro, New Jersey, USA.

21 APRIL 1949

First flight of the first successful ram-jet aeroplane: the Leduc 010, in France.
See figure A

26 APRIL 1949

World endurance record, flight-refuelled of 1008 hours 1 minute (six weeks) is established in the United States: by Dick

Reidel and Harold Harris in an Aeronca Chief light aircraft refuelled from a ground vehicle while flying.

12 MAY 1949

End of the Berlin Blockade. The airlift is continued until October 1949.

27 JULY 1949

First flight of the first production jet-airliner: the de Havilland D.H.-106 Comet.
See figure B

30 JULY 1949

British South American Airways Corporation absorbed into BOAC.

1 OCTOBER 1949

Cape Canaveral (later Cape Kennedy) rocket range established, in Florida, USA.

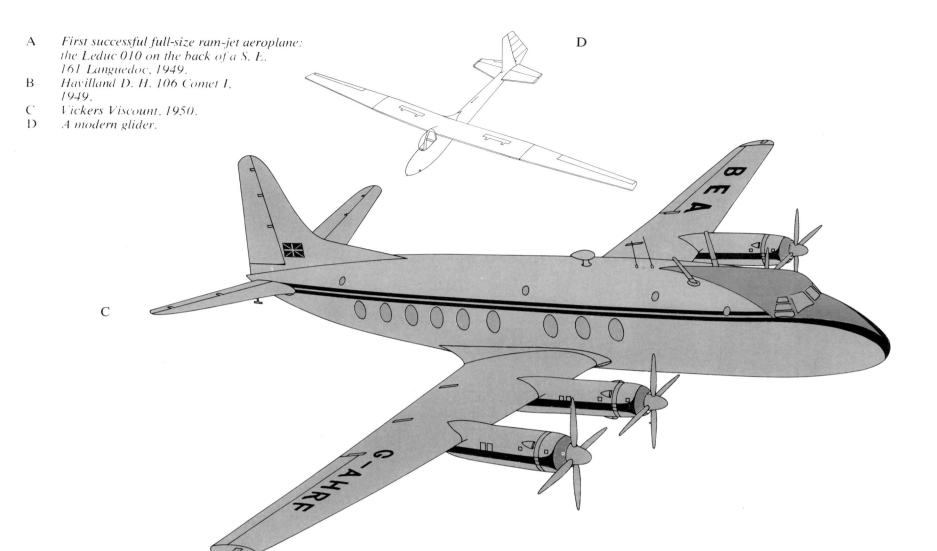

A First successful full-size ram-jet aeroplane: the Leduc 010 on the back of a S. E. 161 Languedoc, 1949.
B Havilland D. H. 106 Comet I, 1949.
C Vickers Viscount, 1950.
D A modern glider.

1950

First flight of the first practical helicopter with a torqueless, ram-jet-propelled rotor: the Hiller Hornet, in the United States.

31 JANUARY—18 FEBRUARY 1950

The first International Antarctic Expedition, composed of British, Swedes and Norwegians, uses two Auster light aircraft for a number of flights of exploration.

12 APRIL 1950

L. Welch crosses the English Channel in the first-ever soaring flight from London to Brussels.

1 JUNE 1950

In the United States, J. Robinson is the first

sailplane pilot to win the Diamond C for a flight of over 500 km (c. 310 miles), a gain of height of more than 5000 m and of distance to a declared goal of more than 300 km (c. 186 miles).

25 JUNE 1950

The start of the Korean War. Two days later President Truman orders the United States Air Force to assist South Korea.

29 JULY—22 AUGUST 1950

The start of the first experimental scheduled gas-turbine-powered airline service with turbine aircraft. British European Airways (BEA) operate the Vickers V.630 Viscount prototype on the London—Paris and London—Edinburgh routes.
See figure C

31 SEPTEMBER 1950

Philip A. Wills is awarded the Britannia Trophy for winning the British Gliding Championships four times (1939, 1947, 1949 and 1950).
See figure D

25 SEPTEMBER 1950

Pan American Airways acquire American Overseas Airlines.

8 NOVEMBER 1950

First jet-aircraft to be shot down by another. Lieutenant Russell J. Brown, USAF, flying a Lockheed F-80C, shoots down a Russian MiG-15 jet fighter of the Chinese People's Republic Air Force over the Yalu river, Korea.

A   *Boeing B-52 Stratofortress long-range bomber, 1952.*
B   *The Goodyear non-rigid airship, ZPN-1, 1952.*
C   *Avro Vulcan jet bomber, 1952.*
D   *Douglas DC-6 passenger airliner, 1952.*

A

18 DECEMBER 1950

North American F-86 Sabre jet-fighters first go into action against Russian-built MiG-15 jet-fighters over the Yalu river, Korea.

5 FEBRUARY 1951

The United States and Canada announce the setting up of the DEW early-warning system for North America.

23 FEBRUARY 1951

First flight of the prototype Dassault Mystère jet fighter, in France.

15 MARCH 1951

First flight across the South Pacific, from Sydney, Australia, to Valparaiso, Chile, by P. G. Taylor, an American, in the

Consolidated Catalina flying-boat *Frigate Bird II.*

18 MAY 1951

First flight of the first prototype of the Vickers Valiant four-jet bomber, the first of the British V-bombers, which will provide the British nuclear deterrent into the 1960s.

29 MAY 1951

First solo trans-Polar flight is made by C. Blair, an American, from Bardufoss in Norway to Fairbanks, Alaska, flying a North American P-51 Mustang.

20 JULY 1951

First flight of the prototype Hawker Hunter swept-wing jet fighter, which is later to

become one of the most successful British military aircraft of the 1950s.

15 AUGUST 1951

Major William Bridgeman, USAF, flying the Douglas D-558-2 Skyrocket research aircraft, reaches a speed of 1238 mph (c. 1990 km/h).

1 OCTOBER 1951

The USAF's first guided missile squadron, equipped with Martin Matadors, is formed at Banana River Air Force Base in the Bahamas.

5 DECEMBER 1951

The eleven airlines operating on the North Atlantic route decide to introduce tourist class air fares.

B

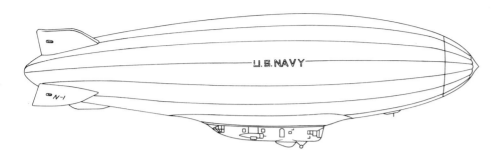

C

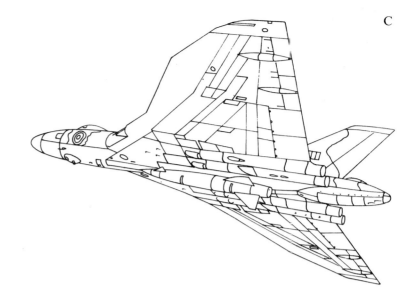

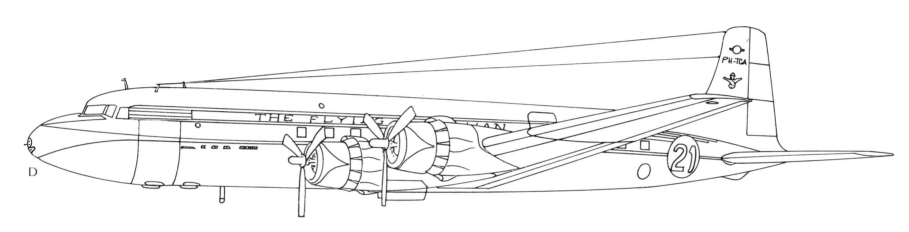

D

5 JANUARY 1952

Pan American Airways inaugurate the first all-cargo service across the North Atlantic, using Douglas DC-6s.
See figure D

15 APRIL 1952

First flight of the Boeing B-52 Stratofortress long-range jet bomber, piloted by A. M. Johnson. It is destined to be the main instrument of the American nuclear deterrent during the next two decades.
See figure A

2 MAY 1952

First turbo-jet airliner to enter airline service is the de Havilland D. H. 106 Comet 1 with British Overseas Airways Corporation on the London to Johannesburg route.

3 MAY 1952

First landing at the North Pole: by Lieutenant Colonel William P. Benedict and Lieutenant Colonel J. O. Fletcher on a ski-equipped USAF Douglas C-47.

17 JUNE 1952

The Goodyear ZPN-1, the largest non-rigid airship ever built, enters service with the US Navy.
See figure B

15—31 JULY 1952

First crossing of the North Atlantic by helicopter (in stages): by Captain Vincent H. McGovern and Lieutenant Harold Moore in two Sikorsky S-55s, in 42 hours and 25 minutes flying time, from Westover, Massachusetts to Prestwick, Ayrshire.

11 AUGUST 1952

A civil agreement is signed in Tokyo for air services between the United States and Japan.

30 AUGUST 1952

First flight of the prototype Avro Vulcan jet bomber, the first large bomber to have a delta-wing plan-form. It is the second of Britain's trio of V-bombers
See figure C

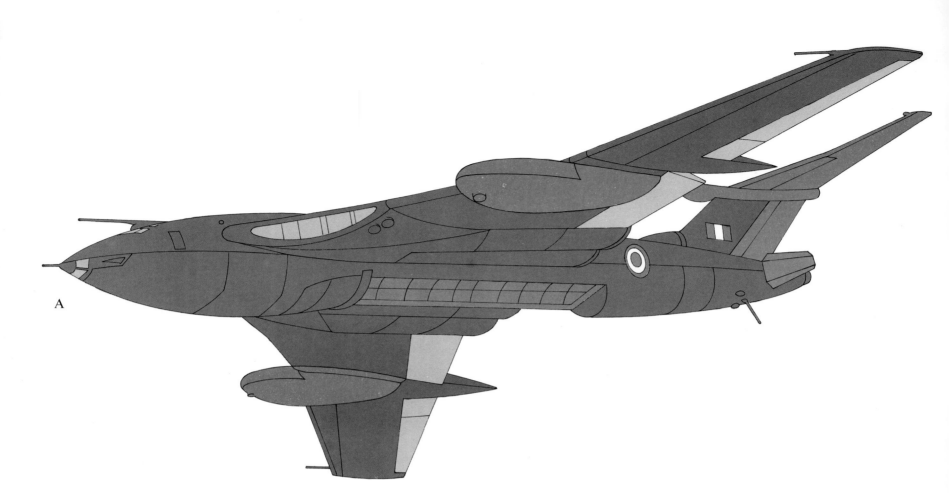

A

6 SEPTEMBER 1952

The prototype de Havilland D. H. 110, flown by John Derry, breaks up in the air while demonstrating at high speed during the SBAC Display at Farnborough, England, killing both members of the crew. Thirty-two people in the crowd die and 63 are injured.

3 OCTOBER 1952

The first British atomic bomb is exploded, at the Monte Bello Islands off north-west Australia.

19—20 NOVEMBER 1952

First commercial flights direct over the polar regions between Europe and North America are made by SAS using Douglas DC-6B airliners. Regular services over the North Pole will start in 1954.

24 DECEMBER 1952

First flight of Handley Page Victor jet bomber. The Victor, with the Valiant and Vulcan, comprise the British V-bombers

which provide the British nuclear deterrent for the next decade.
See figure A

19 APRIL 1953

First turbo-prop airliner enters regular scheduled service: the Vickers V.701 Viscount with BEA.

23—24 MAY 1953

First trans-Arctic charter flight, via Anchorage and Shemya, from Oslo to Tokyo by SAS in a Douglas DC-6B. Elapsed time is 52 hours 58 minutes.

25 MAY 1953

First flight of the XF-100 prototype of the North American Super Sabre, the world's first production supersonic fighter.

1 SEPTEMBER 1953

First scheduled international helicopter services start, operated by SABENA from Brussels in Belgium, to Lille in France, and Rotterdam and Maastricht in Holland.

8—10 OCTOBER 1953

Christchurch Centenary Air Race from England to New Zealand is won by Squadron Leader R. L. E. Burton and Flight Lieutenant D. H. Gannon of the RAF in an English Electric Canberra: a distance of 11,792 miles (*c.* 18,975 km) in 23 hours 50 minutes 42 seconds.

12 DECEMBER 1953

A speed of 2½ times the speed of sound is achieved with an air-launched rocket-propelled experimental aircraft: Major Charles E. ("Chuck") Yeager, USAF, in the Bell X-1A, flies at 1650 mph (*c.* 2655 km/h) at 70,000 ft (*c.* 21,330 m).

29 DECEMBER 1953

The ICAO announces that, for the first time, the number of passengers carried by the world's airlines (excluding USSR and China) has exceeded 50 million (52,400,000).

10 JANUARY 1954

A BOAC de Havilland Comet jet airliner,

A   *Handley Page Victor jet bomber, 1952.*
B   *Boeing 707 passenger airliner, 1954.*

B

on the final stage of a flight from Singapore to London, falls into the Mediterranean with the loss of all 35 occupants. Comet passenger services are temporarily discontinued.

10 JANUARY 1954

The post-war Japanese air force is established, with three separate arms known as the Air, Ground and Maritime Self-Defence Forces.

7 FEBRUARY 1954

First flight of the prototype Lockheed XF-104 Starfighter, a jet-fighter which is to be widely used by the United States and other Western countries and later to be built under licence in Europe. Pilot: A. W. (Tony) LeVier.

1 MARCH 1954

The first hydrogen bomb is exploded by the United States, during tests in the Marshall Islands in the Pacific.

1 MARCH 1954

The ban on the production of military aircraft in Japan, imposed after the Second World War, is lifted. An agreement is signed between USA and Japan—the Lockheed Aircraft Corporation and the Kawasaki Aircraft Company—to allow Japan to manufacture Lockheed F-94C Starfire jet-fighters and T-33A jet trainers.

1 APRIL 1954

Last operational sortie by a Supermarine Spitfire fighter: a photographic reconnaissance flight from RAF Seletar, Singapore, against bandits in the Johare jungle in Malaya.

8 APRIL 1954

A second BOAC de Havilland Comet jet airliner, flying from London to Johannesburg, falls into the Mediterranean after leaving Rome, killing all 21 occupants. Comet services, which had been resumed on 23 March, were completely discontinued when the Minister of Transport and Civil Aviation withdrew the Comet's British Certificate of Airworthiness.

MAY 1954

First British aircraft with jet deflection is tested in flight: a Gloster Meteor, piloted by L. De Vigne.

15 JULY 1954

First flight of the Boeing 367-80 prototype four-engined jet transport, from which is developed the Boeing 707 series—the most successful and widely used subsonic jet airliner of the 1960s.
See figure B

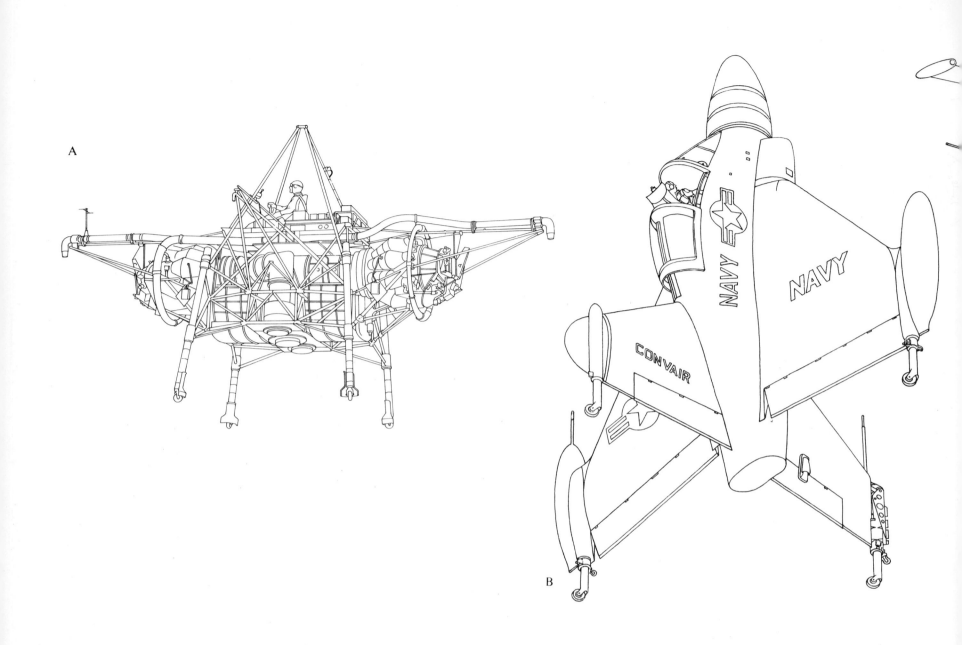

A

B

3 AUGUST 1954

First free flight at Hucknall in Nottinghamshire, England, of the Rolls-Royce TMR (Thrust Measuring Rig) "Flying Bedstead" jet-lift vehicle, piloted by Captain R. T. Shepherd. It had previously flown tethered on 9 July 1953. This rig leads to the development of the Short S.C.1 VTOL flatriser.
See figure A

4 AUGUST 1954

First flight at Boscombe Down, Wiltshire, England, of the prototype English Electric P. 1, piloted by Roland P. Beamont. From this research aircraft will be developed the Lightning, the RAF's first supersonic jet fighter.

26 AUGUST 1954

A height of about 90,000 ft (c. 27,430 m), the greatest then attained by a human being, is reached by the Bell X-1A above the Mojave Desert, California, after being launched at 30,000 ft from a B-29 motherplane. Major Arthur Murray, USAF, is the pilot.

2 NOVEMBER 1954

First full translation from vertical to horizontal flight of the first experimental tailsitter VTOL turbo-prop fighter, the Convair XFY-1, piloted by J. F. Coleman, in the United States.
See figure B

15—16 NOVEMBER 1954

Opening flights for the world's first regular trans-Arctic air route: by SAS between Copenhagen and Los Angeles with Douglas DC-6Bs.

10 JANUARY 1955

Pakistan International Airlines Corporation established, following the nationalisation of commercial air transport in Pakistan.

11 FEBRUARY 1955

A Court of Inquiry into the accidents of the two de Havilland Comet jet airliners, which fell into the Mediterranean in 1954, concludes that both accidents were caused

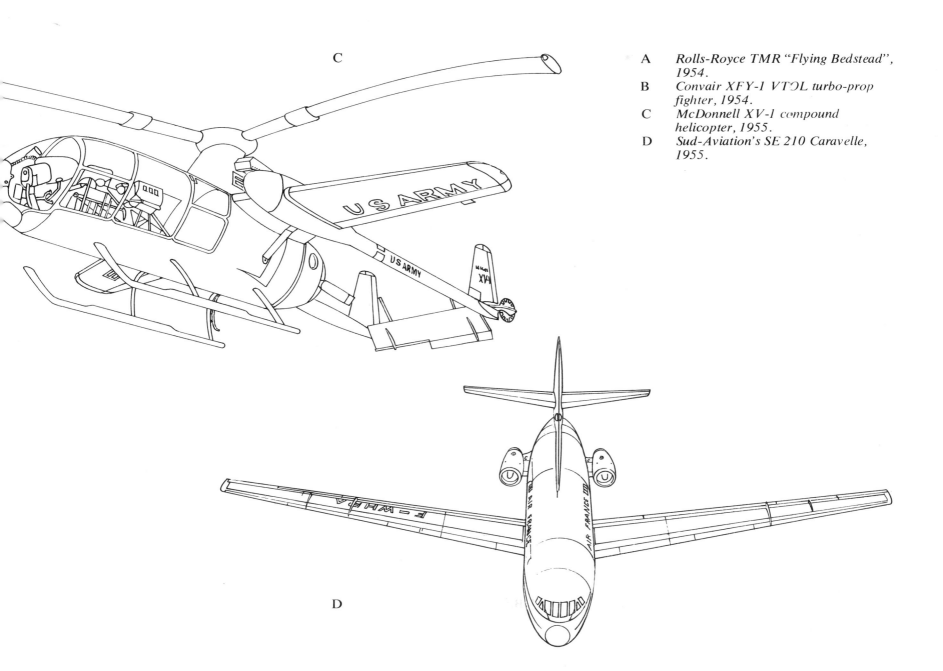

C

D

A   *Rolls-Royce TMR "Flying Bedstead",
1954.*
B   *Convair XFY-1 VTOL turbo-prop
fighter, 1954.*
C   *McDonnell XV-1 compound
helicopter, 1955.*
D   *Sud-Aviation's SE 210 Caravelle,
1955.*

by structure failure due to metal fatigue of
the fuselage shell.

1 APRIL 1955

First regular service by Lufthansa, the re-
formed German airline, is flown from
Hamburg to Dusseldorf and Frankfurt using
a twin-engined Convair 340 captained by a
British pilot.

10 APRIL 1955

Final ratification of the Treaty of Paris,
lifting the ban imposed in 1945 on the
building of powered aircraft in Germany and
permitting the formation of defence forces.

20 APRIL 1955

First authenticated full translation from
helicopter to gyroplane flight by a compound
helicopter, the McDonnell XV-1.
See figure C

5 MAY 1955

United States and Canadian governments
sign an agreement for the construction and
operation of the DEW (Distant Early
Warning) line of radar stations in northern
Canada.

16 MAY 1955

Lufthansa, the West German airline, begins
to operate European services.

27 MAY 1955

First flight of the Sud-Aviation SE 210
Caravelle, at Toulouse, France. This
becomes the first short-haul jet airliner to go
into widespread service, and also sets a new
design trend by adopting a rear-mounted
engine configuration.
See figure D

20 AUGUST 1955

First supersonic world absolute speed record
is set up, in a North American F-100 C
Super Sabre at Edwards Air Force Base,
California, by Colonel H. A. Hanes of the
USAF: 822.135 mph (1323.103 km/h).

A

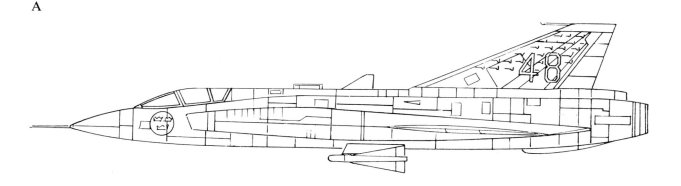

B

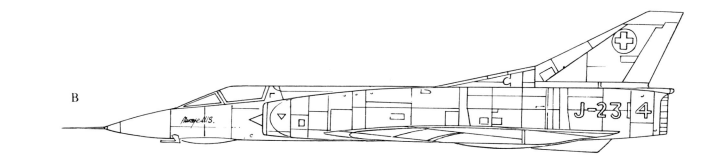

3 SEPTEMBER 1955

First successful demonstration of the use of an ejection seat from an aircraft travelling at speed on the ground is made by Squadron Leader J. S. Fifield from a Gloster Meteor 7 at Chalgrove Airfield, Oxfordshire, England. The pilot is Captain J. E. D. Scott.

13 OCTOBER 1955

Pan American Airways orders both the Douglas DC-8 and Boeing 707 jet airliners and so starts the jet-buying spree which heralds the airline subsonic jet era.

25 OCTOBER 1955

First flight of the prototype Saab 35 Draken "double-delta" Mach 2 Swedish fighter. Hundreds of these are to go into service in the 1960s and on into the 1970s, performing interceptor, reconnaissance and tactical strike rôles.
See figure A

1 NOVEMBER 1955

A United Airlines Douglas DC-6B airliner is destroyed by a time-bomb after take-off from Denver, Colorado, killing all 44 occupants. The FBI later arrests J. G. Graham, who had taken out a high insurance on his mother, who was one of the passengers. Graham is subsequently sentenced to death.

15 DECEMBER 1955

The North Atlantic Council approves a co-ordinated air defence and radar system covering Western Europe, including Britain.

1 FEBRUARY 1956

The Air Planning Group of the German Ministry of Defence initiates a pilot training scheme, making the beginning of the new post-war Luftwaffe.

10 MARCH 1956

First world speed record of more than 1000 mph (1609 km/h) is established by Peter Twiss in a Fairey Delta 2 with a speed of 1132 mph (c. 1822 km/h) between Chichester and Ford, Sussex, England.

21 MAY 1956

First United States hydrogen bomb to be released from an aircraft is dropped by a Boeing B-52B, piloted by Major David Critchlow, USAF, and explodes over Bikini atoll in the Pacific Ocean.

1 JUNE 1956

The Douglas DC-7C long-range piston-engined airliner enters service. This is the last of the famous DC-4 family and the first airliner capable of non-stop crossings of both the Atlantic and the Pacific. For the next two years it is to provide the most advanced standards of airline operation.

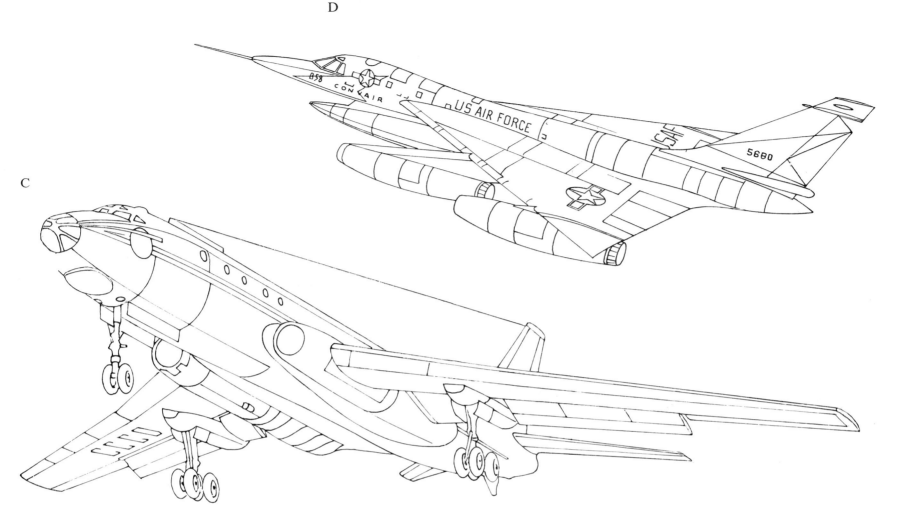

D

C

30 JUNE 1956

All 128 occupants of a TWA Super Constellation and of a United Air Lines DC-7 are killed when the two aircraft collide over the Grand Canyon, Arizona, USA.

26 JULY 1956

President Nasser of Egypt nationalises the international company controlling the Suez Canal, a step leading to British and French military intervention in the area later in the year.

12 SEPTEMBER 1956

First swept-wing jet airliner enters service—the Tupolev Tu-104 with the Russian airline, Aeroflot. Evolved from the Tu-16 twin-jet bomber, its first flight had been made in early 1955.
See figure C

27 SEPTEMBER 1956

First piloted aeroplane exceeds three times the speed of sound: the Bell X-2, flown by M. G. Apt. The aircraft crashes after reaching a speed of 2100 mph (*c.* 3380 km/h).

11 OCTOBER 1956

First British atomic bomb is dropped from a Vickers Valiant jet bomber flown by Squadron Leader E. J. G. Flavell at Maralinga, Southern Australia.

31 OCTOBER—6 NOVEMBER 1956

British and French air forces are involved in the Suez incident. Extensive use is made of parachute and helicopter-landed troops.

11 NOVEMBER 1956

In the United States, the first flight of the General Dynamics B-58 Hustler supersonic bomber. This was the first supersonic bomber to enter service.
See figure D

17 NOVEMBER 1956

First flight of Dassault Mirage III-C jet fighter, which becomes the most successful European aircraft in this category throughout the 1960s and early 1970s.
See figure B

A   *Saab 35 Draken jet-fighter, 1955.*
B   *Dassault Mirage III-C, 1956.*
C   *Tupolev Tu-104 swept-wing jet airliner, 1956.*
D   *General Dynamics Convair B-58 Hustler, 1956.*

SECTION V

FROM THE FIRST SATELLITE TO SKYLAB, 1957 TO THE PRESENT TIME

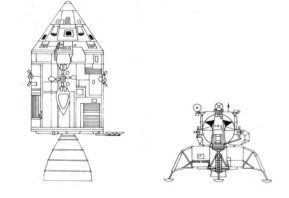

The Boeing 707 went into service in 1958 and is still one of the most widely used long-range jet airliners. It is shown here above the Apollo 11 Command and Service Module and Lunar Module which were used in man's first Moon landing, in 1969.

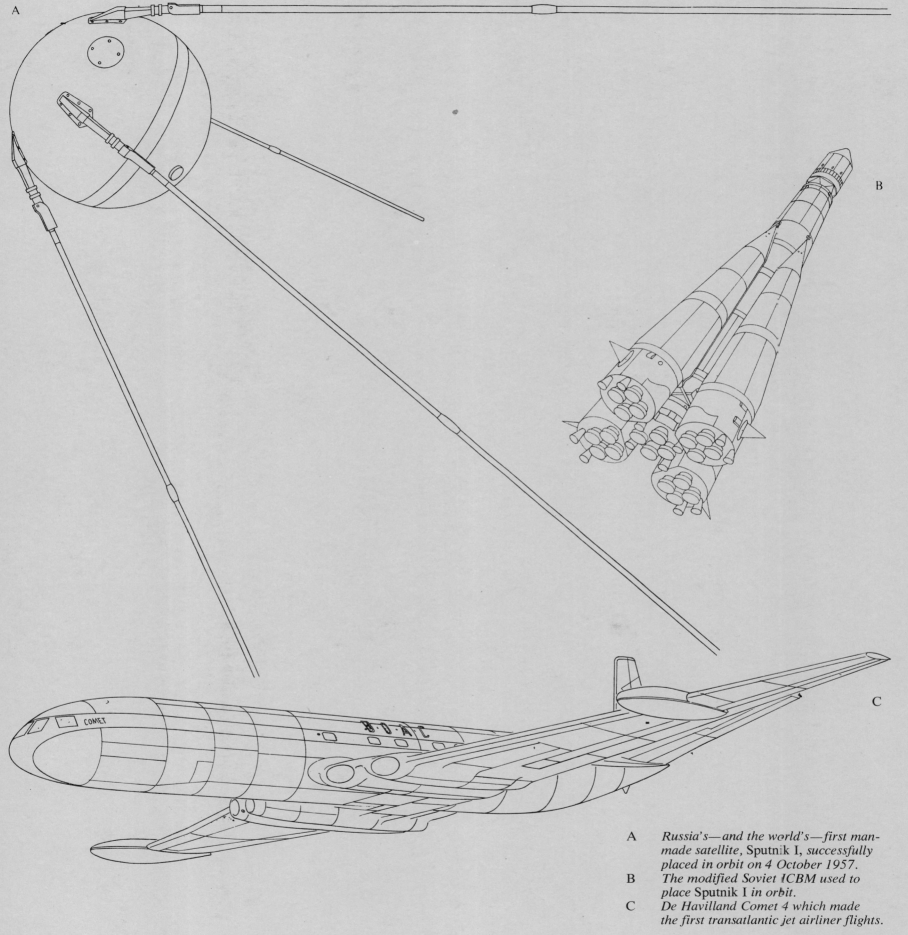

A   *Russia's—and the world's—first man-made satellite,* Sputnik I, *successfully placed in orbit on 4 October 1957.*

B   *The modified Soviet ICBM used to place* Sputnik I *in orbit.*

C   *De Havilland Comet 4 which made the first transatlantic jet airliner flights.*

A

B

On October 4th and November 3rd, 1957, the Space Age was born when Russia sent her first two satellite vehicles into orbit round the Earth; they were named *Sputnik I* and *II*. These pilotless machines were lifted into the sky by giant rockets—directly derived from the German V-2 rocket-bomb—and propelled around the Earth at about 18,000 mph (28,968 km/h); and the world gazed in astonishment as it glimpsed them speeding across the night sky. In 1959, the Russians even landed an unmanned rocket on the Moon. Then, on April 12th 1961, the Soviet Union capped these achievements by placing the first man in orbit round the Earth: Major Yuri Gagarin.

On August 6th of the same year, another Russian "pilot" circled the Earth. The United States soon rose up to rival the Russians, and on February 20th, 1962, Colonel John Glenn was placed in orbit, to be followed on June 16th 1963 by the first woman astronaut, Lieutenant Valentina Tereshkova of Russia. On December 21st 1968, Americans Frank Borman, James Lovell and William Anders took the next decisive step by moving out of the Earth's neighbourhood and circling the Moon. Everyone now realised that sooner or later human beings would achieve the seemingly impossible and that one of our species would actually set foot on the Moon.

But the ordinary man and woman were more concerned with what went on down here on Earth; and in the years since 1957, air transport has grown so enormously that the aeroplane is now the common carrier of mankind, and travel by air is still growing by leaps and bounds. In 1957, the number of passengers carried by the world's airliners (excluding those of Russia and China) was 90 million—thirty-six times as many as in 1937 and four and a quarter times as many as in 1947. By 1971 the annual total had risen to 325 million.

Today the so-called "Jumbo" jet, the Boeing 747, can carry up to 500 passengers

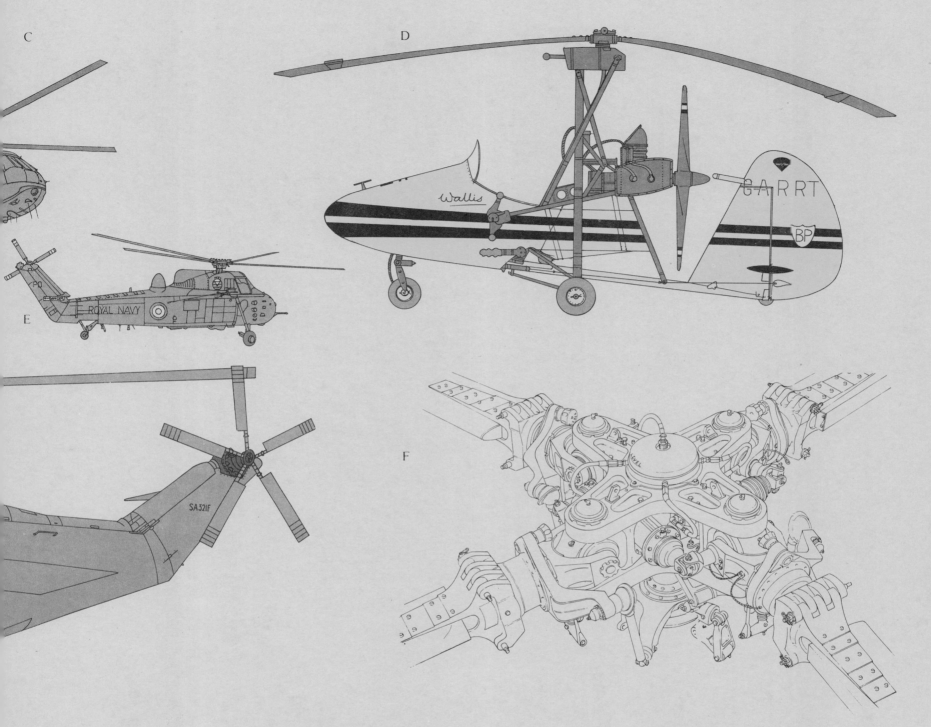

and can fly at nearly 600 mph (965 km/h) for over 6000 miles (9656 km) and there are already more than 200 Jumbos flying. This giant machine is one of the biggest transports which our generation is likely to see. But many millions of travellers still fly in such excellent machines as the Boeing 707, which carries up to 200 passengers at some 600 mph (965 km/h) for 4000 miles, or the British Super VC10, with 175 passengers and a range of 4000 miles (6437 km) at 550 mph (885 km/h). Then, down the scale, come every kind of in-between type of aircraft for long, medium, or short-haul work, ending in small passenger aircraft for pleasure or busi-

ness flying, and training, as well as many types of engineless gliders, flown for the pure love of the sport.

Meanwhile, safety in the air has become daily more and more pressing a problem, with air routes multiplying faster than bus routes on the ground, and the danger of collision growing ever more serious. But the safety devices have mercifully kept pace with this development, and the use of radio, radar, and the computer ensure that the machines are kept flying safely along the millions of miles of air routes above our globe. Even the threat of night, and of bad visibility, has now been conquered, aeroplanes

A   *The huge Mil Mi-10 "flying crane" helicopter, designed by the Mikhail Mil bureau in the Soviet Union, is capable of lifting great loads.*

B   *Largest European helicopter, the Aérospatiale Super Frelon.*

C   *Westland Sea King anti-submarine helicopter, developed from a Sikorsky design.*

D   *A very successful modern autogyro, the record-breaking Wallis Wa-116.*

E   *Westland Wessex helicopter, based on the Sikorsky S-58 and powered by a gas-turbine.*

F   *A modern rotor head assembly.*

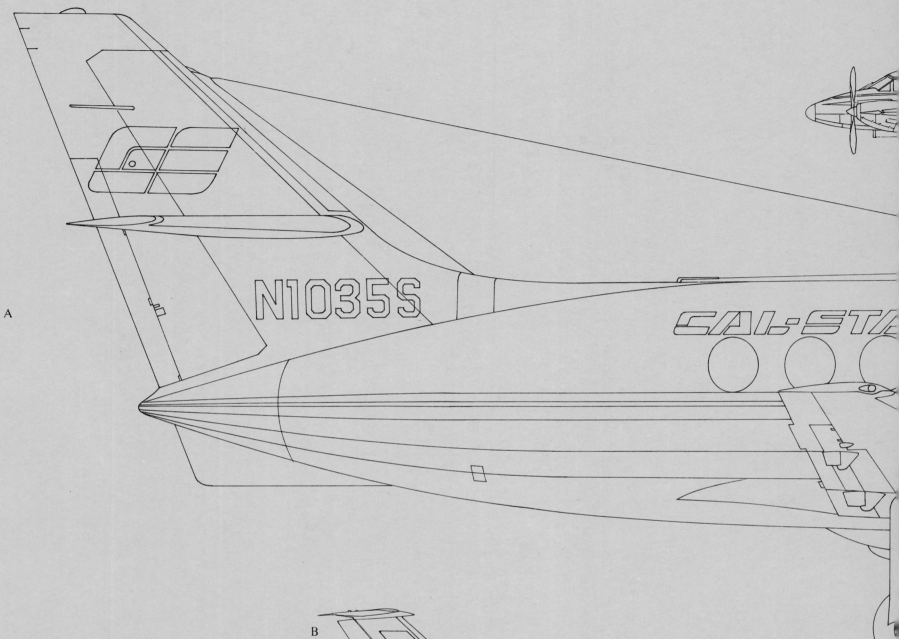

A

B

A   *Jetstream business aircraft, designed
    by the former Handley Page company
    and now built by Scottish Aviation.*
B   *Yakovlev Yak-40, a small tri-jet short-
    haul transport aircraft used widely in
    the Soviet Union and elsewhere.*
C   *Beechcraft Model 99, 17-seat "mini-
    airliner" for local services.*
D   *The Twin Otter STOL "bush
    transport" designed and built by de
    Havilland Canada.*

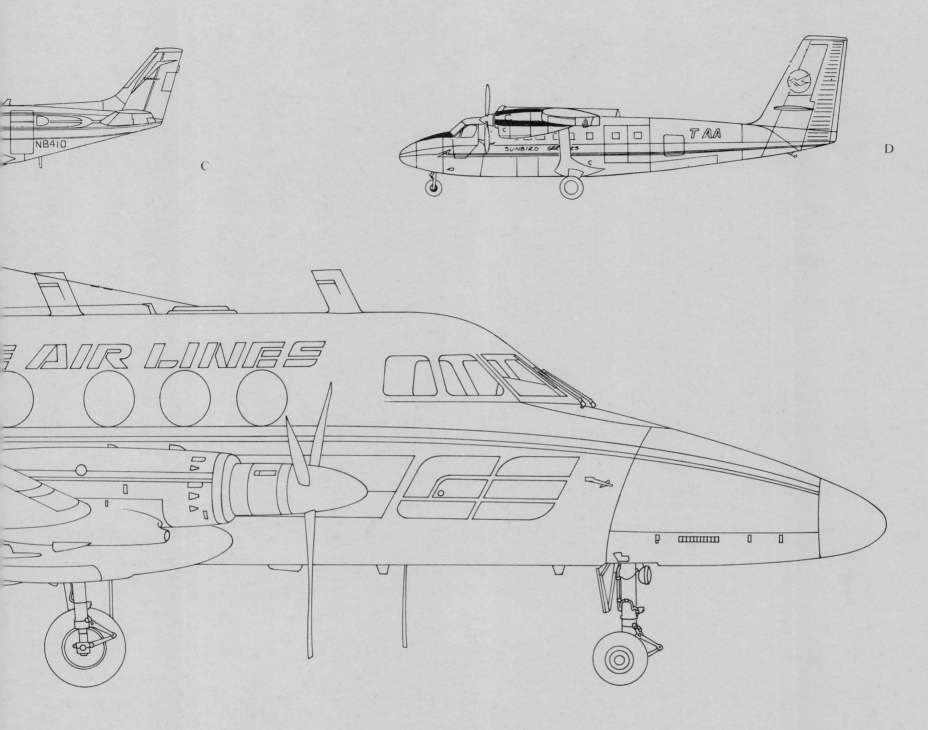

being brought safely to earth automatically, with the pilot sitting in his cockpit and only keeping an eye on the complex machinery which will land his aeroplane even in dense fog.

In the military sphere, the United States has led the way with the huge eight-engined Boeing B-52 subsonic bomber, which has a range of 12,500 miles (20,116 km); but it has become increasingly necessary to protect large and costly aircraft by a variety of electronic countermeasures (ECM) devices to jam or divert any missiles that are sent up to intercept them. Major warplanes of each side nowadays can carry a bewildering array of devices, each trying to outwit the other, and the struggle for supremacy is as much between the wizards of electronics as between those who design the aeroplanes which carry their trickery.

Strike aircraft are, of course, built by many nations, and these machines have maximum speeds of anything up to 1600 mph (2 574.5 km/h), which at 33,000 feet (10,058 m) is over twice the speed of sound. Superiority in these extreme forms of military aeroplanes is a ding-dong business, with the Russians and Americans alternately sharing the lead. Britain has contributed one unique strike aircraft, the Hawker Siddeley Harrier, a fixed-wing machine which can take off or land vertically by directing its jets downwards; it can also fly horizontally and attain a speed of more than 735 mph (1183 km/h). This makes it an ideal type of aircraft to operate in wooded or mountainous country, or from ships at sea, since it needs no conventional runways.

The other form of conventional air transport which has become indispensible in the modern world is the helicopter. A proper helicopter—as opposed to an autogyro—can rise vertically, fly backwards, forwards, or sideways, in any way it wishes; and of course it can also land vertically. Helicopters now

185

A

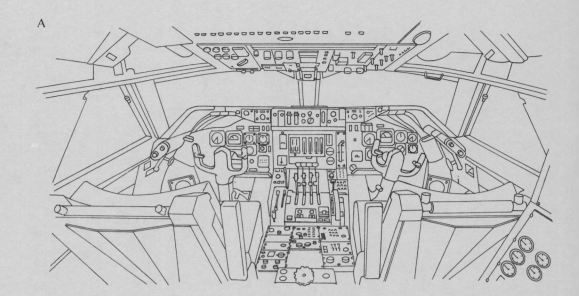

B

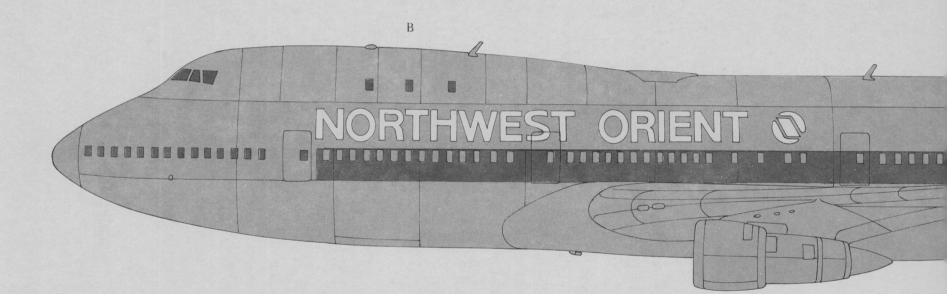

come in every variety of shape, size, and ability, from small two-seaters with a speed of some 140 mph (225 km/h) to the great "flying-crane" species which can lift a 15,000-20,000 lb (about 6000-9000 kg) weight on its hoist. Helicopters are used for every kind of transport duty; for life-saving at sea or in dangerous land situations; for communications with lighthouses or oil-rigs; for police and traffic surveillance; for crop-dusting or fire-fighting; and of course as military vehicles, where one of their most valuable roles is in penetrating enemy territory to rescue air crews who have crashed. They are as at home lifting a new church

spire into position as they are at taking the crew off a sinking ship, or rescuing a climber in the Alps.

Now also taking an important place in transport, and likely to prove ever more vital in the years to come, is a completely new sort of vehicle which literally rides on a cushion of air, and is then propelled either by air-screws or jets. This is the air-cushion vehicle (ACV), or hovercraft, first pioneered in practical form in Britain in 1959 by Christo-pher Cockerell and now being used all over the world. The unique feature of the hover-craft is that it can "fly" over any sea or land surface that does not rise up to more than

eight or ten feet: this means that it is useful for reasonable weather at sea, and ideal for lakes and swamps, and even fast-flowing rivers; while, on land, all it needs is a roughly hewn and levelled path without any road-making. The machine is equipped with skirts all round it, and air is blown down beneath the fuselage: it there builds up an enormous cushion of air, and lifts the craft off the sur-face, the compressed air beneath always being replaced more quickly than it escapes from under the skirts. At present, a typical passenger-carrying hovercraft can take up to 250 passengers and 30 cars, or over 600 passengers without cars, and ride them across

C

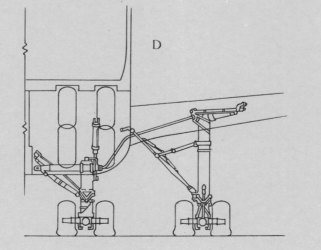

the English Channel, for example, at over 50 mph (80 km/h), even into wind. There are also small hovercraft for police or patrol use, and simple two-seat "runabouts" for sporting use. Before long there may be many private owners with machines taking three or four people, as well as the family car. The world has been inexplicably slow in exploiting this wonderful vehicle, but the hovercraft is now beginning to catch on as a transport, as it is an almost completely safe vehicle. The worst that can happen is for its skirts to rupture, whereupon the craft simply sinks back onto the water, and floats there like a ship.

D

A   *Boeing 747 flight deck.*
B   *Boeing Model 747 "Jumbo" jet, first of the wide-bodied airbus-type transport aircraft, 1969.*
C   *Part of the passenger cabin of the Boeing 747.*
D   *One of the main-wheel undercarriage bogies of the Boeing 747.*

One of the greatest events in the history of our world took place on July 20th—21st, 1969, when America's Neil Armstrong and Edwin Aldrin walked upon the Moon for the first time. Five hundred million of their fellow humans watched them on television as they did it—watched breathless with excitement, and almost as breathless with fear, lest these pioneers would never be able to leave the Moon's surface. The facts and figures of this almost incredible enterprise are so large and so bewildering that many of us still find it hard, when we look up at the Moon on a clear night, to accept that members of our own race have actually travelled the quarter of a million miles which separates us, and landed there and carried out scientific experiments; then taken off again, joined up with the orbiting space-ship waiting for them, and finally flown safely back to Earth and arrived here literally within a few seconds of the scheduled time. To think that this performance has now been carried out no fewer than six times, without any casualties, is enough to make the mind reel!

Although American manned expeditions to the Moon have now ceased, probably until the next century, there are still many programmes of the utmost importance to be carried out, even within the remainder of this decade. One which has already begun centres around *Skylab 1*, the United States manned experimental workshop in space. Launched in May 1973, it now orbits the Earth at about 270 miles (435 km) out, and has been manned successively by three sets of three-man crews, the third of which returned to Earth in February 1974. This repeated performance means that the aeroplane will also come into its own in space; for the vehicle which carries up later space crews to Skylab and similar space stations will be the Space Shuttle, a fixed-wing aeroplane which will ride piggy-back on a huge booster. Once in space, it will leave the booster and use its own engines to go into orbit and link up with *Skylab*, where it will put aboard the new crew and take off the old crew. It will then coast back to Earth and be able to land on a runway similar to that used by modern airliners.

There is also the beginning of co-operation between the United States and Russia, one of the best outcomes yet of the space "race", in the joint Apollo-Soyuz rendezvous and docking experiment planned for 1975. We do not know what the Russians are planning independently, but they will undoubtedly carry out valuable missions, both manned and unmanned.

Other exciting projects already under way are those aimed at improving our knowledge of other members of the solar system. Already, by the end of 1973, America's splendidly successful unmanned Mariner 9 had sent back nearly 7000 photographs covering some 85 per cent of the Martian surface, from which a landing site will be chosen for the 1976 Viking robot explorer; another Mariner probe was well on its way towards a very close pass-by of Venus and Mercury; and *Pioneer 10* had sent back our first close-up colour pictures of the giant Jupiter, before continuing on to leave the solar system altogether and venture into limitless space.

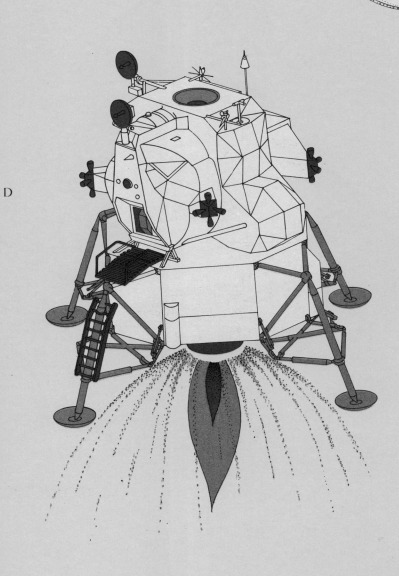

C

D

E

A   *Space suit worn for working on the Moon by the astronauts of Apollo 15.*
B   *Apollo spacecraft and launch rockets on the gantry and crawler vehicle which carries them from the assembly building to the launch pad.*
C   *Apollo CSM (Command and Service Module) in which all three Apollo crew members travelled between Earth and Moon orbit.*
D   *Apollo Lunar Module descending to the Moon's surface.*
E   *Ascent stage of Lunar Module taking off from the Moon to rejoin the CSM in orbit for the return to Earth.*

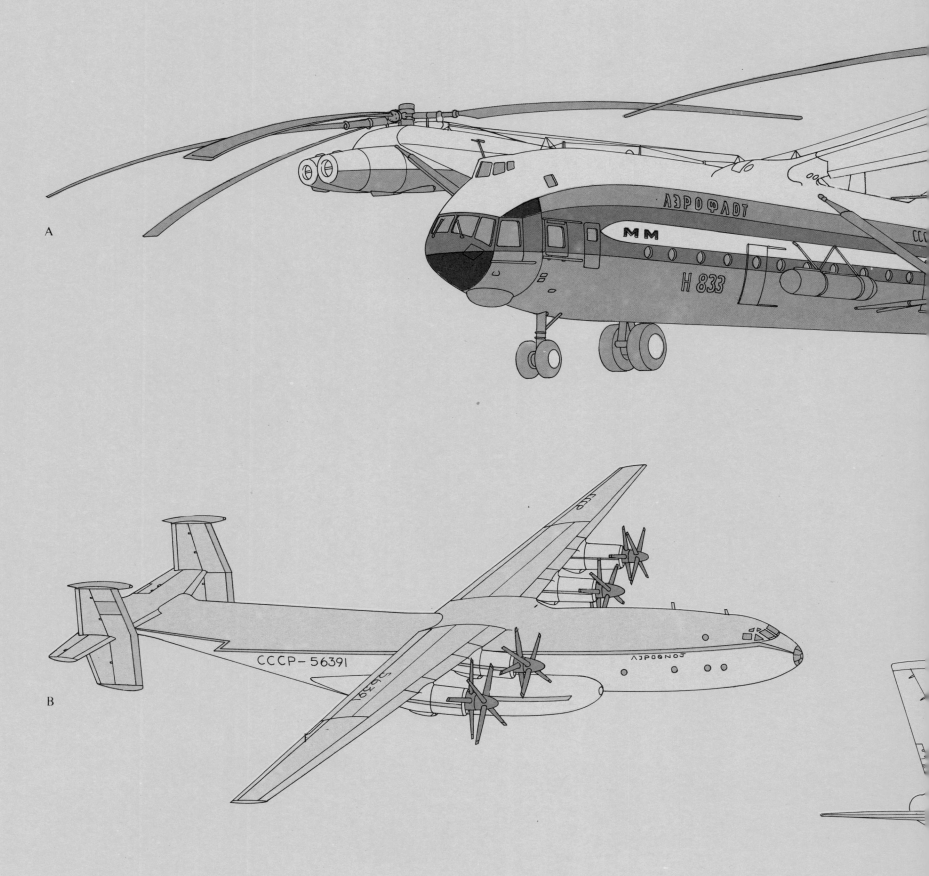

A   The V-12 (Mi-12) four-engined twin-rotor helicopter, designed by the Mil bureau in Russia and the largest rotorcraft yet to fly.

B   Antonov An-22 four-turboprop cargo transport, which can carry up to 176, 350 lb of freight.

C   Much-modified production version of the Tupolev Tu-144 which in December 1968 was the world's first supersonic airliner to fly.

D   Tupolev's Tu-114 airliner shares a common ancestry with the Tu-95 bomber, having the same wings, engines and tail unit combined with a larger-section fuselage.

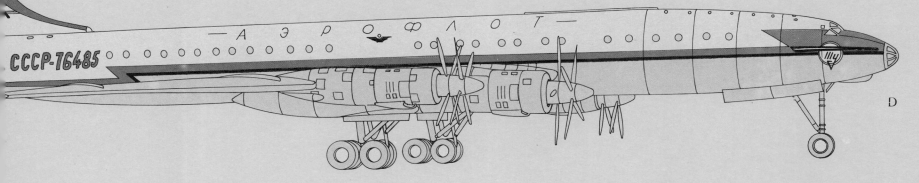

A

B

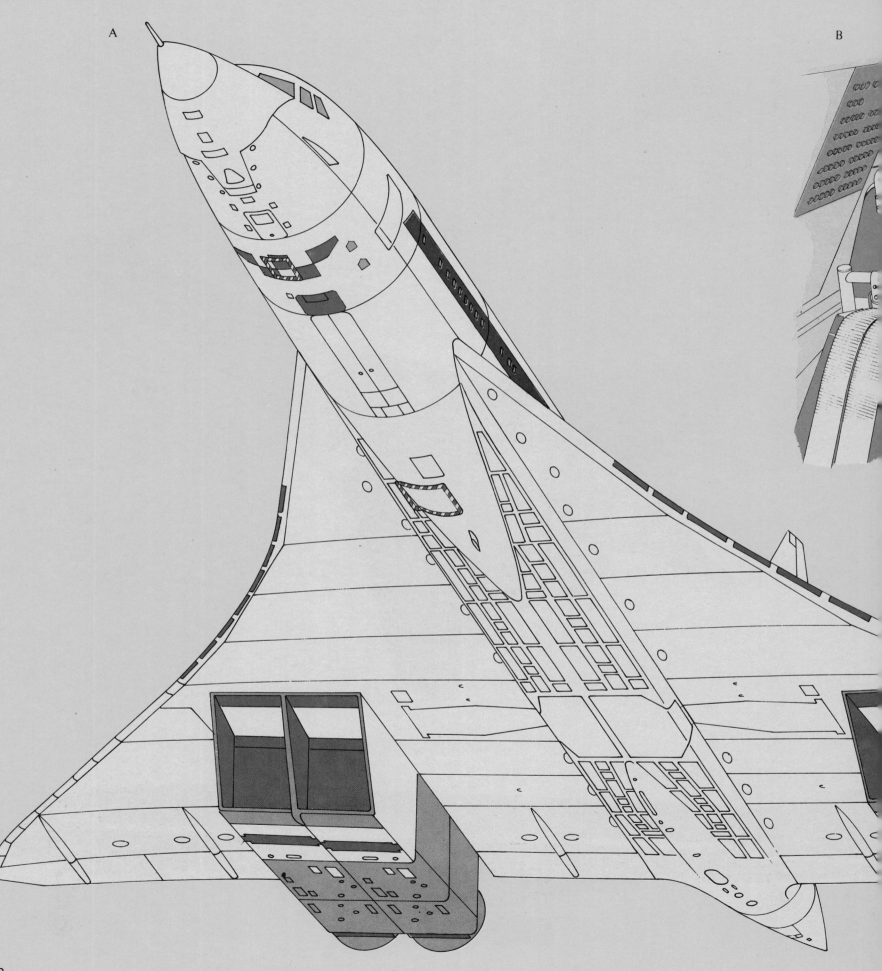

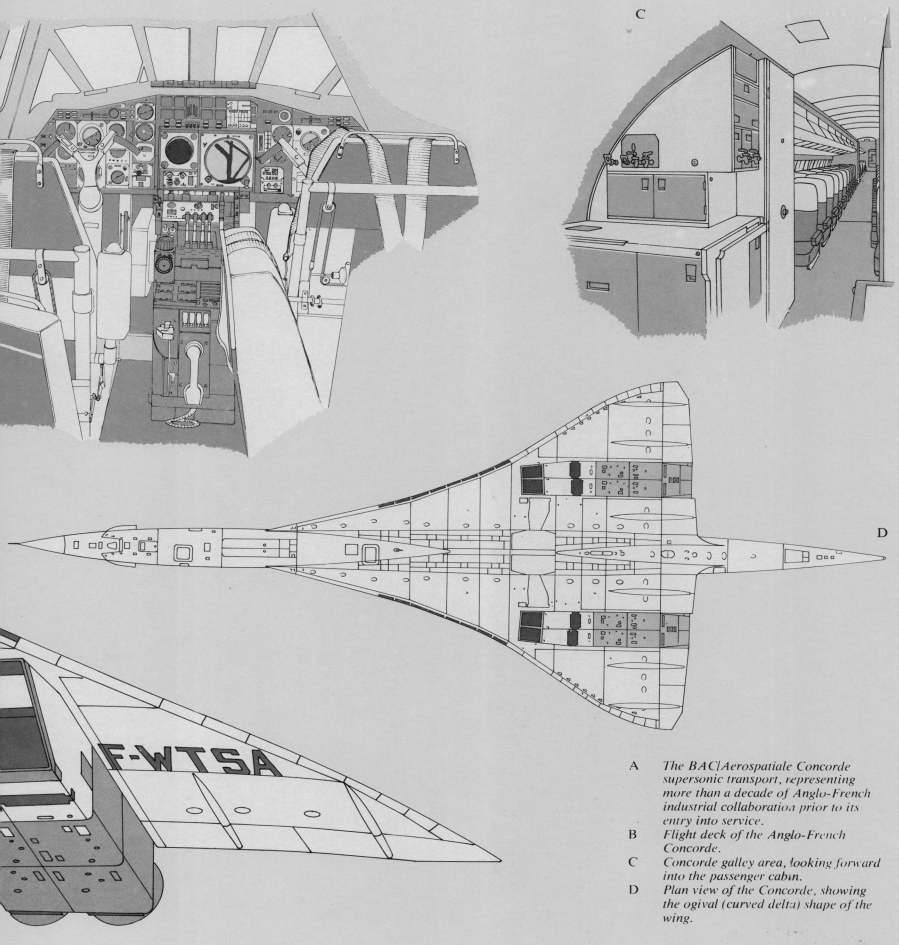

A   The BAC/Aerospatiale Concorde supersonic transport, representing more than a decade of Anglo-French industrial collaboration prior to its entry into service.

B   Flight deck of the Anglo-French Concorde.

C   Concorde galley area, looking forward into the passenger cabin.

D   Plan view of the Concorde, showing the ogival (curved delta) shape of the wing.

A

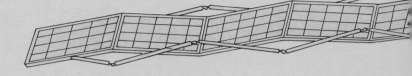

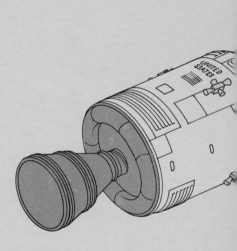

It is fashionable to decry the American space programme, and to say that it has meant billions of dollars of wasted money which could have been better spent elsewhere. This is not a valid view. From time immemorial, human endeavour has flourished without reference to other, and possibly more socially desirable, aims; and although our civilisation has thus grown up so lop-sided in many respects, we must look at each achievement on its own, and in its own right. It is true to say that the advantages reaped by innumerable departments of science and technology, which have followed as a direct result of the multi-sphere research necessary for the conquest of space, have been immense, and will continue to spread. They have already paid off handsomely, including dramatic advances in medical and other humanitarian activities. The American space organisation (NASA) has indeed been slow in publicising

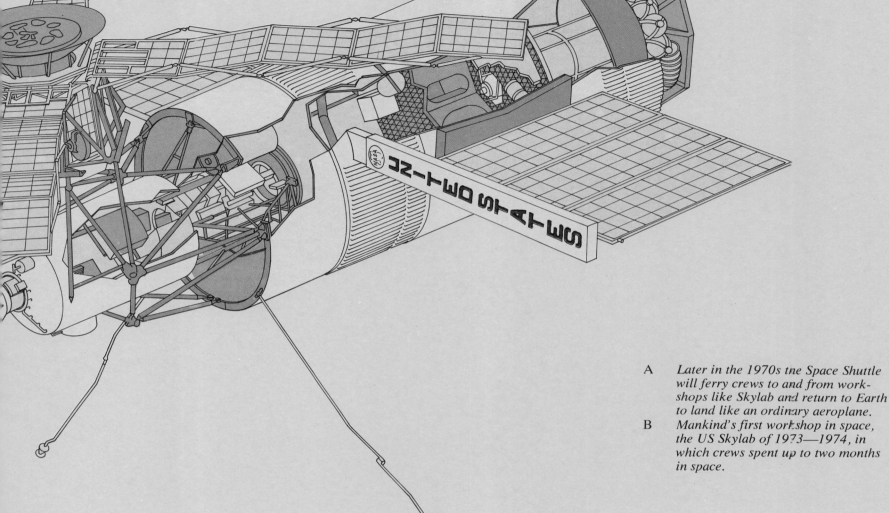

A Later in the 1970s the Space Shuttle will ferry crews to and from workshops like Skylab and return to Earth to land like an ordinary aeroplane.

B Mankind's first workshop in space, the US Skylab of 1973—1974, in which crews spent up to two months in space.

manifold and constructive benefits to the world; but benefits there are, in their thousands, and they will continue to appear the world over for generations to come.

There is also the question of how such almost incredible technological achievements have been made possible. It is so often thought that the success should be laid exclusively at the doors of the various technologies connected with space science. Much credit must, of course, lie there; but it is well to remember that the space programme could never even have "got off the ground" had it not been for the modern miracle of the computer, and the brilliant men who have invented and constantly improved this most essential of modern scientific tools. Computers can work out solutions to problems in a matter of seconds which before would have taken expert mathematicians months, or even years, to perform. So, without the

computer, the devotion and extreme bravery of the astronauts themselves would not have been given a chance to go into action. The space programme has blossomed in a gigantic series of successes as a result of thousands of talented and dedicated men, from the top scientists down to the men on the workshop floor, who have put together the giant rockets and the space ships which have carried them safely heavenward.

I will end this brief account of man in air and space with two quotations. The first is from Sir George Cayley who, in 1809, wrote as follows:

"I may be expediting the attainment of an object that will in time be found of great importance to mankind; so much so, that a new era in society will commence from the moment that aerial navigation is familiarly realised. I feel perfectly confident, however, that this

noble art will soon be brought home to man's convenience, and that we shall be able to transport ourselves and families, and their goods and chattels, more securely by air than by water, and with a velocity of from 20 to 100 miles per hour."

In 1930, Lord Birkenhead wrote:

"Our descendants will certainly attempt journeys to other members of the Solar System . . . By 2030 the first preparations for the first attempt to reach Mars may perhaps be under consideration. The hardy individuals who form the personnel of the expedition will be sent forth in a machine propelled like a rocket."

Some men, as Shakespeare truly says, "can look into the seeds of time, and say which grain will grow and which will not."

What struck me most remarkably was how near the Earth seemed, even from a height of 187 miles.

MAJOR YURI GAGARIN (1961)

I believe that this nation should commit itself to achieving the goal, before the decade is out, of landing a man on the Moon and returning him safely to Earth.

JOHN F. KENNEDY,
ADDRESS TO CONGRESS (25 MAY 1961)

I feel we are on the brink of an area of expansion of knowledge about ourselves and our surroundings that is beyond description or comprehension at this time. Our efforts today and what we've done so far are but small building blocks on a very huge pyramid to come... The more I see, the more impressed I am not with how much we know but with how tremendous the areas are that are as yet unexplored.

Lieutenant Colonel JOHN GLENN (1961)

The case for developing a supersonic airliner appears at this point to be a good one. Unless this nation begins such development, it will not only lose aviation supremacy but international prestige as well... Since the nation has accepted speed as a basic and valid premise, the concept of a supersonic transport must be accepted as inevitable.

N. E. HALABY, PRESIDENT OF THE US FEDERAL AVIATION AGENCY (1962)

CHAPTER TWELVE

FROM 1957 A.D. TO 1962 A.D.

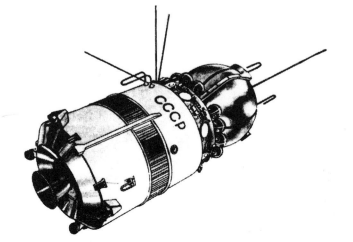

During the late 1950s, the space race became a reality. Here we see a view of the activity in the Mission Operations Control Room in the Mission Control Center at Houston in Texas. It was from Operation Centers such as this that the manned flights to the Moon were to be controlled.

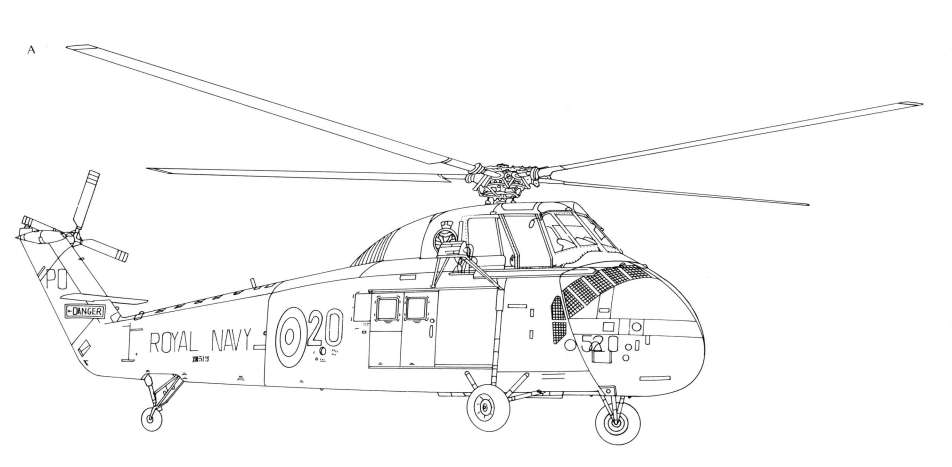

A

18 JANUARY 1957

Three USAF B-52 jet bombers land at March Air Force Base having completed a circuit of the world without landing: a total distance of 24,325 miles (*c.* 39,147 km) in 45 hours 19 minutes. The flight is commanded by Major General Archie J. Old, Jnr.

19 FEBRUARY 1957

First flight by a deflected-jet flat-rising VTOL aircraft, the Bell X-14, in the United States.

3 MARCH 1957

SABENA inaugurates the first international helicopter scheduled service between capital cities—Brussels and Paris—using Sikorsky S-58 helicopters.
See figure A

4 MARCH 1957

US naval airship ZPG-2 *Snowbird*, captained by Commander J. R. Hunt, completes a double crossing of the North Atlantic and establishes an endurance record of 264 hours 14 minutes 18 seconds.

2 APRIL 1957

First flight by a jet-lift flat-rising VTOL aircraft, the Short S.C.-1, flown by Tom Brooke-Smith, in England.

A   *Sikorsky S-58 helicopter, 1957.*

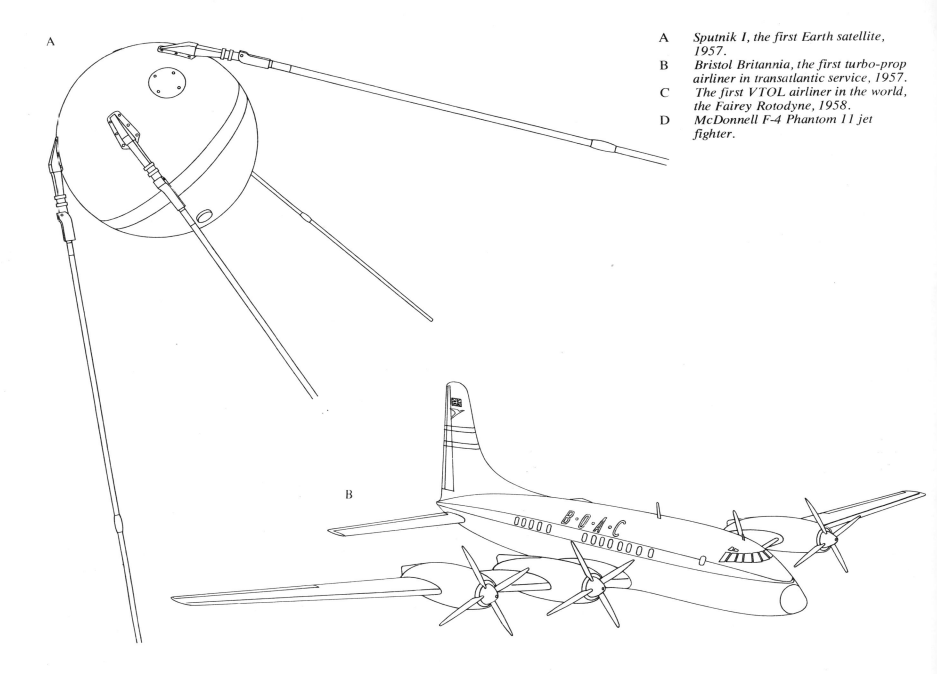

A   *Sputnik I, the first Earth satellite, 1957.*
B   *Bristol Britannia, the first turbo-prop airliner in transatlantic service, 1957.*
C   *The first VTOL airliner in the world, the Fairey Rotodyne, 1958.*
D   *McDonnell F-4 Phantom 11 jet fighter.*

11 APRIL 1957

First tail-sitting VTOL aircraft completes translation from vertical to horizontal flight: the Ryan X-13 Vertijet, in the United States.

19 APRIL 1957

First launch of an American Douglas Thor rocket, the first Intermediate-Range Ballistic Missile to be deployed operationally in Europe.

19 AUGUST 1957

The balloon *Manhigh II*, piloted by D. G. Simons, reaches a height of 101,516 ft (*c.* 37,000 m) in the United States.

4 OCTOBER 1957

Launch of *Sputnik 1* by the USSR, the first artificial satellite in history to be launched into orbit around the Earth.
See figure A

19 DECEMBER 1957

First long-haul turbo-prop airliner enters transatlantic service with BOAC: the Bristol Britannia 312 from London to New York. Its ascendancy is shortlived because the jet airliners begin to take over within a year.
See figure B

10 JANUARY 1958

First flight of the Hiller 12E helicopter.

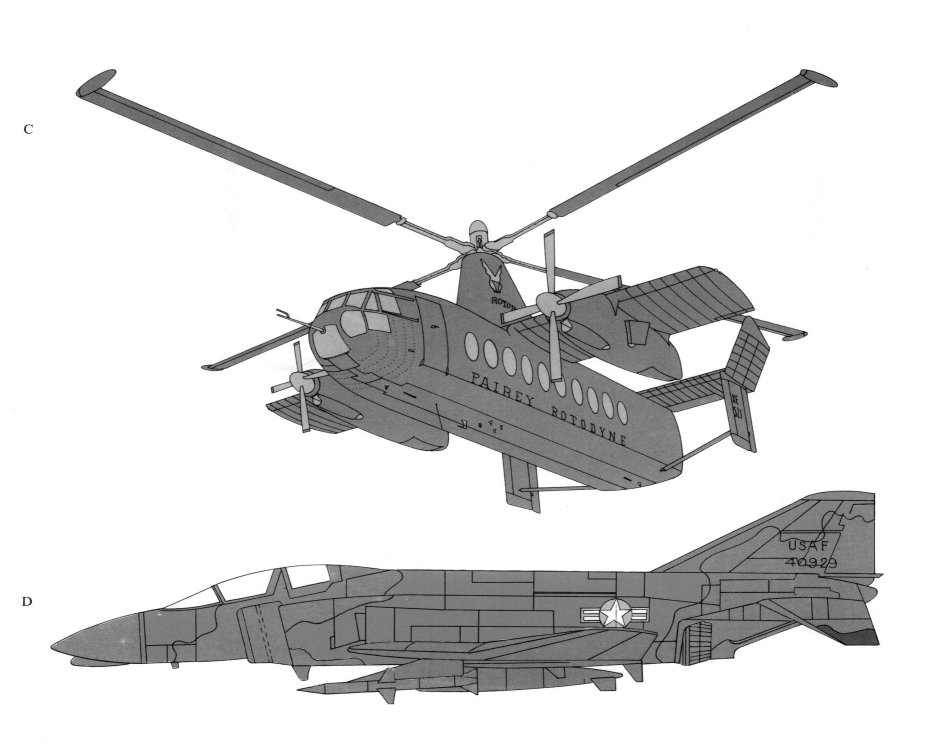

C

D

14 JANUARY 1958

The Australian airline, Qantas, begins the world's first scheduled round-the-world airline service, using Lockheed Super Constellations.

31 JANUARY 1958

Launch of the satellite *Explorer 1*: the first American satellite to be placed in orbit around the Earth.

10 APRIL 1958

In England, the Fairey Rotodyne VTOL airliner first achieves transition from vertical to horizontal flight.
See figure C

27 MAY 1958

First flight of the McDonnell F-4 Phantom II jet-fighter, probably the most successful western fighter of the next decade. More than 4000 F-4s have since been built and

the aircraft is still in production.
See figure D

30 MAY 1958

First flight of Douglas DC-8 long-haul jet airliner, in the United States.

15 JULY 1958

First transition from horizontal to vertical flight of the Vertol 76 tiltwing convertiplane, in the United States.

A   *The Cessna 172 four-seater light aircraft.*
B   *De Havilland D. H. 106 Comet 4 jet airliner, 1958.*
C   *Lift-off of the Martin Titan Inter-Continental Ballistic Missile, 1959.*
D   *The balloon* Small World, *1958.*

A

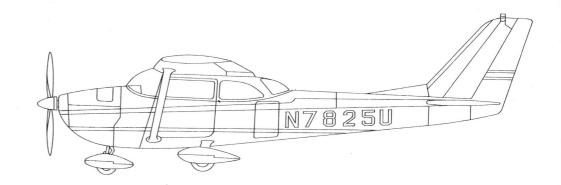

B

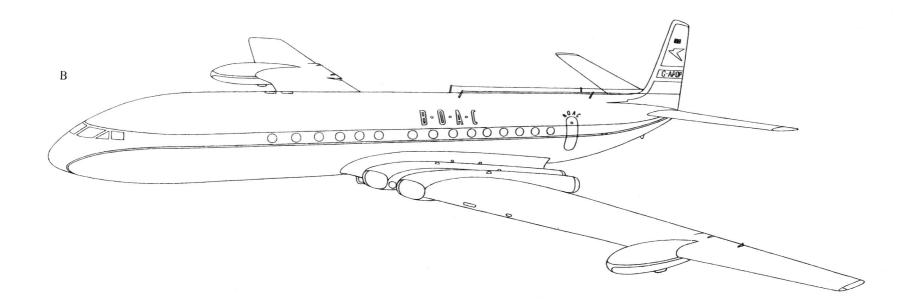

24 SEPTEMBER 1958

First flight by an aircraft designed and built in the Chinese People's Republic, the Beijing No 1 ten-seat twin-engined transport, designed at the Aeronautical Engineering College in Peking.

1 OCTOBER 1958

The American NACA (National Advisory Committee for Aeronautics) becomes NASA (National Aeronautics and Space Administration).

1 OCTOBER 1958

First long-range jet airliner enters trans-atlantic service: the de Havilland D. H. 106 Comet 4 with BOAC. It is followed shortly afterwards by the Boeing 707 with Pan American.
See figure B

28 NOVEMBER 1958

First full-range firing of the Convair Atlas InterContinental Ballistic Missile from Cape Canaveral, Florida, USA. This is to be the

first ICBM in the West to go into service. The equivalent Russian weapon is believed to have been tested about a year earlier.

4 DECEMBER 1958

In the United States, R. Timm and J. Cook take off from Las Vegas in a Cessna 172 and establish an endurance record of 64 days 22 hours 19 minutes 5 seconds.
See figure A

C

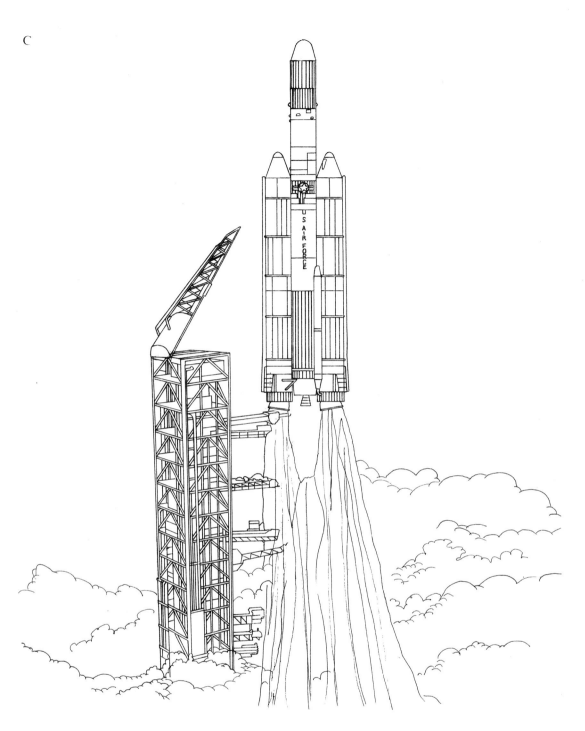

D

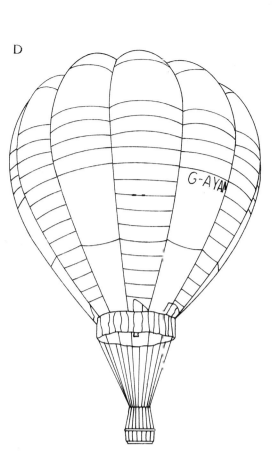

12 DECEMBER 1958

The balloon *Small World*, commanded by
A. B. Elloart, takes off from the Canaries in
an attempt to fly the South Atlantic. It
lands in the sea on 15 December, after
covering 1750 miles (2800 km), and
completes the remaining 1250 miles (2000
km) of the journey on the surface in 20 days.
See figure D

2 JANUARY 1959

Launch of the first spacecraft to escape the
Earth's gravitational field: the Russian
Lunik 1, which goes into solar orbit after a
lunar fly-by.

25 JANUARY 1959

American Airlines inaugurate a transcontinental service between Los Angeles
and New York with Boeing 707s.

6 FEBRUARY 1959

First launch of the Martin Titan ICBM, in
the United States.
See figure C

25 FEBRUARY 1959

In France the world 100 km closed-circuit
speed record of 1018 mph (1638.32 km/h)
set by the Nord Griffon—the first by a
combined turbojet/ramjet-powered aircraft.
The pilot is André Turcat.

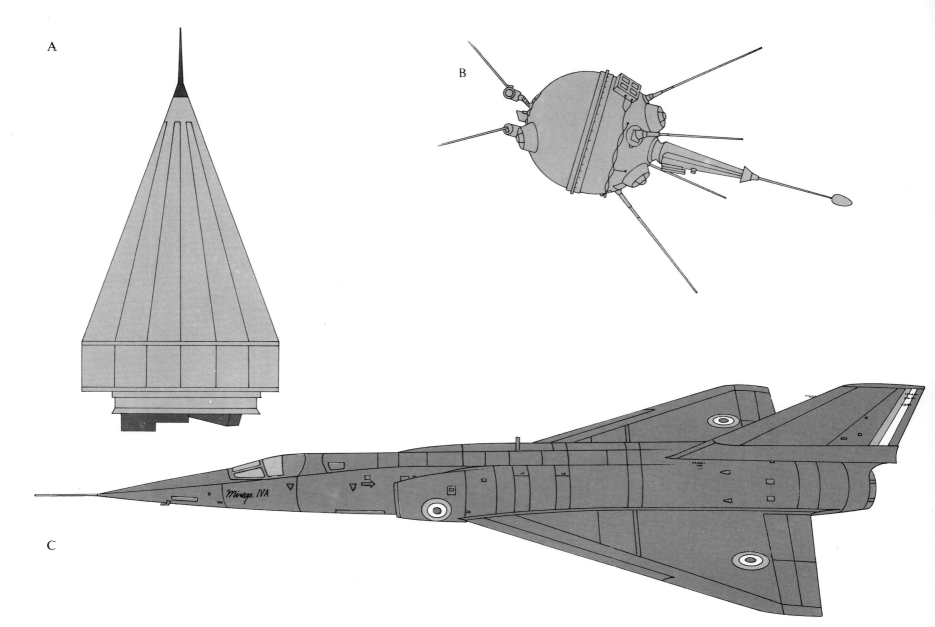

A

B

C

3 MARCH 1959

Launch of *Pioneer IV*, the first American spacecraft to escape the Earth's gravitational field.
See figure A

5 APRIL 1959

First flight of the prototype Aero L-29 Delfin two-seater jet trainer, the first jet aircraft to be designed and built in Czechoslovakia: over 3000 are subsequently produced for Soviet and other Warsaw Pact air forces.

15 MAY 1959

Last operational flight by a RAF Short Sunderland flying-boat, marking the end of the use of seaplanes by the RAF.

17 JUNE 1959

First flight of the Dassault Mirage IV, the first European supersonic jet bomber, in France.
See figure C

25 JULY 1959

The fiftieth anniversary of Louis Blériot's crossing of the English Channel is marked (13—23 July) by Daily Mail London/Paris air race. This is won by Squadron Leader C. G. Maugham, RAF, in 40 minutes 44 seconds flying a Hawker Hunter jet fighter on the main leg of the journey.

13 SEPTEMBER 1959

First man-made object to hit the Moon:

the Russian spacecraft *Lunik II*, launched on 12 September.
See figure B

17 SEPTEMBER 1959

First powered flight of the North American X-15 research aircraft, air-launched from a Boeing B-52 mother-plane from Edwards Air Force Base, California. This programme later achieves speeds of over Mach 6 and attains heights of over 67 miles (c. 107 km).
See figure D

18 SEPTEMBER 1959

In the United States, the Douglas DC-8 four-jet airliner enters service with United and Delta Air Lines. The DC-8 becomes the second most successful first-generation subsonic jet transport.

D

E

F

4 OCTOBER 1959

Launch of the Russian spacecraft *Lunik III,*
which passes round the back of the Moon
and transmits photographs back to Earth.

1 APRIL 1960

First weather satellite is launched: *Tiros I,*
in the United States.

1 MAY 1960

A Lockheed U-2 reconnaissance aircraft,
piloted by Colonel Francis Gary Powers,
USAF, is shot down over the USSR,
resulting in the breakdown of the subsequent
Summit Conference in Paris.
See figures E and F

A   *The American* Pioneer IV *spacecraft,
1959.*
B   *The Russian Lunik II spacecraft.*
C   *Dassault Mirage IV supersonic jet
bomber.*
D   *North American X-15 manned
research aircraft, 1959.*
E   *Colonel Francis Gary Powers.*
F   *The Lockheed U-2 reconnaissance
aircraft first flew in 1955.*

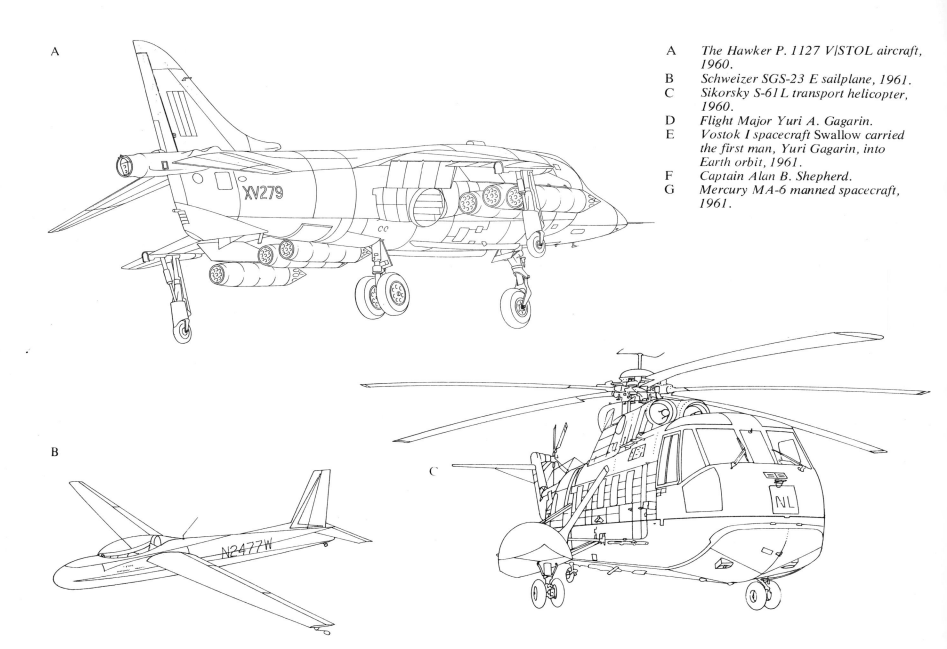

A The Hawker P.1127 V/STOL aircraft, 1960.
B Schweizer SGS-23 E sailplane, 1961.
C Sikorsky S-61 L transport helicopter, 1960.
D Flight Major Yuri A. Gagarin.
E Vostok I spacecraft Swallow carried the first man, Yuri Gagarin, into Earth orbit, 1961.
F Captain Alan B. Shepherd.
G Mercury MA-6 manned spacecraft, 1961.

9—28 JULY 1960

Airlift by SABENA airline from the Congo to Belgium in which 25,711 Belgian nationals are evacuated to safety.

20 JULY 1960

First firing of a Lockheed Polaris test missile from a submerged submarine, the USS *George Washington*.

15 NOVEMBER 1960

Commissioning of submarine USS *George Washington*, the first submarine to be equipped with Polaris missiles.

19 NOVEMBER 1960

First free flight by a swivel-jet fixed-wing V/STOL aircraft, the Hawker P.1127, designed by Sir Sidney Camm and flown by A. W. (Bill) Bedford, in England. This is later developed into the Hawker Siddeley Harrier strike aircraft for the RAF.
See figure A

6 DECEMBER 1960

First flight of the Sikorsky S-61L transport helicopter, in the United States.
See figure C

25 FEBRUARY 1961

In the United States, P. F. Bickle in a

Schweizer SGS-23E sailplane achieves an absolute height of 46,300 ft (14,102 m) representing a gain in height of 42,300 ft (12,894 m).
See figure B

13 MARCH 1961

First vertical flight of the Hawker P.1127 swivel-jet V/STOL fighter, from which was developed the Harrier strike aircraft for the RAF.

12 APRIL 1961

Flight Major Yuri A. Gagarin of the Soviet Air Force, in the *Vostok 1* spacecraft *Swallow*, is the first man to be launched

D

F

G

E

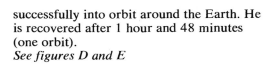

successfully into orbit around the Earth. He is recovered after 1 hour and 48 minutes (one orbit).
See figures D and E

5 MAY 1961

Captain Alan B. Shepard, US Navy, in the Mercury capsule *Freedom* 7, achieves the first American sub-orbital flight around the Earth, lasting 15 minutes 22 seconds.
See figures F and G

27 MAY 1961

First crossing of the English Channel by a VTOL aircraft, the Short S.C.1, which is flown by A. Roberts from England to Paris for the Paris air show.

7 JUNE 1961

First flight of the Breguet Br 941 STOL transport aircraft, a four-engined high-wing monoplane, in France.

21 JULY 1961

Captain Virgil Grissom, in the Mercury capsule *Liberty Bell* 7, makes the second American sub-orbital flight, lasting 15 minutes 37 seconds.

6 AUGUST 1961

Major Gherman S. Titov, in the Russian *Vostok 2* spacecraft *Eagle*, makes the second manned orbital flight (17 orbits), lasting 25 hours 18 minutes.

A

B

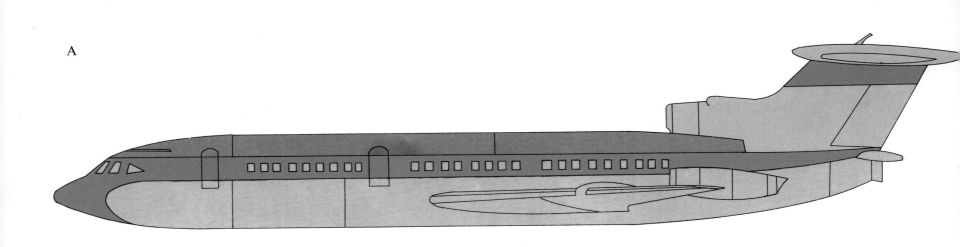

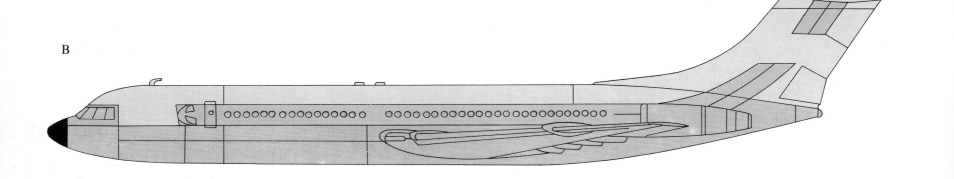

C

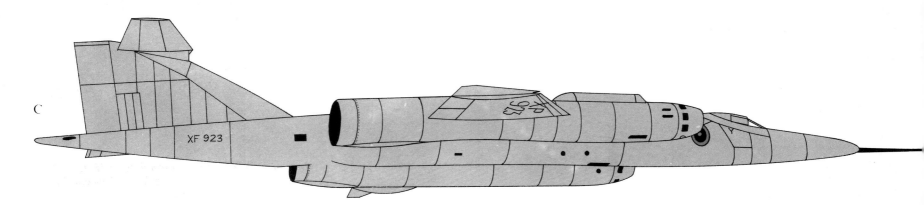

XF 923

D

E

9 JANUARY 1962

In England, the first flight of the Hawker Siddeley Trident tri-jet airliner, which pioneers the three-rear-engine layout with a T-tail.
See figure A

20 FEBRUARY 1962

Launch of the first manned American spacecraft to go into orbit: the Mercury capsule *Friendship 7,* piloted by Lieutenant Colonel John H. Glenn, USMC. He orbits the Earth three times in 4 hours 55 minutes 23 seconds.
See figure D

4 MARCH 1962

A Douglas DC-7C of Caledonian Airways crashes near Doula in the Cameroons killing all 111 occupants. This is the largest number of victims lost up to that time in a single civil accident.

14 APRIL 1962

In England, the first flight takes place of the Bristol 188 high-speed research aircraft, which has a steel airframe.
See figure C

2 MAY 1962

First man-powered aeroplane to make an authenticated straight flight of over half a mile; the Hatfield Man-Powered Aircraft Club's *Puffin,* flown by John C. Wimpenny, in England.
See figure E

6—7 JUNE 1962

World closed-circuit distance record is established by a Boeing B-52H Stratofortress bomber: 11,337 miles (c. 18,245 km) from Seymour Johnson Air Force Base, out and back via Bermuda, Sondrestrom, Anchorage, March Air Force Base and Key West. The flight commander is Captain William M. Stevenson, USAF.

27 JUNE 1962

North American X-15A rocket research aircraft attains a speed of 4104 mph (6604.77 km/h), more than six times the speed of sound. The pilot is Joseph Walker, the chief test pilot of NASA.

29 JUNE 1962

First flight of the British Aircraft Corporation's (BAC) Vickers VC-10 long-haul jet airliner, piloted by G. R. Bryce.
See figure B

A *Hawker Siddeley Trident tri-jet airliner, 1962.*
B *The Vickers-designed BAC VC-10 four-engined intercontinental jet airliner.*
C *Bristol 188 high-speed research aircraft, 1962.*
D *Lieutenant Colonel John H. Glenn.*
E *The 118 lb (53.5 kg) balsa-wood man-powered* Puffin, *1962.*

10 JULY 1962

Launch of *Telstar 1,* first operational tele-communications (TV) satellite. The first TV transmission between the United States and Europe takes place the following day during satellite's fifteenth orbit.

17 JULY 1962

North American X-15A-3 rocket research aircraft attains height of 314,750 ft (nearly 60 miles or 96 km). It is flown by Major Robert M. White, USAF, who thus qualifies for his astronaut's "Wings" for reaching a height greater than 50 miles (*c.* 80 km).

11 AUGUST 1962

Major Andrian G. Nikolayev, in the Russian spacecraft *Vostok 3 Falcon*, establishes a new orbital record of 64 orbits in 94 hours 22 minutes.

19 SEPTEMBER 1962

First flight of the Aero Spacelines Pregnant Guppy outsize transport aircraft, based on the Boeing Stratocruiser, in the United States.
See figure F

14 DECEMBER 1962

The United States spacecraft *Mariner II,* launched on 27 August, passes 21,600 miles (34,762 km) from Venus and investigates the planet's atmosphere for 42 minutes.

9 FEBRUARY 1963

In the United States, the first flight of the three-jet Boeing 727, the civil jet transport destined to be built in the greatest numbers. It is to be used in both cargo and cargo-passenger versions.
See figure B

16 JUNE 1963

Launch of the Russian spacecraft *Vostok 6 Sea Gull*, piloted by the first woman cosmonaut, Junior Lieutenant Valentina Vladimirovna Tereshkova, who makes 48 orbits in 70 hours 50 minutes.
See figure A

30 AUGUST 1963

In England, G. R. Bryce pilots the first

flight of the BAC One-Eleven. This is the first of the second generation of short-haul jet airliners.

1 OCTOBER 1963

First direct flight to Antarctica from another continent by a US Navy Lockheed C-130 Hercules transport, piloted by Commander G. R. Kelly.
See figure C

7 OCTOBER 1963

First flight of the Gates Learjet executive jet aircraft, in the United States.
See figure D

26 OCTOBER 1963

First firing of a Polaris A3 missile from a submerged submarine, the USS *Andrew Jackson.*
See figure E

A   *Junior Lieutenant Valentina Tereshkova.*
B   *Boeing 727 tri-jet civil airliner, 1963.*
C   *Lockheed C-130 Hercules four-turbo-prop high-wing general-purpose freighter, 1963.*
D   *Gates Learjet 24 D executive aircraft carries up to 7 passengers.*
E   *Polaris A-3 missile being fired from a submerged submarine.*
F   *Aero Spacelines Guppy.*

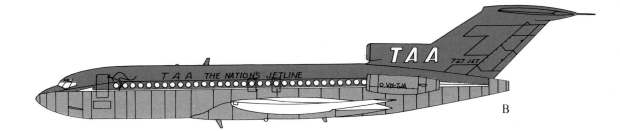

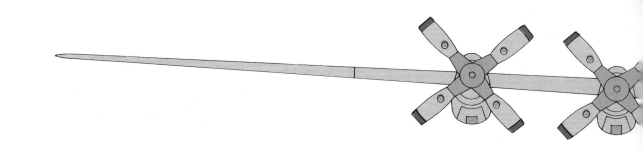

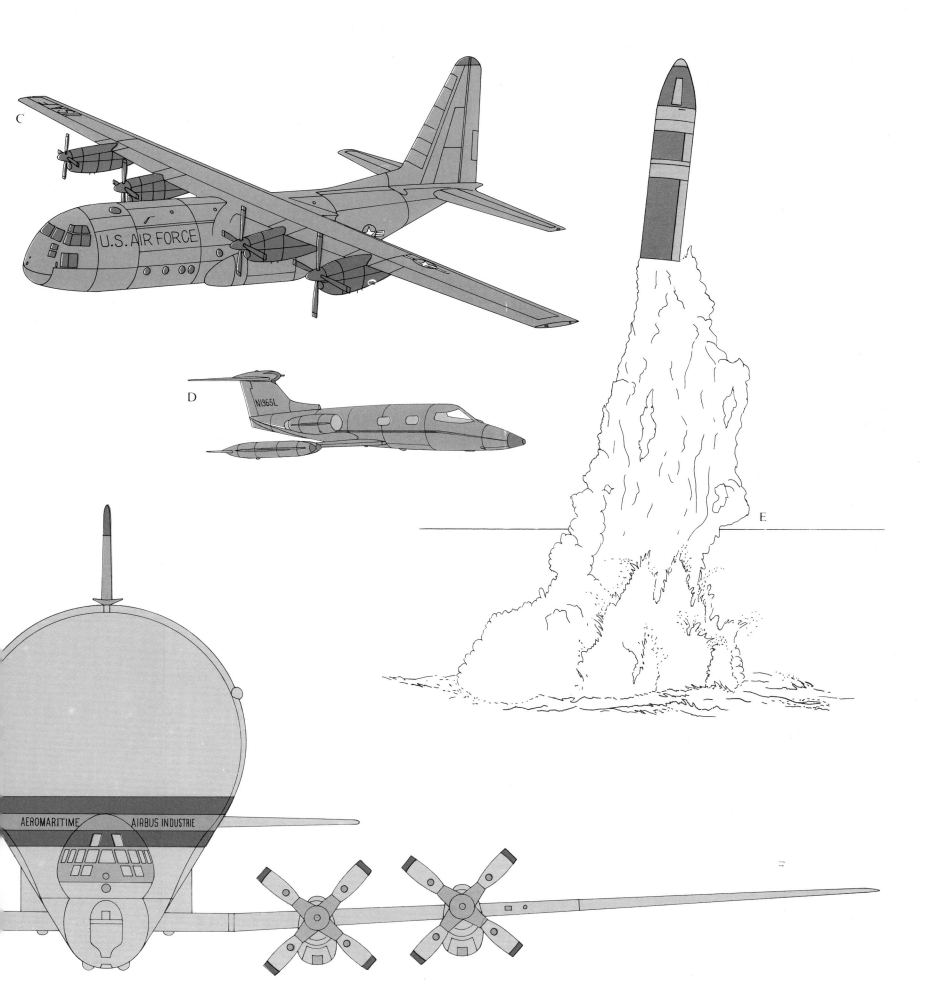

C

D
N1965L

E

AEROMARITIME   AIRBUS INDUSTRIE

That's one small step for man, one giant leap for mankind.

NEIL ARMSTRONG, FIRST MAN TO SET FOOT UPON THE MOON
(21 JULY 1969)

Here men from the planet Earth first set foot upon the Moon, July 1969 A. D. We came in peace for all mankind.

INSCRIPTION ON PLAQUE LEFT BY CREW OF APOLLO 11 IN
THE SEA OF TRANQUILITY (1969)

Clouds disguised Paris and the English Channel but I caught a glimpse of the "White Cliffs" of Dover telling me I was home after circling the earth.

Sheila Scott, *ON TOP OF THE WORLD* (1973)
(WRITING OF HER TRANS-POLAR FLIGHT OF 1971)

Soon there will only be two kinds of airlines... those with Concorde and those without it.

BAC/AEROSPATIALE ADVERTISEMENT (1973)

CHAPTER THIRTEEN

FROM 1963 A.D. TO THE PRESENT TIME

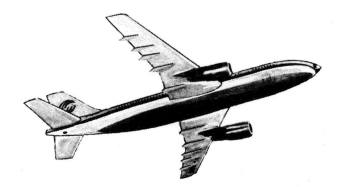

A historic footprint. Left by the first men to land on the Moon, 1969. (Courtesy of NASA and Hasselblad Cameras).

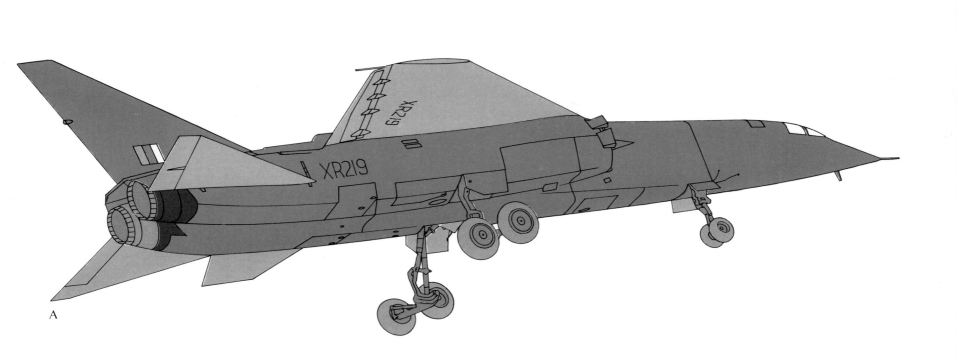

A

A   *BAC TSR-2, 1964.*

28 MAY 1964

First space vehicle of the Apollo programme is launched into space, by a Saturn SA-6 rocket.

5 JUNE 1964

First launching of the de Havilland Blue Streak IRBM from Woomera, Australia. It was not successful.

6 JUNE 1964

The one millionth motor car ferried across the English Channel by Silver City Airways. This service was started in June 1948.

31 JULY 1964

A. H. Parker establishes a world distance record for sailplanes, covering 647 miles (*c.* 1040 km) from Odessa, Texas, to Kimball, Nebraska, in a Sisu-1A sailplane:

the first time more than 1000 km is covered non-stop in a sailplane.

21 SEPTEMBER 1964

First flight of BAC TSR-2, XR219, piloted by Wing Commander Roland P. Beamont, in England.
See figure A

10 OCTOBER 1964

The *Syncom III* satellite allows the transmission, on Eurovision, of the opening ceremony of the 1964 Olympic Games, held in Tokyo, Japan.

12 OCTOBER 1964

The launch of the Russian spaceship *Vostok 1 Ruby*, the first capable of carrying three people. The crew consists of Colonel Vladimir Komarov, Konstantin Feoktistov and Lieutenant Boris Yegorov.

A

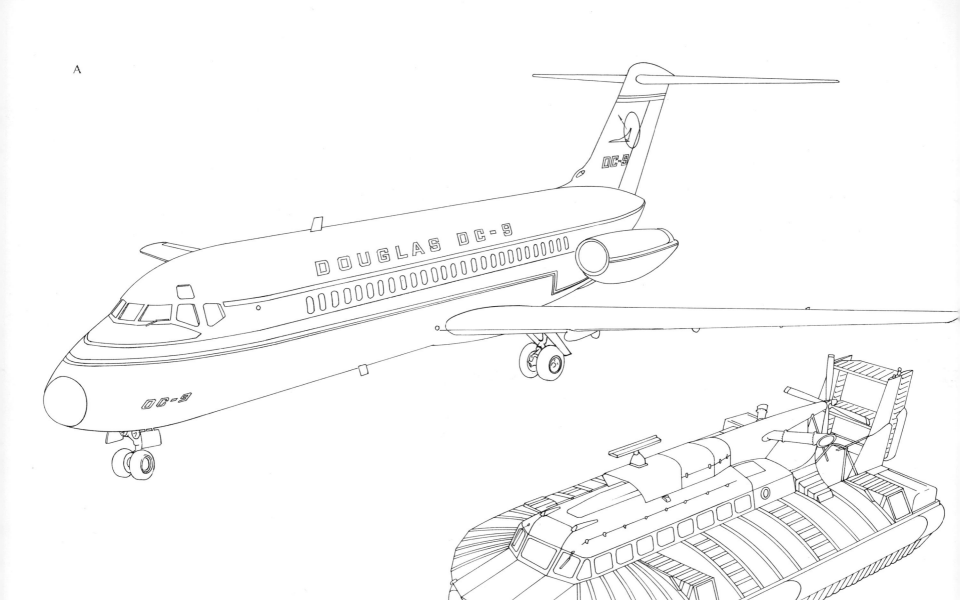

B

21 DECEMBER 1964

First flight of the General Dynamics F-111,
the world's first variable-geometry aircraft.
It is intended as the standard USAF strike
fighter.
See figure C

22 DECEMBER 1964

First flight of the Lockheed SR-71 long-
range reconnaissance Mach-3 aircraft,
piloted by B. Gilliland, in the United States.

13 JANUARY 1965

The LTV-Hiller-Ryan XC-142A tilt-wing
V/STOL experimental aircraft makes its

first transition from vertical to horizontal
flight, in the United States.

27 JANUARY 1965

For the first time, radio communication is
established between an aircraft in flight and
a ground station via a satellite in orbit. The
aircraft is a Pan American Boeing 707 under
the command of J. H. Kelly; the ground
station is Camp Roberts; and the satellite
is *Syncom III*.

12 FEBRUARY 1965

First flight of the Dassault Mirage III-V
VTOL aircraft, piloted by R. Bigand, in
France.

25 FEBRUARY 1965

First flight of the Douglas DC-9 short-haul
twin-jet airliner, which is to be produced
in quantities for many airlines.
See figure A

6 MARCH 1965

First non-stop crossing of the North
American continent by helicopter: Sikorsky
SH-3A flown by J. R. Williford.
See figure D

6 APRIL 1965

Launch of *Early Bird*, the first commercial
telecommunications satellite, in the United
States.

C

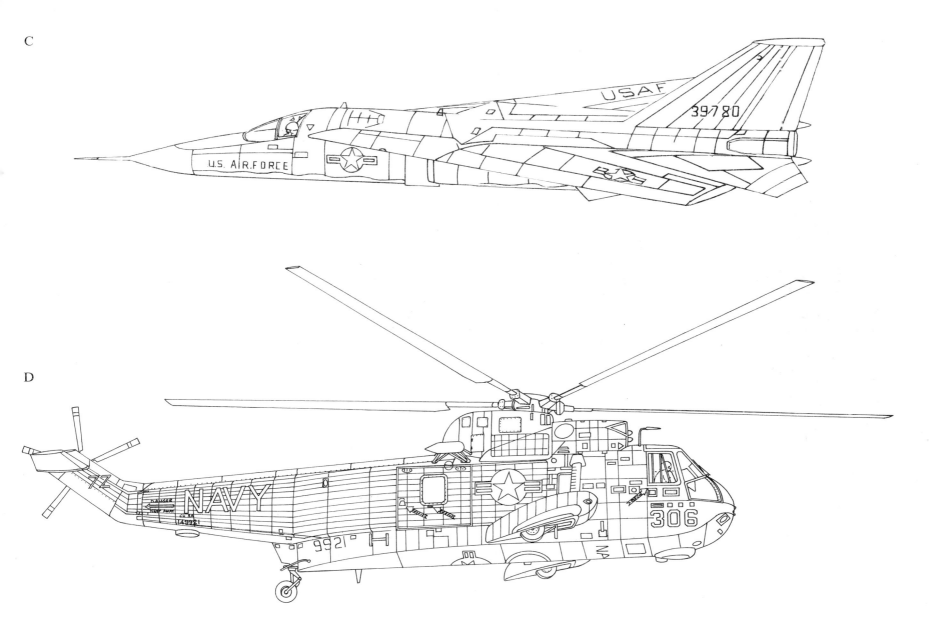

D

1 MAY 1965

World absolute speed record of 2070 mph
(3331.35 km/h) is established over a 15/25
km course by a Lockheed YF-12A, at
Edwards Air Force Base, California, crewed
by Colonel Robert L. Stephens, USAF, and
Lieutenant Colonel Daniel Andre, USAF.
On the same date another YF-12A with the
same crew also establishes an absolute
record, for height in sustained horizontal
flight, of 80,258 ft (24,462.64 m).

9 MAY 1965

Launch of the Russian spacecraft *Luna 5*
which achieves the first-ever soft landing on
the Moon, in the Sea of Clouds, on 12 May.

18 JUNE 1965

First action by USAF Boeing B-52 heavy
bombers in Vietnam.

4 AUGUST 1965

Earl Mountbatten inaugurates the first
hovercraft service between Gosport, Hamp-
shire, and the Isle of Wight, in England.
See figure B

13 SEPTEMBER 1965

The FAI (Féderation Aéronautique Internationale) recognises for the first time an
official height record for a hot-air balloon:
the pilot is B. Bogan and the altitude is

9780 ft (2978 m). The ascent takes place in
the United States.

15 NOVEMBER 1965

A Boeing 707, *Polecat*, of the Flying Tiger
Line, achieves the first flight around the
world overflying both Poles, Captain J. L.
Martin in command.

A   *Douglas DC-9 twin-jet airliner, 1965.*
B   *The first hovercraft in service, 1965.*
C   *General Dynamic F-111 A "swing-
    wing" multi-mission combat aircraft,
    1965.*
D   *Sikorsky SH-3A helicopter, 1965.*

A

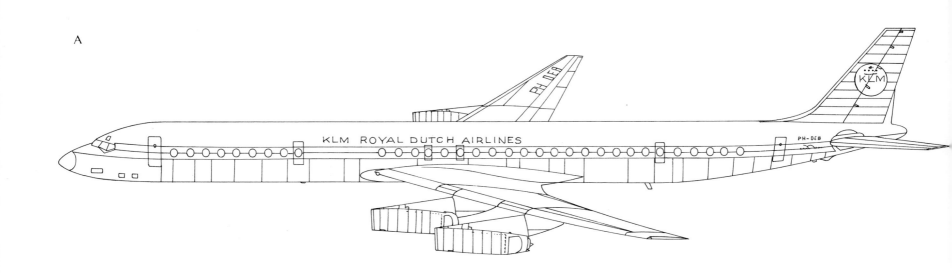

B

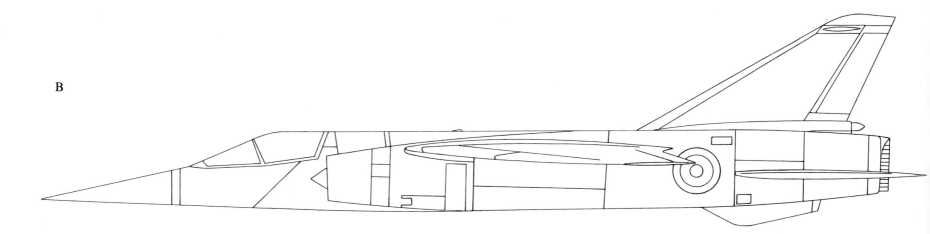

25 NOVEMBER 1965

France launches her first earth satellite *Asterix A-1* by means of a Diamant four-stage rocket.

31 JANUARY 1966

Launch of the Russian spacecraft *Luna 9*, which makes a soft-landing on the Moon on 3 February and sends back photographs for a period of three days.

14 MARCH 1966

First flight of the "stretched" Douglas DC-8-61 airliner, with capacity for 251 passengers.
See figure A

18 MAY—20 JUNE 1966

Round-the-world solo flight by Sheila Scott, in the Piper Comanche *Myth Too*, of over 29,000 miles (*c.* 46,670 km)—first ever by a woman and first by a British pilot of either sex.

30 MAY 1966

The American spacecraft *Surveyor 1* is launched. It soft-lands on the Moon on 2 June and televises pictures of the surface back to Earth.
See figure C

26 AUGUST 1966

Hermann Geiger, most famous of mountain rescue pilots, is killed in a flying accident at Sion. He had made about 500 landings in the high Alps.

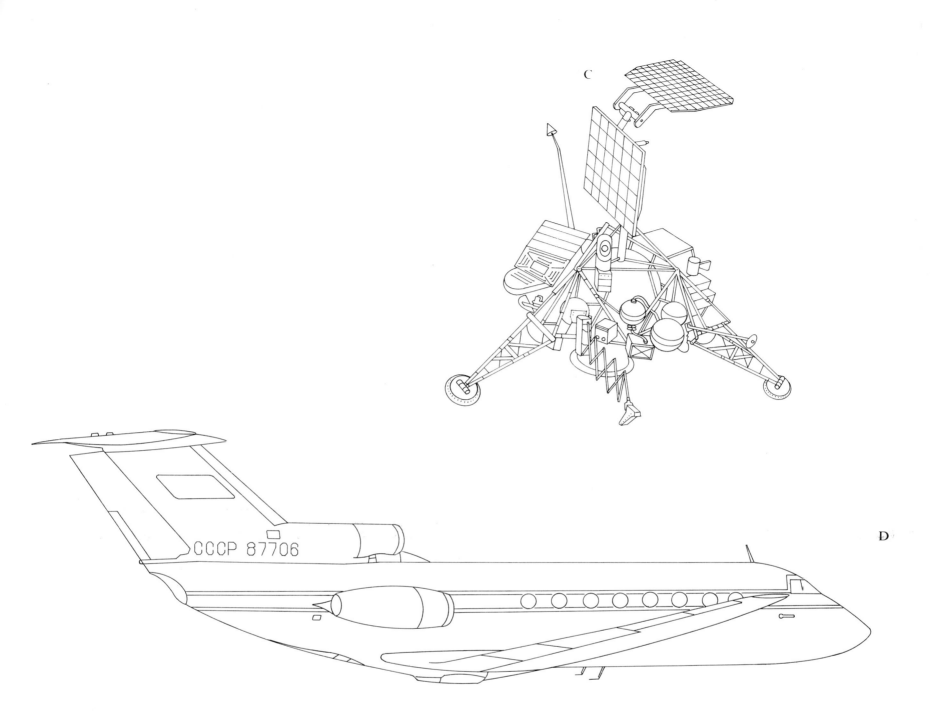

21 OCTOBER 1966

First flight of the Yakovlev Yak-40 tri-jet light transport, the first jet transport in the "DC-3 replacement" category to fly. Yakovlev intends it to be a short-haul cargo-transport aircraft capable of flying in and out of grass and inferior airfields.
See figure D

10 NOVEMBER 1966

A Boeing 707 of Pan American Airways completes the 150,000th crossing of the North Atlantic by the airline.

18 NOVEMBER 1966

The North American X-15A-Z, flown by Major Pete Knight, USAF, achieves a speed of 4250 mph (Mach 6.33 or 6840 km/h).

23 DECEMBER 1966

First flight of the Dassault Mirage F1 fighter aircraft, in France.
See figure B

A   *Douglas DC-8-61 long-range high-density airliner, 1966.*
B   *Dassault Mirage F 1 fighter, 1966.*
C   Surveyor 1, *1966.*
D   *Yakolev YAK-40 tri-jet short-haul light transport, 1966.*

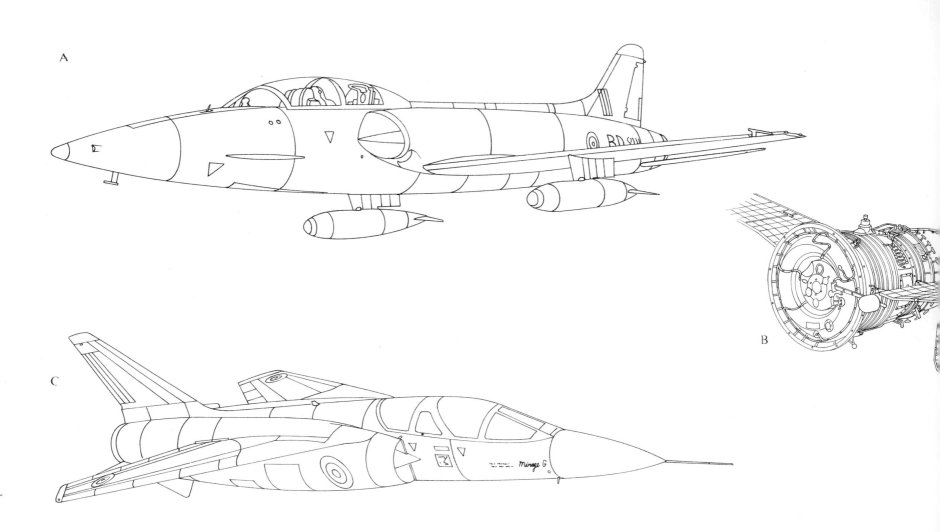

A

C

B

27 JANUARY 1967

An accident on the ground to the Apollo spacecraft (012) results in the deaths of its three astronauts, Virgil Grissom, Edward White and Roger Chaffee. This delays the first Apollo manned orbital flight until October 1968.

29 MARCH 1967

First flight of the Hindustan Aeronautics Marut jet-fighter at Bangalore: India's first home-designed fighter.
See figure A

6 APRIL 1967

Trans World Airlines becomes the first American airline to have a fleet composed entirely of jet aircraft.

23 APRIL 1967

The Russian *Soyuz 1* manned spacecraft makes 17 orbits but its pilot, Colonel

Vladimir Komarov, is killed when landing after re-entry—the first man known to have died during a space flight.
See figure B

20 APRIL 1967

The American *Surveyor 3* space probe soft-lands on the Moon near the Ocean of Storms.

1 MAY 1967

First known rescue at sea by an air-cushion vehicle: SR N6 *Swift*, of Hoverlloyd, rescues two French people from drowning off Calais.

31 MAY—1 JUNE 1967

First non-stop helicopter crossing of the North Atlantic (New York—Paris), by two Sikorsky HH-3Es in 30 hours 46 minutes. Each helicopter refuels nine times en route.

5 JUNE 1967

Outbreak of the Six-Day War between Israel and the Arab countries. The Israeli air force annihilates its enemy by means of a pre-emptive strike and gives a remarkable demonstration of the use of air power. The war ends on 10 June.

17 JUNE 1967

The Chinese People's Republic explodes its first hydrogen bomb.

8 JULY 1967

First Russian variable-geometry fighters (MiG-23 and Su-7B) are revealed publicly for the first time, at an air display at Moscow's Domodedovo airport. Also shown was the Yak-36 prototype fixed-wing V/STOL aircraft.

7 AUGUST 1967

Aerolineas Argentinas and Iberia jointly

launch services on the world's longest non-stop air route: 6462 miles (c. 10,400 km) between Buenos Aires and Madrid.

3 OCTOBER 1967

North American X-15A-2, flown by Major William Knight, USAF, reaches its highest speed: 4534 mph (Mach 6.72 or 7296.79 km/h).

5 OCTOBER 1967

World closed-circuit speed record is established by a Mikoyan E-266 (MiG-25): 1852 mph (2980.52 km/h), at Podmoskovnoe, USSR. The pilot is M. Komarov.

14 OCTOBER 1967

First flight of the Dassault Mirage G prototype, the first European variable-geometry aircraft to fly.
See figure C

18 OCTOBER 1967

First soft-landing on the planet Venus, by the Russian *Venus 4* probe (launched 12 June). Data is transmitted continuously to Earth for 1 $^1/_2$ hours.

19 OCTOBER 1967

The American *Mariner 5* space probe (launched 14 June 1967 from Cape Kennedy) makes a fly-by of Venus at 2480 miles (c. 3990 km) and confirms a surface temperature of about 500°F (268.89°C).

30 OCTOBER 1967

Soviet *Cosmos 186* and *188* spacecraft become the first to locate one another in space, manoeuvre, berth and dock under entirely automatic control.

16 DECEMBER 1967

First transition from vertical to horizontal flight by the Dornier Do 31 E experimental twin-engined jet-lift military transport. This aircraft employs both lift-jets and swivel-jets.
See figure E

DECEMBER 1967

In the United States, the 10,000th Cessna 150 light aircraft is delivered.
See figure D

21 JANUARY 1968

A B-52 Stratofortress of the Strategic Air Command crashes on sea ice off Greenland, on approach to Thule Air Force Base, while carrying four nuclear bombs.

A   *Hindustan Aeronautics Marut jet-fighter, 1966.*
B   Soyuz I *manned spacecraft, 1967.*
C   *Dassault Mirage G "swing-wing" jet aircraft, 1967.*
D   *Cessna 150 light aircraft.*
E   *Dornier Do 31 E twin-engined V/STOL military transport, 1967.*

A

B

22 JANUARY 1968

The Apollo Lunar module is successfully launched into orbit for the first time, by an uprated Saturn I booster, from Cape Kennedy, Florida, USA.

27 MARCH 1968

Colonel Yuri A. Gagarin, the first man in space, is killed in an air crash at Kirzhatsk, north of Moscow.

30 JUNE 1968

First flight of Lockheed C-5A Galaxy, the world's largest aeroplane. The pilot is Leo Sullivan. It is to be used as a military transport by the USAF.

15 SEPTEMBER 1968

Launch of the Russian *Zond 5,* the first spacecraft to be recovered from a near-lunar orbit. It carries turtles, flies and wheat seeds.

11 OCTOBER 1968

The first manned Apollo spacecraft, *Apollo 7*, is launched by a Saturn 1B rocket. This is the first American three-man space flight, the crew being Captain Walter M. Schirra, Major Donn Eisele and R. Walter Cunningham. Splashdown takes place on 22 October after 163 orbits and 260 hours in flight.

16 NOVEMBER 1968

The Russian *Proton 4,* the world's largest unmanned spacecraft to this date, is launched into Earth orbit.

5 DECEMBER 1968

First European deep-space probe, HEOS-1, is launched from Cape Kennedy, Florida, USA, by a Thor-Delta rocket.

21 DECEMBER 1968

Colonel Frank Borman, Commander James

Arthur Lovell and Major William A. Anders become the first men to break free from the Earth's gravitational pull and also the first to orbit the Moon (10 orbits), when their *Apollo 8* spacecraft is launched by a Saturn-5 rocket. Splashdown takes place in mid-Pacific on 27 December.

31 DECEMBER 1968

First flight of the prototype Tupolev Tu-144, the world's first supersonic jet transport. The test pilot is Eduard Elyan and he is assisted by Mikhail Kozlov. The aircraft is assembled at the Zhukovsky Plant, near Moscow.
See figure A

5 JANUARY 1969

The unmanned Russian spacecraft *Venus 5* is launched. It will soft-land on Venus four months later, on 16 May 1969.

9 FEBRUARY 1969

First flight from Paine Field, Seattle, USA,

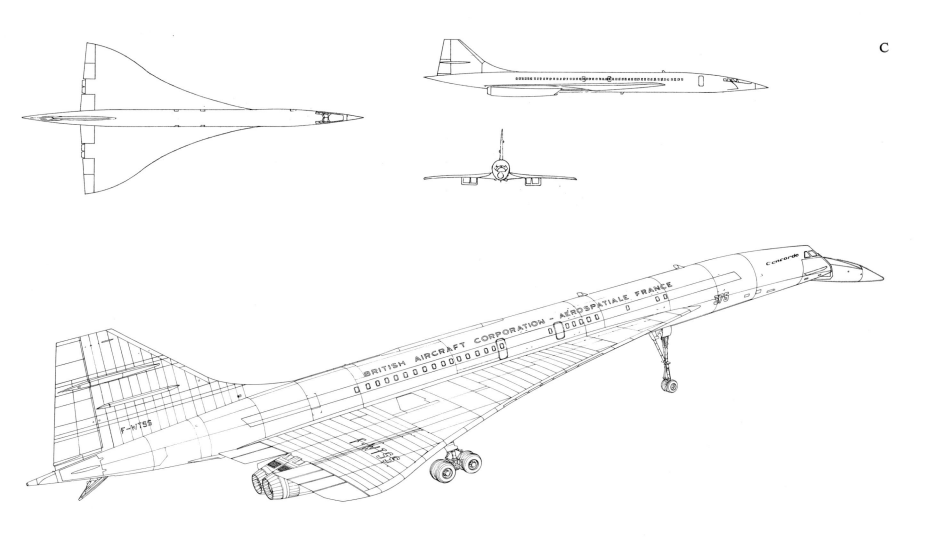

of the Boeing 747 "Jumbo jet" airliner, a
wide-bodied, long-range transport capable
of carrying 360 passengers, thus becoming
the largest aircraft in commercial airline
service in the world. The test pilot is Jack
Waddell. It will enter service first with Pan
American World Airways in January, 1970.
See figure B

9 FEBRUARY 1969

World's largest commercial satellite to this
date, *Tacomsat*, is launched from Cape
Kennedy by a Titan IIIC rocket. It has a
capacity for 10,000 two-way telephone
conversations.

12 FEBRUARY 1969

First announcement of the Russian Mil Mi-12,
the world's largest helicopter, with news of
a record payload of 68,410 lb (31,030 kg)
lifted to a height of 9678 ft (2950 m). The
pilot is V. P. Koloshenko.

25 FEBRUARY 1969

The American spacecraft *Mariner 6* is
launched. It will later photograph Mars at
the end of July from a height of 2000 miles
(*c.* 3200 km).

2 MARCH 1969

First flight of the BAC/Sud-Aviation
Concorde 001 prototype supersonic
transport from Toulouse in France. The
pilot is André Turcat. The British-assembled
002 prototype flies from Filton, near Bristol,
the following month, on 9 April.
See figure C

3 MARCH 1969

Launch of *Apollo 9*, crewed by Colonel
James A. McDivitt, Colonel David R. Scott
and Russell L. Schweikart. This is the first
trial of a manned lunar module in space.
The crew transfers through an interior
connection. Splashdown takes place in the
Atlantic Ocean on 13 March.

18 MAY 1969

Launch of *Apollo 10*, a "dress-rehearsal"
for the Moon landing. The lunar module is
flown within 9.4 miles (15.13 km) of the
Moon. The crew consists of Colonel Thomas
P. Stafford, Commander John W. Young
and Commander Eugene A. Cernan.
Splashdown takes place on 26 May.

16 JULY 1969

Launch of *Apollo 11*, which makes the first
manned landing on the Moon, in the Sea of
Tranquility, five days later, at 21 hours 17
minutes 42 seconds BST on 21 July. Crew:
Neil A. Armstrong, Edwin E. Aldrin and
Michael Collins (Collins remains in orbit
round the Moon). Capsule and crew return
safely to Earth, with the splashdown on
24 July.

A   *Tupolev Tu-144 supersonic jet*
    aircraft, 1968.
B   *Boeing 747 "Jumbo Jet", 1968.*
C   *BAC/Sud-Aviation supersonic*
    airliner Concorde, 1969.

A

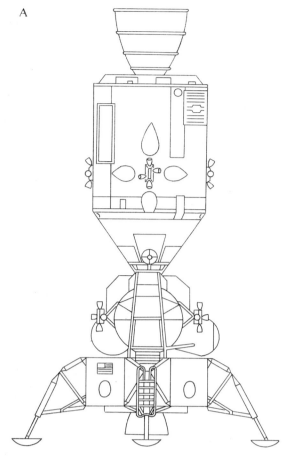

B

C 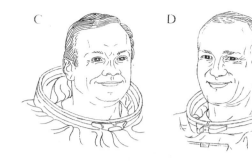 D

F

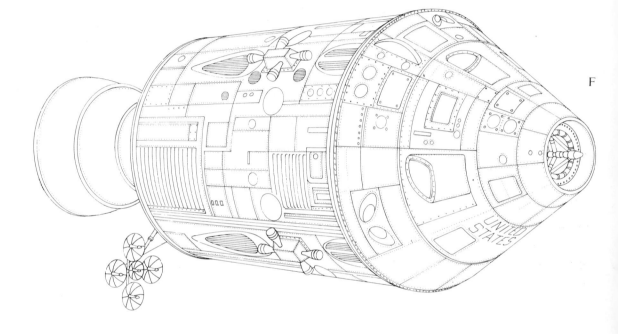

21 JULY 1969

THE FIRST MAN TO SET FOOT ON THE MOON

The American astronaut, Neil A. Armstrong, steps onto the surface of the Moon from the lunar module *Eagle*. He is followed by his colleague, Colonel Edwin E. Aldrin, Jr. The third member of the crew, Lieutenant Colonel Michael Collins, remains in Moon orbit in the command module *Columbia*. Launched from Cape Kennedy, Florida, on 16 July, the capsule splashes down safely on 24 July.
See figures A—F

11, 12 and 13 OCTOBER 1969

Three Soviet spacecraft, *Soyuz 6, 7* and *8*, are launched and rendezvous successfully in space. The crew of *Soyuz 6* (Lieutenant Colonel Georgy Shonin and Valery

Kubasov) conduct welding experiments while in space. The Overall Commander of the three-craft group is Colonel Vladimir Shatalov.

7—10 NOVEMBER 1969

James R. Bede establishes an unrefuelled closed-circuit distance record for a piston-engined aircraft, the Bede BD-2, of 8974 miles (*c.* 14,442 km) between Columbus, Ohio, and Kansas City, Kansas, USA.

14 NOVEMBER 1969

Launch of *Apollo 12*, which makes the second manned landing on the Moon, in the Ocean of Storms. The crew consists of Commanders Charles Conrad, Alan L. Bean and Richard F. Gordon. Splashdown takes place on 24 November.

1 DECEMBER 1969

Introduction of FAR Part 36 regulations for airliners: the first attempt to limit aircraft noise levels at airports by legislation.

11 APRIL 1970

Launch of *Apollo 13* spacecraft which goes around the Moon but cancels landing owing to an explosion in the Service Module on 14 March. The crew, Captain James A. Lovell, Fred W. Haise and John L. Swigert, return to Earth safely, splashing down on 17 April.

24 APRIL 1970

The Chinese People's Republic launches *Chicom 1*, its first satellite, into Earth orbit.

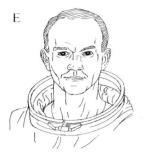

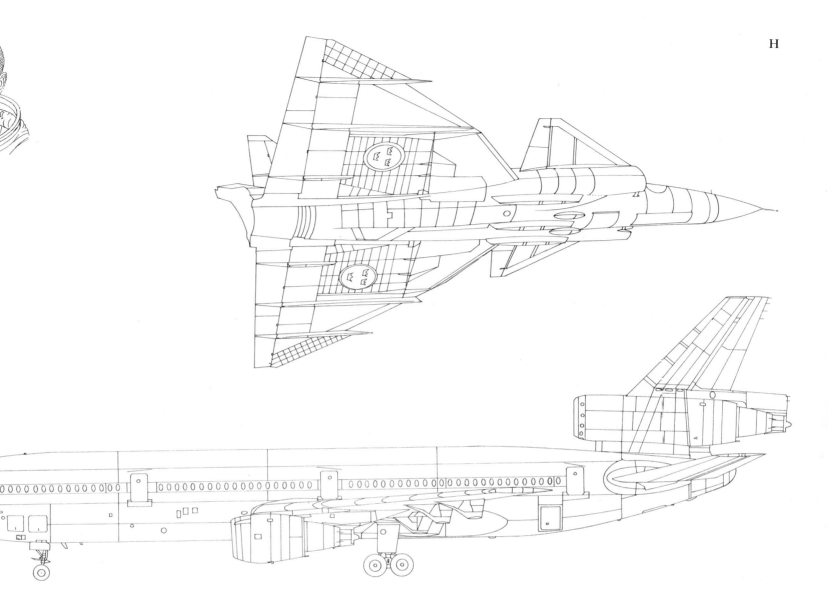

G

25 APRIL 1970

First Soviet multiple launch of eight satellites by a single rocket—they are *Cosmos 336—343*.

1—20 JUNE 1970

Soyuz 9, manned by Colonel Andrian Nikolayev and Vitaly Sevastyanov, establishes a new endurance record by remaining in Earth orbit for 424 hours.

2 JULY 1970

First flight of Saab 37 Viggen multi-purpose combat aircraft, in Sweden. *See figure H*

17 AUGUST 1970

Launch of the American spacecraft *Venus 7*, which soft-lands on the surface of Venus four months later (on 15 December) and transmits temperature data for 23 minutes. This is the first spacecraft to land and operate on another planet.

29 AUGUST 1970

First flight of the McDonnell Douglas DC-10 wide-bodied tri-jet medium-haul airliner, in the United States. *See figure G*

A   *Apollo 11 Lunar Module, 1969.*
B   *Apollo 11 commemorative medallion.*
C   *Neil A. Armstrong.*
D   *Edwin E. Aldrin.*
E   *Michael Collins.*
F   *Apollo 11 Command and Service Module, 1969.*
G   *Douglas DC-10 tri-jet airliner, 1970.*
H   *Saab 37 Viggen multi-purpose combat aircraft, 1970.*

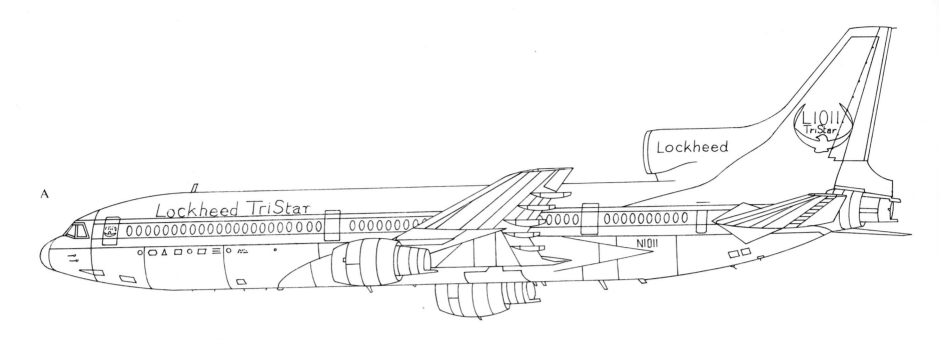

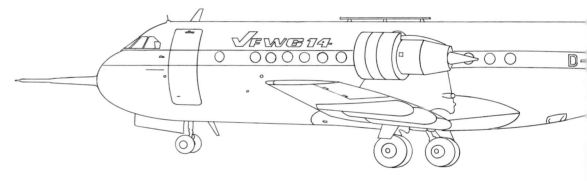

6 SEPTEMBER 1970

An El Al airliner from Amsterdam lands in London after foiling a hijack attempt by Palestinian guerillas. One hijacker is killed during the flight and a steward seriously wounded. A second hijacker, a woman, is arrested.

6—9 SEPTEMBER 1970

Four airliners, a PAA Boeing 747, a Swissair Douglas DC-8, a TWA Boeing 707 and a BOAC BAC VC10, are hijacked by Palestinian guerillas. The 747 is forced to land at Cairo where it is blown up after the passengers are evacuated. The other three aircraft are held captive at Dawson's Field, north of Amman, and are finally blown up on 12 September after the passengers are evacuated.

12 SEPTEMBER 1970

Launch of Soviet *Luna 16* unmanned Moon probe. Controlled entirely from Earth, it soft-lands automatically on the Moon, drills and scoops rock samples, blasts off from lunar surface, re-enters the Earth's atmosphere and soft-lands in Kazakhstan. Recovered on 24 September.

16 NOVEMBER 1970

First flight of the Lockheed L-1011 Tristar wide-body jet airliner.
See figure A

17 NOVEMBER 1970

Russia's remotely-controlled *Lunokhod 1* lunar rover, taken to the Moon on board the *Luna 17* spacecraft, makes its first journey, of 70 ft (*c.* 21 m), on the lunar surface.

21 DECEMBER 1970

First flight of the Grumman F-14 Tomcat variable-geometry jet-fighter for the US Navy.
See figure B

31 JANUARY 1971

Launch of *Apollo 14*, which makes the third successful Moon landing, near the Fra Mauro crater in the Sea of Rains. The crew consists of Captain Alan B. Shepard, Commander Stuart A. Roosa, and Major Edgar J. Mitchell. Splashdown takes place on 9 February.

24 MARCH 1971

The United States Senate decides, by a single vote, not to provide financial backing for prototypes of an American supersonic transport aircraft (the Boeing 2707-300). Congress terminates the project officially on 20 May 1971.

8 MAY 1971

First flight of the Dassault Mirage G8 variable-geometry prototype fighter, in France.

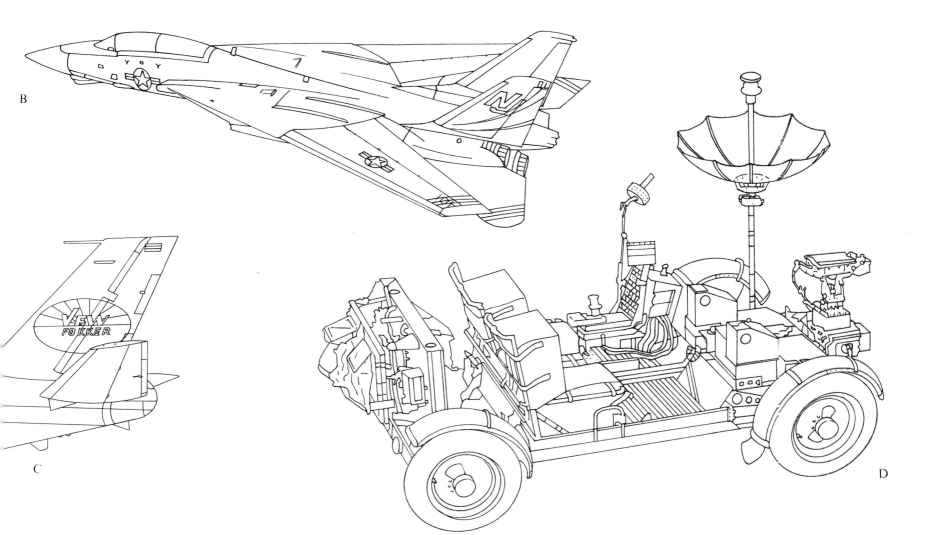

6 JUNE 1971

Launch of *Soyuz 11* which sets the record duration space flight of 24 days. The crew, Lieutenant Colonel Georgi Dobrovolski, Vladislav Volkov and Viktor Patseyev, die of decompression during re-entry 23 days later.

11 JUNE — 4 AUGUST 1971

Sheila Scott, in a Piper Aztec Mythre, makes a 34,000-mile (54,718 km) flight from equator to equator via the North Pole —the first such flight ever made in a light aircraft.

14 JULY 1971

First flight of the VFW-Fokker VFW 614 light jet transport at Bremen, West Germany: the first to use an overwing mounting for jet engines.
See figure C

20 JULY 1971

First flight of the Mitsubishi XT-2 jet trainer, the first supersonic aircraft designed and built in Japan.

26 JULY 1971

A BOAC VC10 en route from London to Khartoum is forced to land at Benghazi by the unprecedented action of the Libyan government whose agents are responsible for this hijacking and who take two high-ranking Sudanese passengers into custody.

26 JULY 1971

Launch of *Apollo 15*, which makes the fourth successful lunar landing, in the Hadley Rill area. The Lunar Roving Vehicle (No 1) is used for the first time. The crew is Major Alfred J. Worden, Colonel David R. Scott, and James B. Irwin. Splash-down takes place 7 August.
See figure D

13 NOVEMBER 1971

NASA's *Mariner 9* goes into orbit around Mars: the first spacecraft to orbit another planet. It is followed by Russia's *Mars 2* on 27 November.

2 MARCH 1972

Launch of *Pioneer 10*, the first spacecraft to travel to (and past) Jupiter and the first to escape from the solar system. It is also the first to have an all-nuclear propulsion system, and has travelled further and faster than any other man-made object.

A   *Lockheed L-1011 Tristar jet airliner, 1970.*
B   *Grumman F-14 Tomcat jet-fighter, 1970.*
C   *VFW-Fokker 614 light jet transport, 1971.*
D   *Lunar Roving Vehicle No 1, the first to carry men on the surface of the Moon, 1971.*

8 MARCH 1972

First flight of the Goodyear advertising airship *Europa* at Cardington, Bedfordshire, England.
See figure A

16 APRIL 1972

Launch of *Apollo 16*, which lands four days later on the Moon and carries out a geological survey of the Descartes Crater. The Lunar Roving Vehicle No 2 is used for the exploration. The crew consists of Captain John W. Young, Lieutenant Commander Thomas K. Mattingly, and Lieutenant Colonel Charles M. Duke. Splashdown occurs on 27 April.

25 APRIL 1972

World distance record for sailplanes is established: 901 miles (1450 km), by Hans-Werner Grosse in West Germany.

24 MAY 1972

President Nixon and Premier Kosygin sign an agreement for a joint American/Russian Earth orbital mission in 1975.

25 MAY 1972

BOAC places an order for five Concordes —the first airline order for a supersonic transport aircraft.

26 MAY 1972

President Nixon and Party Chairman Brezhnev sign SALT (Strategic Arms Limitation Talks) agreement.

26 MAY 1972

Cessna announces the completion, earlier in the year, of its 100,000th aircraft—the first company to reach this figure.

18 JUNE 1972

A BEA Trident crashes after take-off from Heathrow airport with the loss of all 118 occupants.

29 JUNE 1972

Martin-Baker announces that 3000 lives have now been saved by use of its ejection seats.

A

23 JULY 1972

Launch at Vandenberg, California, of the first Earth Resources Technology Satellite.

27 JULY 1972

First flight of the prototype McDonnell Douglas F-15 Eagle air superiority fighter, in the United States.

14 AUGUST 1972

An Ilyushin Il-62 jet airliner crashes after take-off at Berlin with the loss of 156 lives.

22 SEPTEMBER 1972

An order for 14 by Delta Airlines takes Boeing 727 sales past 1000—the first airliner to reach this figure.

13 OCTOBER 1972

Accident to Ilyushin Il-62 jet transport at Moscow killing 176 occupants, the largest number killed in a single airline accident to this date.

28 OCTOBER 1972

First flight at Toulouse, France, of the Airbus Industrie A-300B Airbus, a twin-engined short-haul wide-bodied airliner.
See figure B

7 DECEMBER 1972

Launch of *Apollo 17*, the eleventh manned Apollo flight and the last of the Apollo programme. This sixth manned lunar landing takes place in the Taurus-Littrow area on 11 December when rocks are collected and volcanic evidence is found. Lunar Roving Vehicle No 3 is used for lunar exploration. The crew consists of Eugene A. Cernan, Ronald E. Evans and Harrison H. Schmitt. Splashdown takes place on 19 December.

23 DECEMBER 1972

First flight, at Radlett, Hertfordshire, of the world's first 2-man man-powered aircraft, the HPA *Toucan*. The crew consists of Bryan Bowen and Derek May. On 3 July 1973, with the same crew, it covers 2100 ft (*c.* 1126 m).

4 JANUARY 1973

First flight, at Wantage, Berkshire, of the world's first hot-air airship, the *Cameron D96*. It is crewed by Don Cameron and Dr E. T. Hall.

21 FEBRUARY 1973

Israeli fighter aircraft shoot down a Libyan Boeing 727 airliner which wanders over the Israel-occupied Sinai Desert. 106 occupants of the Boeing are killed.

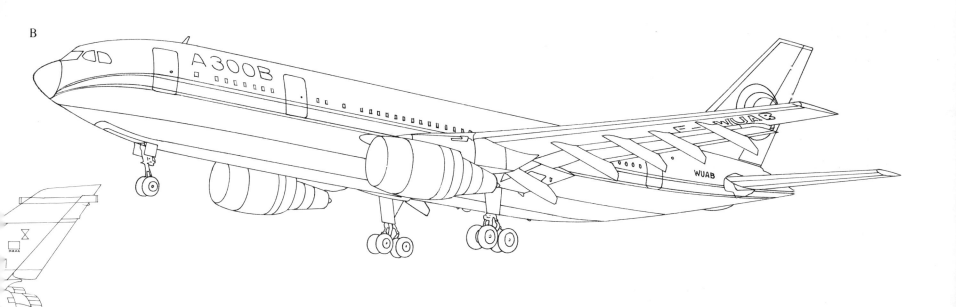

B

C

14 MAY 1973

Launch of *Skylab 1,* orbital workshop. The first crew, Charles Conrad, Dr Joseph P. Kerwin and Paul J. Weitz, is launched in *Skylab 2* on 25 May; their mission ends 22 June after 28 days in orbit.

3 JUNE 1973

Crash of the Tupolev Tu-144 SST (second production aircraft) during a demonstration flight at the Paris Air Show—the first known accident to a supersonic transport aircraft.

25 JULY 1973

New world absolute height record of 118,897 ft (63,782 m) is set up by a Mikoyan E-266 (MiG-25), piloted by Alexander Fedotov, in Russia.

26 JULY 1973

First flight of the Sikorsky S-69 ABC (Advancing Blade Concept) helicopter, which requires no torque-cancelling tail rotor, in the United States.

28 JULY 1973

Launch of second Skylab crew (Alan Bean, Jack Lousma and Dr Owen Garriott) in *Skylab 3.* Mission ends on 25 September after 59 days in space.

6 OCTOBER 1973

Israel is attacked on two main fronts, by Egypt (across the Suez Canal) and Syria (on the Golan Heights), supported by other Arab nations. Subsequent war involves heavy losses of Israeli aircraft to Egyptian SA-6 and other surface-to-air missiles. A provisional cease-fire is arranged by the United States and Russia 18 days later.

3 NOVEMBER 1973

Launch of *Mariner 10* spacecraft for Venus and Mercury fly-by: the first attempt to obtain close-up TV pictures, and the first probe to Mercury. (Due to pass Venus on 5 February and Mercury on 29 March 1974 and then to go into solar orbit, returning for a second Mercury fly-by on 22 September 1974.)

16 NOVEMBER 1973

Launch of third and last Skylab crew (Lieutenant Colonel Gerald P. Carr, Lieutenant Colonel William R. Pogue and Dr Edward G. Gibson) in *Skylab 4.* One of the crew's missions is to observe the comet Kohoutek.

3 MARCH 1974

Turkish Airlines DC-10 crashes near Paris killing all 345 people on board, the highest ever death toll from an aeroplane crash.

A *Goodyear helium-filled advertising airship* Europa, *1972.*
B *Airbus Industrie A-300 B European Airbus, 1972.*
C *Some 800 examples of the internationally conceived MRCA (multi-role combat aircraft) will be built to serve with the British, German, and Italian air forces from the late 1970s.*

BIBLIOGRAPHY

ADER, C. *La Première Etape de l'Aviation Militaire.* London 1907.
ADER, C. *L'Aviation Militaire.* Paris 1909. (2nd ed. 1911.)
ALEXANDER, JEAN P. *Russian Aircraft since 1910.* In preparation.
AMECOURT, PONTON D'. *Collection de Mémoires sur la Locomotion aérienne sans ballons.* Paris 1864—1867.

BABINGTON-SMITH, C. *Testing Time: a Study of Man and Machine in the Test-Flying Era.* London, 1961.
BACON, GERTRUDE. *Balloons, Airships, and Flying Machines.* London, 1905.
BARBER, H. *The Aeroplane Speaks.* London, 1916.
BECKFORD, L. *An ABC of Aeronautics.* London, 1957.
BERGET, A. *La Route de l'Air.* Paris, 1909.
BOFFITO, G. *Il Volo in Italia.* Firenze, 1921.
BORELLI, G. A. *De Motu Animalium.* 2 vols. Roma, 1680—1.
BOURGEOIS, DAVID. *Recherches sur l'Art de voler, depuis la plus haute antiquité jusqu'à nos jours.* Paris, 1784.
BRETT, R. D. *The History of British Aviation, 1908—14.* London, 1934.
BREWER, G., and ALEXANDER, P. Y. *Aeronautics: an Abridgement of Aeronautical Specifications filed in the Patent Office, 1815—91.* London, 1893.
BROOKS, P. W. *The Modern Airliner: its Origin and Development.* London, 1961.
BRUCE, J. M. *British Aeroplanes, 1914—18.* London, 1957.

CANUTE, O. *Progress in Flying Machines.* New York, 1894.
CAYLEY, SIR G. *Aeronautical and Miscellaneous Note-book (c. 1799—1826) of Sir George Cayley.* Cambridge, 1933.
CHAMBRE, R. *Histoire de l'Aviation.* Paris, 1948.
CHICAGO: International Conference on Aerial Navigation, 1893. *Proceedings.* New York, 1894.
CIERVA, J. DE LA. *Wings of To-morrow; the Story of the Autogiro.* New York, 1931.
CYNK, J. B. *Polish Aircraft 1893—1939.* London, 1971.

DAVIES, R. E. G. *A History of the World's Airlines.* London, 1967.
DAVY, M. J. B. Aeronautics: *Heavier-than-air Aircraft. Pt. III, The Propulsion of Aircraft.* London, 1936.
DAVY, M. J. B. *Henson and Stringfellow — their Work in Aeronautics.* London, 1931.
DAVY, M. J. B. *Interpretive History of Flight.* 2 nd ed. London, 1948.
DAVY, M. J. B. Aeronautics: *Heavier-than-air Aircraft, Pts. I and II. Historical Survey; Catalogue of the Exhibits.* 2nd ed. London, 1949.
DEDREUX, D. *La Navigation aérienne en Chine.* Paris, 1863.
DOLLFUS, C. *Les Avions.* Paris, 1962.
DOLLFUS, C., BEAUBOIS, H., and ROUGERON, C. *L'Homme, l'Air, et l'Espace: Aéronautique, Astronautique.* Paris, 1965.

DOLLFUS, C., and BOUCHÉ, H. *Histoire de l'Aéronautique.* London, 1932.
DOLLFUS, E. H. *Petits Modèles d'Aéroplanes.* Paris, 1912.
DORMAN, G. *Fifty Years Fly-past: from Wright Brothers to Comet.* London, 1951.
DUHEM, J. *Histoire des Idées aéronautiques avant Montgolfier.* Paris, 1943.
DUHEM, J. *Musée aéronautique avant Montgolfier: Recueil des Figures et Documents* (etc.). Paris, 1943.
DUHEM, J. *Histoire des Origines du Vol à Réaction.* Paris, 1959.
DUMAS, A. *Stud Book de l'Aviation: Ceux qui ont volé et leurs Appareils.* Paris, 1909.
DU TEMPLE, F. "L'Appareil de Locomotion Aérienne". In *L'Aéronaute*, August 1877.
DUVAL, G. R. *British Flying-Boats, 1909—1952.* London, 1966.

EGE, L. *Balloons and Airships 1783—1973.* Copenhagen and London, 1973.
EMME, E. M. *Aeronautics and Astronautics; an American Chronology of Science and Technology in the Exploration of Space, 1915—1960.* Washington, D.C., 1961.
EMME, E. M. *A History of Space Flight.* Washington, D.C., 1965.
ESTERNO, M. D'. *Du vol des Oiseaux.* Paris, 1864—65.

FALKENBERG, G. VON. *Der Fallschirm* (The Parachute). Berlin, 1912.
FERBER, F. *L'Aviation: ses Débuts, son Développement.* Paris, 1910.
FERRIS, R. *How to Fly; or the Conquest of the Air.* London, 1910.
FRANCILLON, R. J. *Japanese Aircraft of the Pacific War.* London, 1970.
FRANKFURT A. M.: Exhibition, 1909, *Katalog der historischen Abteilung der ersten Internationalen Luftschiffahrts-Ausstellung . . . 1909.* Frankfurt, 1910.
FULLERTON, J. D. *Report on Aerial Navigation.* Chatham, 1904.

GABLEHOUSE, C. *Helicopters and Autogiros: a chronicle of rotating-wing aircraft.* Philadelphia and New York, 1967.
GAMBLE, C. F. S. *The Air Weapon: being some Account of the Growth of British Aeronautics from the Beginnings in the Year 1783 until the End of the Year 1929.* Vol. I. London, 1929.
GARRIGA-JOVÉ, X. (Gen. Ed.) *Enciclopedia de Aviacion y Astronautica* (8 vols). Barcelona, 1973—74.
GATLAND, K. W. *Development of the Guided Missile.* 2nd ed. London, 1954.
GATLAND, K. W. *Pocket Encyclopaedia of Spaceflight in Colour* (4 vols.). London, 1967—1974.
GÉRARD, L. J. *Essai sur l'Art du vol aérien.* Paris, 1784.
GIACOMELLI, R. *Gli Scritti de Leonardo da Vinci sul Volo.* Roma, 1936.
GIBBS-SMITH, C. H. *A History of Flying.* London, 1953.
GIBBS-SMITH, C. H. "The Origins of the Aircraft Propeller". In *Quarterly Review (Rotol and British Messier Journal).* London, 1959.
GIBBS-SMITH, C. H. "The Birth of the Aeroplane"; BROOKS, P. W. "The Development of the Aeroplane"; MENSFORTH, E. "The Future of the Aeroplane." (The three Cantor

Lectures for 1958, reprinted in the *Journal of the Roy. Soc. of Arts.* London, January 1959.)
GIBBS-SMITH, C. H. *The Aeroplane: an historical Survey* (Science Museum publication). London, 1960. (For 2nd ed., see *Aviation: an historical Survey.* London, 1969.)
GIBBS-SMITH, C. H. *Sir George Cayley's Aeronautics, 1796—1855* (Science Museum publication). London, 1962.
GIBBS-SMITH, C. H. *The Wright Brothers: a Brief Account of their Work* (Science Museum publication). London, 1963.
GIBBS-SMITH, C. H. *The invention of the Aeroplane, 1799—1909.* London, 1966.
GIBBS-SMITH, C. H. *A Directory and Nomenclature of the First Aeroplanes, 1809 to 1909* (Science Museum publication). London, 1966.
GIBBS-SMITH, C. H. *Leonardo da Vinci's Aeronautics* (Science Museum publication). London, 1967.
GIBBS-SMITH, C. H. *Clément Ader: his Flight-Claims and his Place in History* (Science Museum publication). London, 1968.
GIBBS-SMITH, C. H. *Aviation: an Historical Survey from its Origins to the End of World War II* (Science Museum publication). London, 1969.
GIBBS-SMITH, C. H. *Early Aviation History: Studies and Problems.* (Companion volume to *Aviation: an Historical Survey.*) (Science Museum publication: in preparation.)
GOLDSTROM, J. *A Narrative History of Aviation* (i.e. from the Wrights to 1929). New York, 1930.
GOUPIL, A. *La Locomotion Aérienne.* Paris, 1884.
GRAHAME-WHITE, C., and HARPER, H. *The Aeroplane, Past, Present and Future.* London, 1911.
GRAND-CARTERET, J., and DELTEIL, L *La Conquête de l'Air vue par l'Image (1495—1909).* Paris, 1910.
GREEN, W. *Warplanes of the Third Reich.* London, 1970.
GREEN, W. and CROSS, R. *The Jet Aircraft of the World.* London, 1955.
GREEN, W., and POLLINGER, G. *The Aircraft of the World.* Revised ed. London, 1956. (3rd ed. 1965).
GREGORY, H. F. *The Helicopter.* London, 1948.
GREY, C. G. *History of the Air Ministry.* London, 1940.

HADDOW, G. W., and CROSZ, P. M. *The German Giants: the German R-Planes, 1914—1918.* London, 1962.
HALLE, G. *Otto Lilienthal.* 2nd ed. Düsseldorf, 1956.
HALLE, G. *Otto Lilienthal und seine Flugzeug-Konstruktionen.* Munich (Deutsches Museum), 1962.
HART, C. *Kites: an Historical Survey.* London, 1967.
HART, I. B. *The World of Leonardo da Vinci.* London, 1961.
HARVIE, E. F. *Venture the Far Horizon: the Pioneer Long-Distance Flights in New Zealand.* Christchurch (N.Z.), 1966.
HAVILLAND, SIR G. DE. *Sky Fever.* London, 1961.
HÈBRARD, J. A. L. *L'Aviation des Origines à nos Jours.* Paris, 1954.
HEINMULLER, J. P. V. *Man's Fight to Fly: famous World-record Flights and a Chronology of Aviation.* New York, 1944.

231

HILDEBRANDT, A. *Airships Past and Present*, etc. (translated from Die Luftschiffahrt, etc., 1907). London, 1908.
HODGSON, J. E. *The history of Aeronautics in Great Britain*. London, 1924.
HUNSAKER, J. C. *Aeronautics at the Mid-Century*. Yale, 1952.

JACKSON, A. J. *British Civil Aircraft, 1919—1959*. 2 vols. London, 1959, 1960.
JACKSON, R. *Airships in Peace and War*. London, 1971.
JANE, F. T. *All the World's Air-Ships: Aeroplanes and Dirigibles*. London, 1909, 1911.
JANE, F. T. *All the World's Air-Craft: Aeroplanes and Dirigibles*. London, 1912, 1913, 1914.
JANE, F. T. *All the World's Aircraft*. Edited by C. G. GREY and others. London, 1916 to date (no issue in 1921).
JOHNSTON, S. P. *Horizons Unlimited: a Graphic History of Aviation*. New York, 1941.
JONES, H. A., and RALEIGH, SIR W. *The War in the Air*. (The official history.) 6 vols., with appendix, 1922—1937.

KELLY, F. C. *The Wright Brothers*. London, 1944.
KING, H. F. *Aeromarine Origins*. London, 1966.
KING, H. F., and TAYLOR, J. W. R. *Jane's 100 Significant Aircraft 1909—1969*.

LANA TERZI, F. DE. *Prodromo overo Saggio* (etc.). Brescia, 1670.
LANCHESTER, F. W. *Aerodynamics*. London, 1907.
LANGLEY, S. P. *Experiments in Aerodynamics*. (Smithsonian Institution publication.) Washington, D.C., 1891.
LAUFER, B. *The Prehistory of Aviation*. (Field Museum publication.) Chicago, 1928.
LAUNOY and BIENVENU. *Instruction sur la nouvelle Machine inventée par MM. Launoy . . . & Bienvenu*. Paris, 1784.
LA VAULX, H. DE (Comte). *Le Triomphe de la Navigation Aérienne*. Paris, 1912.
LA VAULX, H. DE (Comte), and TISSANDIER, P. *Joseph et Etienne de Montgolfier*. Annonay, 1926.
LECORNU, J. *Les Cerfs Volants* (Kites). Paris, 1902.
LECORNU, J. *La Navigation Aérienne: Histoire documentaire et anecdotique*. Paris, 1903.
LENT, H. B. *The Helicopter Book*. New York, 1956.
LEWIS, P. *British Aircraft, 1809—1914*. London, 1962.
LEWIS, P. *The British Fighter since 1912*. London, 1965 (2nd ed. 1966).
LEWIS, P. *The British Bomber since 1914*. London, 1967.
LEY, W. *Rockets, Missiles and Space Travel*. 2nd ed. London, 1951.
LILIENTHAL, O. *Der Vogelflug als Grundlage der Fliegekunst*. Berlin, 1889. (English translation from the second ed. of 1910, as *Bird Flight as a Basis of Aviation*, 1911.)
LINDBERGH, C. A. *The Spirit of St. Louis*. London, 1953.
LIPTROT, R. N., and Woods, J. D. *Rotorcraft*. London, 1955.
LOUGHEED, V. *Vehicles of the Air*. London, 1909.
LOUP, M. *Solution du Problème de la Locomotion aérienne*. Paris, 1853.

MAGOUN, F. A., and HODGINS, E. *A History of Aircraft*. New York, 1931.
MASON, F. K. *Battle over Britain*. London, 1969.
MAXIM, SIR H. S. *Artificial and Natural Flight*. London, 1908.
MAXIM, H., and HAMMER, W. J. *Chronology of Aviation*. New York, 1931.
MEANS, J. H. *James Means and the Problem of Manflight during the Period 1882—1920*. Washington, D.C., 1964.
MILBANK, J. *The First Century of Flight in America*. Princeton, 1943.
MORRIS, L., and SMITH, K. *Ceiling Unlimited: the Story of American Aviation from Kitty Hawk to Supersonics*. New York, 1953.
MOUILLARD, L.-P. *L'Empire de l'Air: Essai d'Ornithologie appliquée à l'Aviation*. Paris, 1881.
MUNSON, K. *Pocket Encyclopaedia of World Aircraft in Colour*. (14 vols.) London, 1966—1973.
MURPHY, C. J. V. *Parachute*. New York, 1930.

NADAR (pseud. of F. TOURNACHON). *Le Droit au Vol*. Paris, 1865. (Translated as *The Right to Fly*, 1866.)
NAYLER, J. L., and OWER, E. *Aviation: its technical Development*. London, 1965.
NICOLSON, M. H. *Voyages to the Moon*. New York, 1948.

PARKIN, J. H. *Bell and Baldwin: their Development of Aerodromes and Hydrodromes at Baddeck, Nova Scotia*. Toronto, 1964.
PATENT OFFICE (London). *Abridgments of Specifications relating to Aeronautics, A. D. 1815—1866*. London, 1869.
PÉNAUD, A. "Aeroplane Automoteur: Equilibre automatique." In *L'Aéronaute*, Paris, January 1872.
PÉNAUD, A. "Un Brevet d'Aéroplane." In *L'Aéronaute*, Paris, October 1877.
PENROSE, H. J. *British Aviation: the Pioneer Years (1903—1914)*. London, 1967.
PEYREY, F. *L'Idée aérienne: Aviation: Les Oiseaux artificiels*. Paris, 1909.
PILCHER, P. *Gliding*. London, 1890.
PRICE, A. *Instruments of Darkness: the struggle for radar supremacy*. London, 1967.
PRITCHARD, J. L. "The Wright Brothers and the Royal Aeronautical Society." In *Journal of the Roy. Aeron. Soc.* London, December 1953.
PRITCHARD, J. L. "The Dawn of Aerodynamics". In *Journal of the Roy. Aeron. Soc.* London, March 1957.

ROBERTSON, B. *Sopwith: The Man and His Aircraft*. Letchworth, 1970.
ROLFE, D., and DAWYDOFF, A. *Airplanes of the World, from Pusher to Jet, 1490 to 1954*. New York, 1954.
ROOT, A. I. "Our Homes — What hath God wrought?" In *Gleanings in Bee Culture*. London, January 1st 1905.
RUMPLER, E. *Die Flugmaschine*. Berlin, 1909.

SCHULZE, H. G., and STIASNY, W. *Flug durch Muskelkraft*. Frankfurt a. M., 1936.
SCHWIPPS, W. *Otto Lilienthals Flugversuche*. Berlin, 1966.
SEIFERT, K. D. *Otto Lilienthal: Mensch und Werk*. Neuenhagen-bei-Berlin, 1961.
SHRADER, W. A. *Fifty Years of Flight: a Chronicle of the Aviation Industry in America, 1903—1953*. Cleveland, 1953.

SMITH, G. G. *Gas Turbines and Jet Propulsion*. 6th ed. London, 1955.
SMITH, J. R., and KAY, A. *German Aircraft of the Second World War*. London, 1972.
STEVENS, J. H. *The Shape of the Aeroplane*. London, 1953.
STEWART, O. *Aviation: The Creative Ideas*. London, 1966.
STINTON, D. *The Anatomy of the Aeroplane*. London, 1966.
STROUD, J. *European Transport Aircraft since 1910*. London, 1966.
SWANBOROUGH, F. G., and BOWERS, P. M. *United States Military Aircraft since 1909*. (2nd ed.). London, 1972.

TAYLOR, J. W. R. *A Picture History of Flight*. London, 1955 (2nd ed. 1960).
TAYLOR, J. W. R. (Ed.) *The Lore of Flight*. Göteborg, 1970.
TAYLOR, J. W. R., and MUNSON, K. (Eds.) *History of Aviation*. London, 1973.
TAYLOR, J. W. R., and MUNSON, K. *History of Aviation Aircraft Identification Guide*. London, 1973.
THETFORD, O. *Aircraft of the Royal Air Force since 1918*. London, 1962.
THETFORD, O., and GRAY, P. *German Aircraft of the First World War*. London, 1962.
THETFORD, O. G., and RIDING, E. J. *Aircraft of the 1914—1918 War*. New ed. Marlow, 1954.

UCCELLI, A. *I Libri del Volo di Leonardo da Vinci*. Milano, 1952.

VIVIAN, E. C., and MARSH, W. LOCKWOOD. *A History of Aeronautics*. London, 1921.

WALKER, P. B. *Early Aviation at Farnborough (1878—1910)*. London, 1971.
WALLACE, G. *The Flight of Alcock and Brown*. London, 1955.
WALLACE, G. *Flying Witness: Harry Harper and the Golden Age of Aviation*. London, 1958.
WEISS, J. B. *Gliding and Soaring Flight*. London, 1922.
WENHAM, F. H. *Aërial Locomotion*, 1866. (Reprinted as no. 2 of the *Aeronautical Classics*, 1910.)
WENHAM, F. H. "Report of the First Exhibition." Appended to *Annual Report* (of the Aeronautical Society) *for 1868*. London, 1869.
WEYL, A. R. *Fokker: the Creative Years*. London, 1965.
WHITTLE, SIR F. *Jet*. London, 1953.
WISSMAN, G. *Geschichte der Luftfahrt von Ikarus bis zur Gegenwart*. Berlin, 1960.
WRIGHT, O., and A. (Special combined number of the *Aeronautical Journal*, July—September, 1916 on the Wright brothers.)
WRIGHT, ORVILLE. *How we invented the Aeroplane*. Edited by F. C. Kelly (Orville Wright's deposition in the Montgomery trial). New York, 1953.
WRIGHT, W., and O. *Miracle at Kitty Hawk: the Letters of Wilbur and Orville Wright*. Edited by F. C. Kelly. New York, 1951.
WRIGHT, W. & O. *The Papers of Wilbur and Orville Wright*. Edited by Marvin W. McFarland. 2 vols. New York, 1953.

YOUNG, PEARL I. (ed.) *The Chanute-Wenham Correspondence, September 13, 1892 to January 23, 1908*. Lancaster, 1964.

GLOSSARY

AERODROME (as aircraft). The word mistakenly first used by S.P. Langley, then by others, for their aeroplanes: the Greek word *dromos* can mean a course, a race, or running, or the place where such activities take place; but never the man, animal, or machine that runs or races.

AERODROME (as airfield). This good old-fashioned word (see also above for etymology) is now disappearing in favour of AIRFIELD for all military aerodromes, and for the small civilian aerodromes; and AIRPORT for the medium and large civilian aerodromes from which scheduled airlines are operated.

AERODYNAMICS. That field of dynamics concerned with the motion of air and other gaseous fluids; a branch of fluid mechanics.

AEROFOIL. A body designed to obtain an aerodynamic reaction normal to its direction of travel through the air (e.g. a wing, propeller blade, fin, etc.).

AERONAUT. Literally an "air sailor": today generally confined to either pilot, crew member, or passenger in a balloon or dirigible airship, especially the former: but the word has, in the past, been applied to airmen in heavier-than-air machines.

AERONAUTICS. The whole field of man-made aircraft, of whatever type.

AEROPLANE (AIRPLANE in USA). A heavier-than-air aircraft supported by the dynamic reaction of air flowing over or about fixed or rotating plane surfaces; the term has slowly become synonymous with "powered aeroplane", and most people today would understand it in that sense. Historically, it is used in the first sense. "Aeroplane" orginally meant simply a fixed wing, i.e. an *aero*-plane.

AEROSTATION. The whole field of lighter-than-air aircraft; as opposed to aviation. A lighter-than-air aircraft is an AEROSTAT, and the science is that of AEROSTATICS.

AILERONS. Movable surfaces to control the rolling movements of an aeroplane, now generally set in or by the trailing edges of wings (near the tips). Some early aeroplanes had between-wing ailerons. See also DIFFERENTIAL AILERONS; WING-WARPING.

AIRCRAFT. Any kind of man-made airborne vehicle. The word is often used loosely as a synonym for aeroplane, which can be misleading if the machine in question is not identified at first.

AIRFLOW. The relative flow of air around an object in flight.

AIRFRAME. An aeroplane without its engines and their accessories.

AIRLINER. An unsatisfactory word connoting a medium or large transport aeroplane.

AIRPLANE. The American spelling of "aeroplane". This form of the word was officially adopted in the USA in 1911, and also strongly advocated at the time for use in Britain.

AIRSCREW. A screw to effect propulsion through the air: an alternative word to propeller (which see). "Airscrew" is sometimes the word of choice when discussing the early history of the device, to distinguish it from the marine propeller.

AIRSHIP. A power-driven lighter-than-air aircraft; but often used before 1912 for any kind of powered aircraft, including aeroplanes.

ALTIMETER. A flight instrument for indicating altitude, usually an aneroid barometer calibrated to read feet or metres in a standard atmosphere.

ALTITUDE. The elevation of an object above a given level: with aircraft a given altitude is generally taken to be that above sea level.

AMPHIBIAN. An aircraft equipped to take off and land on either land or water.

ANHEDRAL. The generally accepted term for negative dihedral, although etymologically the word "anhedral" should mean "positive dihedral": it is not clear how this contradiction arose. See DIHEDRAL.

ASTRONAUT. The pilot or crew member of a spacecraft. ASTRONAUT'S "WINGS" are conferred on anyone who has flown higher than 50 miles (80 km) in any kind of aircraft.

ASTRONAUTICS. The field of space travel.

ATTACK (ANGLE OF). The American term for INCIDENCE (which see).

AUTOGIRO. A trade name (the Cierva Autogiro) for the first successful type of gyroplane (which see). The name is often loosely applied to other gyroplanes.

AVIATION. The whole field of heavier-than-air aircraft, as opposed to aerostation. It is becoming increasingly used as a synonym for aeronautics (to include all "man-made" flying), which is to be deplored.

AVIATOR. The pilot of a glider, powered aeroplane or helicopter.

AVION. The French word for "aeroplane" invented by Clément Ader.

AXIS. A straight line, real or imaginary, that passes through a body and about which that body may revolve. An aircraft is considered to have three mutually perpendicular axes, each of which passes through the centre of gravity. 1. The LONGITUDINAL AXIS, the nose-to-tail axis, about which the aircraft revolves in rolling; 2. the LATERAL AXIS, the side-to-side (spanwise) axis about which it revolves in pitching; and 3. the VERTICAL AXIS, which runs in the plane of symmetry (through top and belly), about which it revolves in yawing.

BALLOON. An unpowered aerostat, generally spherical or near-spherical.

BANKING. Inclining an aircraft laterally, usually when making a turn, to prevent skidding. Sometimes used for "turning".

BIPLANE. An aeroplane with two main sets of wings, one above the other; was occasionally used, in early works on flying, for a tandem-wing monoplane. See also WING(S).

BOX-KITE. A form of kite (see KITE), and applied in the early days of flying to many full-size biplanes, often (and unaccountably) those machines which had no trace of box-kite construction, e.g. the so-called Bristol "Box-Kite".

CAMBER. The curve of an aerofoil section from leading to trailing edge, either the upper surface, lower surface, or mean line between them.

CANARD. The French word for "duck". The unaccountable word applied to a "tail-first" aeroplane with the fuselage and elevator forward of the main wings.

CANTILEVER. A wing (or any other member) supported at one end only without any external bracing.

CENTRE OF GRAVITY. The point at which the combined force (resultant) of all the weight forces in a body are concentrated for any position of the body.

CENTRE OF LIFT. The point at which a body in equilibrium may be said to be supported.

CERTIFICATE OF AIRWORTHINESS (C. of A.). A certificate issued by the Air Registration Board (in Britain) respecting civil aircraft, permitting the machine in question to operate under given conditions, etc. No aircraft may be commercially operated without a C. of A.

CHORD. The straight-line distance between the leading and trailing edges of an aerofoil.

COCKPIT. The compartment from where an aircraft is controlled, seating the pilot and often other crew members: in large aircraft it is sometimes referred to as the "flight deck".

CONTROL COLUMN. The pilot's control for working elevators and ailerons.

CONTROL LEVER(s). An early word for the control column, when one or more levers were sometimes used, or suggested.

CONTROL SURFACE. Generally used to denote one of the main control surfaces of an aeroplane (i.e. rudder, elevator, or ailerons) but including flaps, tabs, etc.

CRUISING SPEED. A level-flight speed resulting from a power-setting recommended by the makers for flying under a given set of conditions, usually the optimum compromise of speed and range.

CYCLIC PITCH CONTROL. A helicopter control by means of which the angle of incidence of the rotor blades is changed, thus producing a horizontal thrust component, and hence horizontal flight in any direction.

DELTA WING. An aeroplane's wings which in plan form resemble an isosceles triangle, with the trailing edges forming the base.

DIFFERENTIAL AILERONS. Modern usage confines this term to the special aileron linkage which results in the up-moving aileron travelling farther than the down-moving one. The mere fact of one aileron moving up whilst the other one goes down is best referred to as "contra-acting".

DIHEDRAL. The upward inclination of an aeroplane's wings from their roots, making a shallow V from the front view: hence DIHEDRAL ANGLE. Strictly speaking this is "positive dihedral", but the "positive" is generally omitted. "Negative dihedral" (downward inclination) is generally called "anhedral" (which see).

DIRIGIBLE. A dirigible airship (i.e. powered).

DRAG. A resistant force exerted by the air upon a body, in a direction opposite to the direction of motion. In the early days of flying, drag was termed "drift", or simply "resistance". PROFILE DRAG is a composite drag produced by the lifting surfaces, and comprises FORM DRAG (due to the shape of the aerofoil) and SKIN FRICTION. INDUCED DRAG is that due to the lift forces produced by the wings. PARASITE DRAG is that produced by parts of the aircraft other than the lifting surfaces. INTERFERENCE DRAG is that induced by the interaction of wings, fuselage, tail, etc.

DRIFT. A lateral divergence of an aircraft or missile from the projected line of its heading. Also an early term for drag.

ELEVATOR. A horizontal control surface to control the climb and descent of an aircraft. In early aviation it was usually called the "horizontal rudder".

EQUILIBRIUM (in flight). The stability achieved when the forces of drag, thrust, lift, and weight are acting so as to produce steady flight. See also STABILITY.

EXOSPHERE. The uppermost layer of the Earth's atmosphere, above the ionosphere, stretching upwards from between approximately 310-620 miles (500-1 000 km).

FAIRING. An auxiliary member or structure shaped to reduce drag.

FIN. A fixed vertical aerofoil for stabilising purposes. The American term is "vertical stabiliser".

FLAP. Any control surface designed to increase the lift, or lift and drag combined, of an aeroplane (as opposed to an AIR-BRAKE which only increases drag): the term is usually applied to those surfaces which either hinge down at the trailing edge of the wings, or are projected to form an extension of the trailing edge, curving downwards (Fowler Flap): the other types are slotted, split, and leading-edge flaps.

FLAPPER. An ornithoptering winglet, or small beating surface, used to effect either propulsion-cum-lift, or propulsion only.

FLATTEN OUT. To level an aircraft after a dive or climb.

FLIGHT DECK. The take-off and landing deck of an aircraft carrier: also used for the cockpit of a large aircraft.

FLIGHT PATH. The path described by an aircraft, etc., in the air; i.e. the hypothetical hole bored by an aircraft through the atmosphere.

FLIGHT SIMULATOR. A device (dummy cockpit, etc.) in which any or all of the conditions and feelings of flight are simulated, for training and other purposes.

FLOATPLANE. A seaplane on a float or floats. See also AMPHIBIAN; FLYING-BOAT; SEAPLANE.

FLYER. The Wrights' name for their powered aeroplanes. The name was widely used for powered aeroplanes of any make until about 1909—1910. It was first used by Cayley in 1813. Curtiss spelled the word "Flier".

FLYING-BOAT. A seaplane with a hull on which it floats, takes off, and lands. See also AMPHIBIAN; FLOATPLANE; SEAPLANE.

FLYING MACHINE. Strictly speaking all aircraft, whether powered or not, are machines; the term has been confined almost exclusively to powered aeroplanes in the past, but is now dying out of general usage altogether.

FUSELAGE. The body or hull of an aeroplane.

GAS TURBINE. A mechanical unit that rotates in reaction to a current of gas passing through or over it.

GLIDER. An unpowered fixed-wing aeroplane, for gliding or soaring. A "hang-glider" is one in which the pilot hangs by his arms, etc., and controls the machine by movements of his body and legs.

GYROPLANE. In British usage a rotorcraft with non-powered rotors, as in the Autogiro, which provide lift, but no propulsion. In American usage "gyroplane" may refer to any rotorcraft.

HANGAR. A building for housing aircraft.

HELICOPTER. A type of rotorcraft that derives all its lift and thrust from engine-driven rotating aerofoils (i.e. rotor blades) mounted about an approximately vertical axis. "Helicopter" is often loosely used for any type of rotorcraft.

HORIZONTAL RUDDER. The early term for "elevator".

HORIZONTAL STABILISER. The American term for "tailplane".

HYDRO-AEROPLANE. An early term for a seaplane (translated from the French hydroavion): sometimes confusingly shortened to "hydroplane".

INCIDENCE (Angle of). (1) The angle between the chord of a wing and the direction of the undisturbed airflow. Also referred to as the ANGLE OF ATTACK. (2) The angle between the chord and the horizontal—now commonly referred to as the RIGGING ANGLE OF INCIDENCE.

IONOSPHERE. The layer of the Earth's atmosphere above the ozonosphere, extending to above 200 miles (322 km).

JOY-STICK. An early term for the control column.

KEEL SURFACE. The effective side surface of an aircraft influencing directional stability.

KITE. The earliest type of heavier-than-air aircraft, in which "propulsion" is supplied by the pull on the "tow-line", and lift is supplied by the kite being inclined to the wind. The box-kite (invented by Hargrave in 1893) comprises two four-sided "cells" joined by booms, or variations of this configuration. The word "kite" has also been used as slang for aeroplane.

LAMINAR FLOW. Non-turbulent airflow over or about an aerofoil (etc.) and made up of thin parallel layers.

LANDING GEAR. See UNDERCARRIAGE.

LEADING EDGE. The edge of an aerofoil (wing, propeller, etc.) which first meets the air in normal flight; as opposed to the "trailing edge" (which see).

LIFT. That component of the total aerodynamic forces acting on an aerofoil (or whole aircraft, etc.) perpendicular to the relative wind; in normal flight, it is exerted in an upward direction, opposing the pull of gravity.

LIFT/DRAG RATIO. The ratio of lift to drag.

LONGITUDINAL AXIS. See AXIS.

LOOPING THE LOOP (or LOOP). A flight manoeuvre in which an aeroplane flies an approximately circular path in a vertical plane; an INSIDE LOOP is the normal form of looping the loop, with the top of the aeroplane inside the circle traced: an OUTSIDE LOOP is a loop in which the top of the aircraft is on the outside of the circle traced.

LOW WING MONOPLANE. One with the wings attached at or near the bottom of the fuselage.

MACH NUMBER. The ratio of the airspeed of an aircraft to the speed of sound in the air surrounding it (the "local speed of sound"). Mach 1 is the speed of sound; Mach 2 is twice the speed of sound; and so on. The CRITICAL MACH NUMBER ("Mach Crit") is that representing the speed of a given aircraft at which a Mach number of 1 is attained at any local point of that aircraft: the term has also been used to denote the point at which control is lost in a non-supersonic aircraft. The speed of sound is approximately 760 mph (1 223 km/h) at sea level and approximately 660 mph (1 062 km/h) in the stratosphere.

MAIN PLANE(S). The main lifting surface(s) of an aeroplane, i.e. the wings.

MISSILE. Any object thrown, dropped, projected or propelled, for the purpose of hitting a target. An AERODYNAMIC MISSILE is one which is in effect an aeroplane with aerodynamically supporting surfaces; a BALLISTIC MISSILE is any missile that becomes a freefalling body in the latter stages of its "flight"; a GUIDED MISSILE is a missile directed to its target either by pre-setting or self-reacting devices, or by radio or wire command from outside the missile; a ROCKET MISSILE is one propelled and supported entirely by rocket power. In practise, missiles may combine the characteristics of all four of these classes.

MONOCOQUE CONSTRUCTION. From the French word meaning "egg-shell": aircraft construction in which the skin bears all or most of the stresses involved. Pure monocoque is almost unknown, as even the presence of bulkheads, or a few longerons, makes it strictly speaking a semi-monocoque. The term STRESSED SKIN is now used to include all types of construction where some or most of the stresses are borne by the skin.

MOVABLE TIPS. An early term for ailerons.

MULTIPLANE. A general term for any aeroplane with two or more sets of wings mounted one above the other.

N.A.C.A. Abbreviation of "National Advisory Committee for Aeronautics" (USA).

ORBIT. To revolve about a point; or the act of revolving, as in the orbit of a comet or Earth satellite, etc., which generally move in elliptical orbits.

ORNITHOPTER. An aircraft sustained and propelled by flapping wings.

OUTRIGGER(S). A projecting structure to support (on an aircraft) such parts as an elevator, rudder, or complete tail-unit, etc. The word "boom" is almost synonymous.

OZONOSPHERE. The layer of the Earth's atmosphere above the stratosphere, between approximately 12 and 31 miles (19 and 50 km) above the Earth.

PARACHUTE. A parasol-like aeronautical device for retarding the movement of whatever is attached to it. The man-carrying parachute is composed of the CANOPY, the RIGGING (or SHROUD) LINES, and the HARNESS: there is often a stabilising VENT in the crown of the canopy. In a rip-cord parachute the main canopy is pulled out of the PACK by a PILOT PARACHUTE. Also used for a glider in the last century.

PARASOL MONOPLANE. One with the wings mounted above, and clear of, the fuselage.

PAYLOAD. That part of the load of a commercial aircraft that produces revenue (i.e. passengers and cargo).

PITCH. The blade angle of a propeller or rotor blade.

PLANE. (a) Short for "aeroplane"; (b) a wing; (c) a flat surface.

PLANE OF SYMMETRY. A vertical plane containing the longitudinal axis of a symmetrical object, such as an aeroplane, where such a plane would cut through the machine from nose to tail leaving the port side and wing on one side of the plane, and the starboard on the other.

PLANOPHORE. Alphonse Pénaud's name for his stable model monoplane of 1871; from the Latin *plano* (plane) and the Greek *phoros* (bearing).

POWER PLANT (or UNIT). In aircraft these terms are generally taken to include the engine, propeller, and accessories.

POWER/WEIGHT RATIO. The ratio of the power of an engine to its own weight; or, when used of the whole aircraft, the ratio of power to total weight.

PRESSURIZATION. The keeping of the interior of an aircraft at a higher air pressure than the atmospheric pressure outside.

PROPELLER. This word, in aeronautical and marine parlance, only became synonymous with "airscrew" from about 1845—1855. Prior to that it referred to any propelling device.

PROPELLER (Constant-speed). One that tends to maintain the engine revolutions under any flight conditions by automatically increasing or decreasing the pitch of the blades.

PROPELLER (Contra-rotating). A twin unit comprising two co-axial propellers rotating in opposite directions. "Counter-rotating" is generally applied to two propellers on separate axes, or to two propellers on the same axis but driven independently by two engines.

PROPELLER. (Reversible-pitch). One whose blades can be turned to negative pitch to produce reverse thrust to retard an aircraft when landing.

PROPELLER (Variable-pitch). Any propeller the pitch of whose blades can be altered in operation.

PROTOTYPE. The first one (or more) complete and working aircraft (or other object) of a new type, class, or series. There may be more than one prototype of a given machine.

PUSHER PROPELLER. A propeller placed behind its engine, and generally behind the main wings of an aeroplane. See also TRACTOR PROPELLER.

PUSH-PULL. An adjective applied to the combination of pusher and tractor propellers.

RADIAL ENGINE. One in which one or more rows of cylinders are arranged radially around a common crankshaft: the cylinders are stationary, as distinct from the "rotary" engine (which see).

RAF. Abbreviation originally of "Royal Aircraft Factory" (Farnborough); later of "Royal Air Force".

RAMJET ENGINE. A type of jet engine, which can operate only at high speeds, in which the air for oxidising the fuel is literally "rammed" in at the front by the forward speed of the engine through the air.

ROCKET ENGINE. A reaction propulsion engine whose fuel includes an oxidiser, thus making it independent of the atmosphere. Rocket engines may use solid or liquid fuels.

ROLL. (a) Any movement about the horizontal axis of an aircraft; (b) a deliberate manoeuvre in which an aeroplane is rolled over: also HALF-ROLL; (c) the American equivalent of "run", i.e. take-off, landing, or taxying, roll; also used thus in the early days of British flying.

ROTARY ENGINE. One in which the crankshaft remains fixed, and the cylinders revolve about it, the propeller revolving with them.

ROTARY or ROTATING WING AIRCRAFT. See ROTORCRAFT.

ROTOR. An assembly comprising generally two or more long narrow wings or aerofoils (called blades) set in a hub on a vertical shaft which provide lift (or lift and thrust) for a rotorcraft.

ROTOR (Anti-torque). A small rotor on a rotorcraft revolving in the vertical plane which generates thrust to oppose the torque effects of the main rotor.

ROTORCRAFT. An aircraft which employs rotating aerofoils to provide lift, or both lift and propulsion. In American usage, a "gyroplane" is the equivalent of a rotorcraft. See also AUTOGIRO; GYROPLANE; HELICOPTER.

RUDDER. A vertical control surface for guiding an aircraft in the horizontal plane.

RUDDER (Horizontal). "Horizontal Rudder" was an early term for elevator.

RUDDER BAR (or RUDDER PEDALS). The foot-operated bar or pedals to which are attached the cables operating the rudder.

RUNNER. An early term for a skid.

SAIL. Word used by Cayley for an aircraft wing.

SAILPLANE. A glider designed especially for soaring.

SATELLITE. A vehicle which is made to orbit the Earth, in an elliptical or circular orbit.

SEAPLANE. Any aeroplane built to operate only from the water. Seaplanes are either FLOATPLANES or FLYING-BOATS. The word was introduced by Sir Winston Churchill in 1913. See also AMPHIBIAN.

SEMI-MONOCOQUE. See MONOCOQUE.

SKID. Flat or curved wooden (or other) member which may be part of an aircraft undercarriage (with or without the addition of wheels); or be in the form of a TAIL SKID.

SHORT TAKE-OFF AND LANDING AIRCRAFT. See STOL.

SKIN FRICTION. The friction of the air particles on a surface in motion. See also DRAG.

SLAT. See SLOT.

SLIPSTREAM. The flow of air driven backward by the propeller.

SLOT. A gap between the wing and a specially formed slat, through which air is directed over the upper surface of the wing to preserve a smooth airflow, generally at high angles of incidence; the same principle applied to ailerons, etc.

SONIC SPEED. The speed of sound. See also SOUND.

SOUND (Speed of). The speed of sound is approximately 760 mph (1223 km/h) at sea level, decreasing with height (owing to decrease in temperature): in the stratosphere it is approximately 660 mph (1062 km/h). Speed below that of sound is called SUBSONIC; at that of sound SONIC; and above, SUPERSONIC. See also MACH NUMBER.

SOUND BARRIER. A popular but misleading term loosely indicating the rapid rise of drag at transonic speeds.

SPAN (of wings). The spread of the wing(s), from tip to tip.

SPAR. A span-wise structural member of a wing, etc.

SPEED. FLYING SPEED is the speed necessary for a fixed-wing aeroplane to attain, or maintain, in order to become or remain airborne. AIRSPEED is the speed of any aircraft through the air, i.e. relative to the air through which

235

it moves. GROUND SPEED is the aircraft's speed in relation to the ground. SONIC SPEED is the speed of sound, i.e. about 760 mph (1223 km/h) at sea level (see SOUND).

SPIN. An aerial manoeuvre, intentional or not, in which an aeroplane descends vertically in autorotation.

SPUTNIK. The Russian word for "satellite".

STABILISER. Any aerofoil to provide stability.

STABILITY AND CONTROL:

STABILITY. There are only two kinds of aircraft stability, longitudinal stability for motion in the plane of symmetry, and lateral stability for motion out of the plane of symmetry; the former concerns rising, falling and pitching movements; the latter, rolling, yawing and side-slipping movements. Colloquially and descriptively, however, one may also speak of "directional stability" which is a component of lateral stability.

CONTROL. Where flight control is concerned, one may speak of "longitudinal control", which is control in pitch; and "lateral control" is often used to refer to control in roll only, and the term "directional control" for control i yaw.

In early aviation (up to 1908) the Europeans were concerned to ensure: (a) LONGITUDINAL STABILITY; via a tailplane at the back; (b) LONGITUDINAL CONTROL; via an elevator for control in pitch; (c) DIRECTIONAL STABILITY; via a keel area and a vertical surface in the rear; (d) DIRECTIONAL CONTROL; via a rear rudder. As the Europeans neglected the proper function and use of warping and ailerons, they found it difficult to control their machines when they attempted to turn them on rudder alone, with the outer wings producing more lift on the turn than the inner; the pilots could only counteract the inwards rolling momentum by putting on opposite rudder to accelerate the lowered wings and lift them, and — in extreme cases — hoping that this rudder action would be in time to stop the machine heeling right over and crashing; (e) STABILITY IN ROLL; via a dihedral angle of the wings. Until Wilbur Wright started flying in France in August 1908, the use of ailerons or warping to effect control in roll was neither properly understood nor practised by the Europeans; this was initially due to their remaining ignorant of the necessity to achieve proper control in roll when turning, and their belief that the main function of ailerons or warping was to maintain lateral balance in level flight; then, as a result of these considerations, it was due to their ignorance of the use of the rudder to counteract aileron (or warp) drag. The Wright brothers, on the other hand, were not concerned with any kind of inherent stability, but much concerned from the first with full lateral control (control in roll, yaw and side-slip).

STALL. (a) "High incidence stalling" is the behaviour of an aeroplane when, owing to insufficient airspeed or other cause, the wing(s) lose(s) lift and fall(s). (b) "Shock stalling" is where an aerofoil designed for subsonic flight loses lift owing to the formation of shock waves, and falls.

STEERING FLAPS (or TIPS). Early terms for ailerons.

STEP ROCKET. A multi-stage rocket.

STOL. Abbreviation of "short take-off and landing"; an aircraft, usually fitted with additional lift-producing aerodynamic surfaces or power units, which can take off and land in extremely short distances.

STRATOSPHERE. The layer of the Earth's atmosphere above the tropopause, extending up to, approximately, 18 miles (29 km).

STREAMLINING. The giving of a specially shaped and smooth contour to an object to decrease its resistance in a fluid flow.

STRESSED-SKIN CONSTRUCTION. The use of the outer skin of a structure to carry primary structural loads in addition to local air pressure. See also MONOCOQUE.

STRUT. Connecting member, generally between the wings of a biplane, etc.; mainly to take compression loads.

SUBSONIC SPEED. Speed below that of sound. See also SOUND.

SUPERCHARGER. A pump or compressor for forcing more air or fuel-air mixture into an engine than it would normally induct at the prevailing atmospheric pressure.

SUPERSONIC SPEED. Speed above the speed of sound. See also SOUND.

TAILPLANE. The fixed horizontal stabilising plane(s) of the tail-unit.

TAIL-UNIT. The rear assembly of an aircraft comprising fin, rudder, tailplane, elevator, etc.

TANDEM. An arrangement of units one behind the other.

TAXI. To drive an aircraft along the ground or water, other than in take-off or landing runs.

THRUST. The driving force exerted on any aircraft, missile, etc., by its propeller, rotor blades, propulsive jet, or other means.

TORQUE. A moment that produces, or tends to produce, rotation, twisting or torsion.

TRACTOR PROPELLER. One that pulls, i.e. in front of its engine and generally to the front of the main wings of an aeroplane.

TRAILING EDGE. The rear edge of an aerofoil, i.e. over which the air passes last.

TRIPLANE. An aeroplane with three main (sets of) planes set one above the other.

TURBOFAN ENGINE. Type of jet engine in which only a part of the inducted air is used to oxidise the fuel, the remainder being discharged directly to the atmosphere through separate propulsive nozzle(s) after by-passing the combustion chamber. A turbofan gives more efficient propulsion at subsonic speeds than a turbojet. The earlier term "by-pass engine" is now seldom used.

TURBOJET ENGINE. The recognised combine-word for a gas turbine jet propulsion engine; or (loosely) an aeroplane propelled by it: as distinct from a TURBOPROP.

TURBOPROP ENGINE. The recognised combine-word for an airscrew/gas turbine engine combination; or (loosely) an aeroplane propelled by it: as distinct from a TURBOJET (which see). The term "propjet" is sometimes used for "turboprop".

TURBOSHAFT ENGINE. Form of turboprop engine in which the rotating shaft drives a mechanical transmission system instead of a propeller, as in a helicopter or certain types of VTOL aircraft.

TURBULENT FLOW. Airflow about an aerofoil in which layers travel at radically different velocities involving lateral movement, with consequent differences in pressure.

ULTRASONIC. Sound frequencies above those affecting the human ear, i.e. above 20,000 vibrations per second.

UNDERCARRIAGE. The collective term for the wheels or other gear supporting an aircraft on land or water, generally the former: also termed "landing gear".

VARIABLE PITCH PROPELLER. See PROPELLER.

V (or VEE) ENGINE. One with banks of cylinders arranged in a V, seen from the end.

VTOL. Abbreviation of "vertical take-off and landing"; an aircraft, other than a rotorcraft, which can take off and land vertically, and also fly horizontally.

WARPING. See WING-WARPING.

WING(S). The main lifting aerofoil(s) of an aeroplane. By bird-derived usage, a monoplane is said to have two wings, even if there is only one connected surface. Hence a biplane has two "sets" of wings. But, occasionally (as in "gull-wing", etc.) the singular is used for convenience. In the last century the word "wings" was often used technically to denote ornithoptering wings as opposed to fixed wings ("aeroplanes"). Cayley called a fixed wing a "sail".

WING-WARPING. A twisting or torsion of a wing to increase or decrease its curvature and thus its angle of incidence, and effect control in roll; used first of the Wright machines. This misleading term ("wing-warping") was invented by Octave Chanute in 1903 as a kind of shorthand word for the helical twisting of the wings according to the Wrights' practice. It was first literally translated into French (1903—1904) by the verb "gauchir", which did not mean a twisting of the wings, but a literal "warping" of them.

YAW. The movement of an aircraft about its vertical axis.

ZOOM. To climb briefly at an angle greater than the normal climbing angle.

INDEX

Page numbers which are italicised indicate that the subject is illustrated.

240

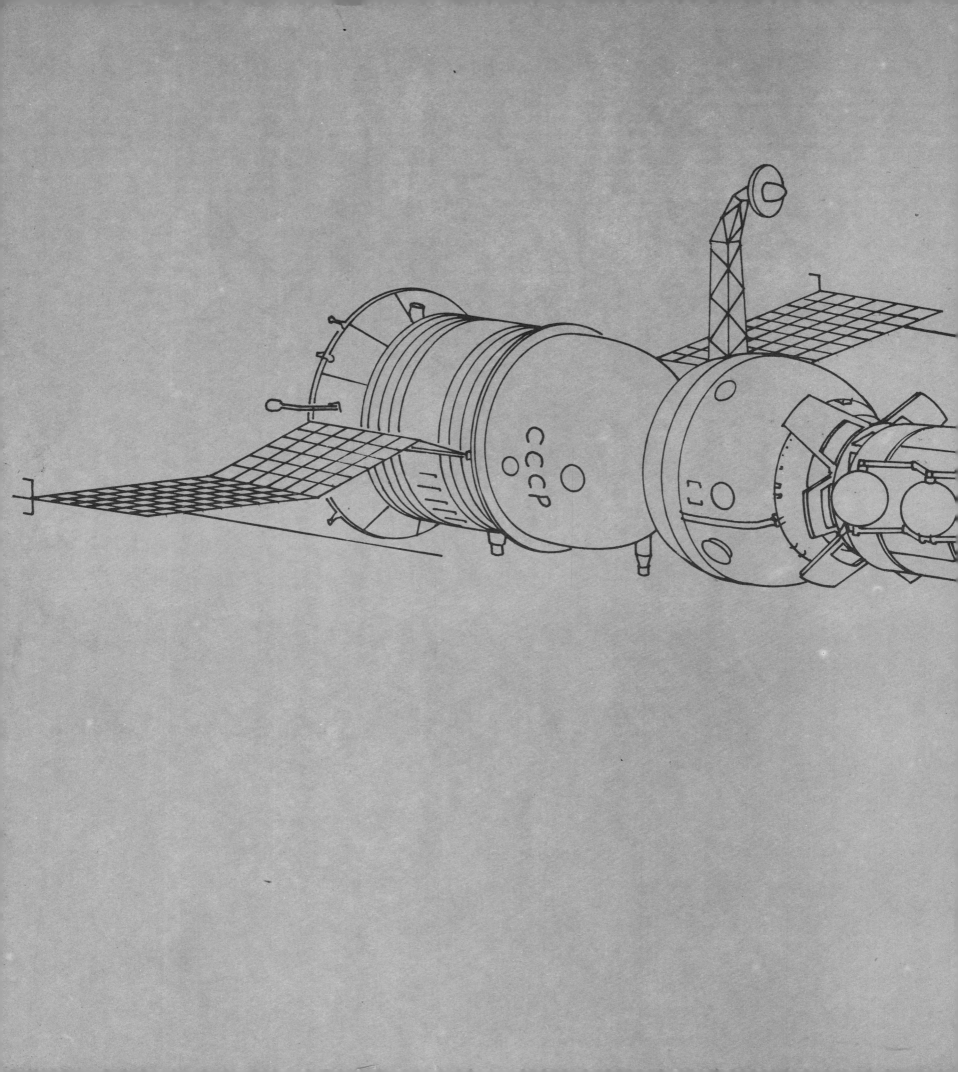